LIFE AND SHAPE

LIFE AND SHAPE

by
RICHARD NEUTRA

All rights reserved. No part of this book in excess of five hundred words may be reproduced in any form without permission in writing from the publisher.

Where persons, places, and circumstances are not specifically named, any resemblance to real persons, places, and circumstances is merely coincidental.

First new edition: September 2009
Published by Atara Press, Los Angeles
Library of Congress Control Number: 2009934983
Copyright © 2009 Dion Neutra on behalf of the Richard and Dion Neutra Papers at the University of California, Los Angeles
Sketches: Department of Special Collections, Charles E. Young Research Library, UCLA
First published in 1962 by Appleton-Century-Crofts, New York
ISBN-13: 978-0-9822251-3-4
Printed in the United States of America
Visit Atara Press on the web: atarapress.com

To DIONE NEUTRA

Acknowledgments

Richard Neutra wishes to thank cordially Diane Amussen, Ted Purdy, Eleanor Crain, his son Raymond, and his faithful collaborator John Blanton, for editorial suggestions. Many who have taken friendly, thorough interest and, unfortunately, cannot all be named and specifically appreciated for their stimulating comments, have in various early stages devotedly read and aided this manuscript slowly to grow in form and spirit.

Contents

Foreword by Dion Neutra	ix
PUZZLEMENT THROUGH LIFE	1
Emergence and Unfolding	9
HAND SKETCHES	15
Glimpses into a Manifold World	15
EARLY INFLUENCES	34
From Floor to Clouds	34
Parents and Siblings	44
Physician and Architect	62
Impressive Clinician	63
Reformer and His Community	68
Unequal Eyes	73
Teacher and Apprentice	84
EXOTIC TRAINING	99
In a Far-Distant Fortress	99
Sea Power in Silhouette	109
Unknown Europe	117
Tropical Malaria	126
FINDING A COMPANION	130
From Albania and Slovakia to Switzerland	130
Encounter and Renewal in Vienna	147

Brandenburg, a Wedding, a Household	151
Berliner Tageblatt	155

WHITE HOPE—U.S.A.? — 162
Loos, Sullivan, Wright	162
Wright's Prairie Chicago	176
How America Builds	191
"California Calls You"	208
Health House, Vintage 1927	222
Through Asia and Africa	228
Back to Europe via the Orient	244
Europe—U.S.A—1929	254
The Van der Leeuw House	265

PROGRAMS AND PROBLEMS — 277
Budget, Mirror of Destiny	285
Pain, Despite Success	292
From a Past Battlefield to a Future Cosmopolitan Scene	304

OUR FATEFUL SETTING — 317
Human Cities	317
Epilogue to a Prelude	357

BIBLIOGRAPHY — 369

INDEX — 372

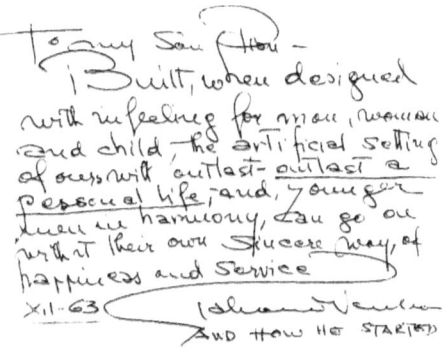

Foreword
to the 2009 Edition

It's been twenty-five years since the last foreword I wrote for the reprinting of *Survival Through Design* in 1984. It seemed like a good time to take another look at another of dad's important books; his autobiography.

Originally published in 1962, some eight years before his death, *Life and Shape* appeared in only one edition, although it was translated into a half dozen other languages. This year, 2009, we ran out of the last hard copies of the first edition and it was suggested that it might be good to offer this in an affordable format. We've expanded the bibliography at the back with some more of the many new books by and about, as well as printed some comments by principal biographer Tom Hines on this occasion.

My personal copy of this book contains the above inscription from October 1, 1963 (maybe a birthday present?):

> To my son Dion—
> Built, when designed with infeeling for man, woman and child, the artificial setting of ours will outlast—<u>outlast a personal life</u>, and, younger men in harmony, can go on with it their own sincere way, of happiness and service.
> Signed Richard Neutra, 'and how he started'.

I think this was his way of telling me he hoped I would do just that, carry on from where he left off.

We decided to save the cover image and reuse it for this edition. I like the imposition of the man-made object onto the sketch of a pine tree as the spirit of life and shape. I was heartened to learn that this stair which we designed in 1955 for the Gemological Institute still stands. I made the design for additions to this project in 1968, and was saddened to see them move to Santa Monica in the eighties hiring new talent for that building. The old headquarters were so drastically remodeled years later that I doubted the stair could still be there. To my amazement only recently I was told it still survives buried in an interior courtyard very difficult to find.

Perhaps that can symbolize my hope that more of our work can survive the inevitable entropy that seems to be the rule.

Browsing through this book again after many years, I'm struck again with the broad intellect and artistry of this man which he brought to his *oeuvre* in so many ways. His prose is not always the easiest, but there is no mistaking his sincere desire to be of service to his clients and his overriding concern with the individual being served in every commission from the simplest single family dwelling to projects serving hundreds of unknown clients. In so many ways, he was the early embodiment of today's 'Green Architect'.

I continue to feel even to this day, when our work has found increasing appreciation, that Neutra's contributions are still to be fully understood and valued.

Enjoy this chance to commune with one of the 20th century's remarkable talents in our field.

Dion Neutra AIA, FISD, son and partner
Los Angeles, July, 2009

LIFE AND SHAPE

PROLOGUE

> Life is so short—you may miss the boat.
> Or: Life is too short—why bother?
> To bother or not to bother, that is the question.

Puzzlement Through Life

THROUGHOUT THEIR LIVES people try planning ahead. I myself have made a living by it. Is planning a must for us? Or is it an illusion? In the long run, things have a way of turning out so differently, and they go on and on "turning out" while life slips by. Maybe, beyond complaining, there *is* a new way to look at it—after looking at it for so long, in the established, disgruntled way?

Recently, while on a professional trip in Greece, some people in whose car I was riding showed me, deep down in a lovely valley, an ancient crossroad. Long ago, like so many thousands of others, a man walked there on his way to the oracle town of Delphi—seeking information on how to avoid fate planfully. At this spot he met, coming from the other direction, a traveler who had already been tipped off—and misunderstood the tip. At any rate, both of them missed the point head on. They had a row, and things went very wrong, as seems typical for oracle seekers.

Can one arrange one's life? For those who believe they can, there is this ancient story of intelligent King Oedipus. It is frustrating and ends in gory detail. That young man had the highest I.Q. in town, no question: he was much admired for turning the tables on the Sphinx and solving the most puzzling quiz in record time. In a jiffy he made a brilliant career and enjoyed himself as efficient manager of a kingdom. Yet, finally, he gouged out his own eyes in despair.

Where did the trouble have its start? Is it ignorance which is our destiny and which no oracle words can help? Intellect does not pay perhaps, and advice fails its purpose? By a fateful trifle of "know-not" the bright young man had unsuspectingly killed his own father, although he had been forewarned and made this whole trip to avoid it.

As long as one follows one's nose and travels ahead, life seems still passable, but when one comes to a tricky traffic intersection, one runs into a dilemma. At just such places there is a great deal of getting emotional, of accident, and ignorance as to who is who, what to do, and who has the right of way. Crossings are classical points for differences of opinion and wrong decisions—for getting cross, and countercrossing oneself.

But, in the old story, one thing soon seemed to be clear. To become King, a man must marry the widowed Queen. It was a package deal according to the rules of the game; yet, when the package was opened, and Oedipus suddenly knew he had wedded his own mother, he did not remain the clever solver of riddles—*he went out of his mind.* It is the human fate and make-up to change inside, and instantly take things to be different, now and the next moment.

The whole, from A to Z, was no accident. The gods had cooked it up. They were known to plan their own way, which can't be fathomed. But, a significant part of their design seems to be that they have created us as "up-and-downers," tumbling between long- and short-range plans which, in the last analysis, we really do not get along with, any more than with our own changing selves. Each of us, billions of firing brain cells called mind and will. Yet, with all our insight the gods mix some blindness. It is a heady cocktail, and after a couple of drinks, we may lose our proud balance. At some unpredictable moment, in subtle irony, they, who tendered us the draught of life, may withdraw, from under our very noses, our so-called self-forged success and happiness—and then even make us feel that it is all our own fault.

They humbled that young blade, born and gifted for royalty, to humble all of us who watch the awesome show. It is not at all a show of punishment for a misdeed—unless we mean the general misdeed of human self-confidence that we steadily stay the same, and of overconfidence that life—our life—is in our power.

Being cut down to size has happened to many a man. There is a large "control group," as the scientists call it, to compare notes on this sort of thing, and there has been a great deal of storytelling about amazing turns of fortune and shocking failures—with a lot of hindsight to explain them.

The Oedipus story is just a saga; but it says something not easily refuted. It is not readily superseded; it has long been listened to, taken into account and to heart. A single life cannot be mapped out in all detail and step by step, no more than group fate; and human civilization is not planned without setbacks.

How stable is intelligence? How lasting, our appetites?

Yet we must go on with this well-announced grand show, called *our plan*, which has been long rehearsed, and a flop so often.

There is the satanically doubtful half-success story of our endless series of seemingly rational "progresses" and inventions. We are often so proud of them, in spite of their taking off each other's fenders in the jam they produce. Do they really jell to insure survival with increased happiness for our shaky species? Or are we maybe ruining our parental background, or *bearing subsoil*, working ourselves only into more of a frazzle, into hectic pressure and a final spectacular explosion? Is *this* the nature of the beast—us superbeasts? Is the subtle human brain which makes all this trouble—a success of creation, or a proof for the Devil's doubt in it? Maybe Lucifer, who is said to have raised his eyebrows and shaken his head about humanity, had something there!

The sixth creation day, like the others, first seemed well conclusive. But was not the Deity, too, disappointed about our behavior soon after, and ever again?

Throughout recorded history, *we humans ourselves* have pondered unceasingly this irksome little thing of our instability, insecurity in earthly life. A lot of dubious evidence keeps piling up right now. Finally of the old molehill has been made a megaton.

Let us hope we have not reached the end of the rope of evolution. It is the best we have. Did we really achieve *anything* salubrious that works automatically, and as per patent applied for? Or is with us inadequacy eternal; a perpetual incentive?

When those who trusted my profession of plan-making laid all they had on the table, hoping for happiness, and later testified it had yielded quite some satisfaction to them, I ought perhaps to have gained some self-confidence in planning to house the lives of others—in building them a house to last. And for a while I did. But, then, just when my own course of life seemed to make sense through the game of anticipating, self-scrutiny was also sharpened enough to make me see that all could topple over, that watertight plans might leak in spite of every shrewd precaution. Was this because indeterminancy starts in the very core of the atom?[*] The unexpected suddenly may ring the doorbell; there is probability for that.

One thing is certain and, for plans, it is always a happy point of departure and return: *human beings will not get out of their*

---

[*]Werner Heisenberg, who said it first, is a lovely calm man to talk to and be with. But his discovery has left us all at uncannily loose ends.

skin, nor, for long, *out of their innate bounds.* Still—they do not "go steady," as consumers. To call them fickle would be slanted language; but because of their colossal complexity, human desires must fluctuate more than those of a cow or a cormorant, or of anything in organic nature before us.

First, and uppermost, the riddles to be respected are within our own skin and make-up. We cannot even foresee our many *inner constellations*, not to speak of external ones. Man is no fixed given quantity, nor self-determined rocket, going through heaven and hell with an inexhaustible fuel supply all his own. Nor is he able to travel those skies unfatigued, guided only by his own navigational controls. From the start there has always seemed to be a long-distance hand to guide the genes as they assemble and make of man a good skyfarer. This force may shrink or stretch our limits, or tamper with the fuel supply we take in for our safari onto higher levels. It may cause sudden swervings from the plotted route, or even amazing changes in the traveler's innermost metabolic rate when he suddenly finds himself out of his element and all his finely figured out altitude gadgets fail him.

But, as a whole, our natural dynamics inside are *amazingly safe:* at least much safer to build on than mere intellectual verbalizations and fickle speculation!

Apart from calculated far-fetched astronautics, we stand, in life on earth, at one crossroad after another—often in dispute with ourselves through all our lives. Shall we and can we be life's licensed architects, or are we just pushed around by words and fashions? (But, after all, an architect also can be pushed around; there are plenty of examples for that!)

Before we may try for any more encouraging conclusion in current terms, new insight must muzzle or muffle those who try prattling us out of possible peace with ourselves. They have a way of disregarding our urgent necessity of the moment because, at that moment, they do not share it with us: their own pattern just then happens to go through a different phase. But *they are not necessarily wiser;* not just because they are, maybe, a little annoyed by our zest—or, perhaps, by our contented drowsiness—as the case might be.

Still, endless good advice goes on: two kinds of it, in keeping with the phase through which the adviser just happens to be going himself and which fits his own mood.

Take it easy!	or?	Better get busy!
Stop worrying!	or?	Watch out!
Don't cross your bridges before you come to them!	or?	Look before you leap!

Yes, look, use your brains. Be human and think! But then, after all, can't you be a little *more* human, relax and for God's sake, enjoy life!

One could go on reviewing all the "philosophical steers, bum and otherwise, given over millennia, and likewise those boring daily reproaches to which we are all addicted and of which we are sick and tired: Why didn't you think about this earlier? Why didn't you tell me, or do something about it while there was time? Listen, didn't you say only yesterday...??

Then again: Why can't you forget about spilled milk? Can't you see that your endless fidgeting has no sense, makes no difference, and makes me sick, and you, too?

Essentially, it's always the same question: Was anything missed? Or is it hit or miss anyway? *Should one plan or should one drift? Drift or direction? Drift or design?*

Failing to use one's brain to GIVE LIFE SHAPE is often looked at as a *moral* issue. But that old story of Oedipus does not tell of "just" punishment, nor of testing a human being, as does the story of Job. No moral stamina was given a trial here.

Now, let us take a naturalist's view. There is no issue about whether a bird *should* fly, since he is born to grow wings. And as to us, we have grown anticipating brains; we simply cannot stop them and "live for the moment," even if Horace and Omar Khayyam have suggested it—except perhaps by having another drink, as they also recommended. That, of course, will, for a while, still or dull our brain's fast and wondrous activity.

Perhaps that whole old fable serves to demonstrate man's limitations, built-in vagaries, impermanency. They *are* characteristics; they are his nature, which must be seen as what it is—not static, but primarily *fluctuating* in the breeze of life.

YET BEYOND THAT INNER WAVERING—WHICH HAS NOT BEFALLEN A BEE IN THREE HUNDRED MILLION YEARS—AND BECAUSE OF OUR BRAIN MOBILITY—THERE IS THE GRAND CHANCE OF BECOMING, OF EVOLVING—ESPECIALLY THIS NOVEL CHANCE TO EVOLVE OUR OWN SETTING. IT IS A WELL-BASED WHITE HOPE, BEYOND DEPRESSING MYTHS THAT ALL WAS "SET" TO START WITH.

A physiological view on all good and silly advice lets us also bypass a bit of bad conscience, guilt, and fear, and lets us begin to believe in our promising potential, beyond any and all stereotyped verbiage. Our biological make-up has space to turn around, space for what may only *look* like conflict when harshly brought together into one moment. Our pattern is, and over a lifetime shows up as, back and forth, bipolar, multiphasic. No advice nor blame will change that. But from time to time, from moment to moment, *fluctuations in vitality* will project the next color slide. It might be a grand one and lead magnificently on. And so, if we want to plan, *we must plan elastically for living beings*—since that is what we are ourselves.

A man, manically exhilarated, may feel like a million and plan for a thousand years; but in the dark, depressive, despondent stage he will just plan to shoot himself in his bunker before sunrise and have it over with. That's an extreme case, but leaving insanity aside, "normalcy" is not monotonously stable either.... Environment may help it more than just talk.

Suddenly the best advice and resolves of an hour ago may, dull and futile, stumble off stage; or on a bright day, which happily marries inside with outside, gloomy prospects may suddenly look brilliant, ebullient, and make us soar. For shadows and brightness we must arrange adaptable surroundings.

The most promising thing for an architect, unless he is specializing in graveyard design, is to shun rigidity. He works for a client who remains organically "in the making," and thus can be aided. This is a very practical view on the matter of housing life, and helping it.

How could architecture be allowed to freeze the music of life, its changes from minor to major? They will go on, back and forth.

The one who made up his mind, soon is no longer "the same." He may be older and weaker, or possibly he may be refreshed and once again a vigorous plan-maker. Like a jack-in-the-box, he goes down and gets up again. Even such an idea of "he-himself" is a good deal of a dangerously oversimplified cliché. To cling to *self-identity*, very consciously, may break one's heart in disappointment.

And yet, treasuring one's self-identity and marveling at it also holds promise! Deep down, it is fed, entertained, by many molecules in a continuing biochemical ballet; figures and configurations follow each other and do repeat themselves, often with ever clearer definition.

Each of us feels single, but seen over time and growth everyone is a series of persons; there acts a manifold crew. *The individual is a whole team, stretched out in time;* a team that may collaborate harmoniously. On other cases it is a mixed-up crew, in which each fellow follows other calls and commands, stimulated from without or within, so that the ship rocks and zigzags through life's tossing sea!

In the long run one must be capable of collaboration with oneself through many weather changes, many stages of the journey. . . . Being faithful to oneself, perhaps, teaches one to remain faithful to others.

Essentially it is a similar thing. Always a *phase* of biologically mobile individuality must neatly fit together with another. Gearing them, matching and happily overlapping them, *tuning passing phases together*, is all.

"Wavering instead of stable" sounds bad, of course. But this is loaded language. Life simply is up and down, not a neat Euclidian, a straight line between two points. And a human brain, *because it is anything but rigid*, appears the top miracle of life—recent and young as it is in natural history. Recognized by science, as yet far from activated in all its potentials, it holds great promise for a happier harmonization yet to come, if we only can keep going and evolve. . . .

Deserved comfort to the Reader: Books are easier reading than their prefaces. But this is not really a preface; it is "part and parcel"—the planner's problematics.

Emergence and Unfolding

A life runs through its phases while the globe spins through the hours of the day, revolves through the seasons of the year, and while the hands of mechanically ticking clocks move steadily.

But the organic growth and maturation of a life is not so evenly spread over time. It has its own emotional clock, driven by that inner chemistry.

There are creative moments. There are inconspicuous but birth-giving seconds—perhaps fractions of seconds—which decide. As in world history, there are unfoldings and witherings in amazingly rapid succession. And there is sometimes a sudden bursting forth, from God knows what unexpected resources, slowly accumulated. What an undertaking to build walls around it all! It's like confining life between book covers.

If one were to write one's own life story, wistfully and curiously, it would seem pedantic not to give more emphasis to currents, rapids, and falls, passed over in perilous moments but echoing for decades, or for a lifetime.

One must not merely engage in an engineered chronology. One cannot look at time as an arithmetical table of dates, nor at space experience as if it were a dry geometric abstraction. Time, space, their intervals and distances, are differently measured, as we take them in, not by the calendar, nor by meters or millimeters. It is our *organic responses*, senses, moving limbs, that really count. They have kept "counting" their way through a long human and prehuman past. They themselves measured time and space long before mathematics were invented or wrist watches began gauging life for us.

Once at a London party the hostess asked G.B.S., "Are you enjoying yourself, Mr. Shaw?"

He replied, "Yes, but that is the only thing I am enjoying."

Mr. Shaw's pun notwithstanding, it is essentially true, and by no means only at that party. The reciprocal verb tells it. We always enjoy *ourselves*. This is not mere egoism, but simply an organic function. Only through ourselves can we enjoy everything else. Or we fail to do so—the pleasure may miss—because our vital endowment at that particular stretch of "living time" may be failing. And even a small failure here makes a big difference, may cause a long silent pause.

A good life means full and far-reaching absorption by ourselves of all our manifold life happenings, from inception and while still in the womb. Then, if I understand Lewis Mumford right, "at a singular point," as the mathematician

Clerk Maxwell dubbed it, under this or that impact or at a lucky moment, our being may suddenly deviate from what it was before. Perhaps it may turn into some newly expressive and fertile form, undergo an unpredictable change—let us now call it a mutation, or a mystery.

Setting down merely a mechanical or purely "reasonable" order of events, one after the other, gives little true guidance for reliving a life story. There are overlapping after-sounds, crowdings, and sudden stillnesses. Life seems sometimes rather vacant, and at other times pregnant, replete with newly emerging higher ideas and lower emotive swells. Or again it shows itself reverberant of earlier currents which have really never died down. Perhaps light particles and shreds are the best flotsam; they float best and do not sink.

Travel sketches reflect recurrent "tonuses," which a physiologist may see in the sketcher. Tendencies and attitudes of a man, more than his abstract concepts or "plans," are his lasting essentials. How things are formed by him or flow out of his biological individuality might long remain a puzzle, but perhaps this puzzle may be made legible to some minds through empathy—in-feeling. Sometimes we can, with lightning speed, be stirred to the firm illusion that we are now projecting ourselves into the shoes of another individual. True artists reach us this way.

At any rate, without empathy, that subconscious in-feeling, no architect-planner (who is an artist, too) can produce anything but a stillborn environment for his clients, however logically and carefully worked out and consistently constructed.

Without such in-feeling the listener or reader can hardly partake in the mneme, the collective, baked-together memories of another human being, who inevitably must tell of them in the outwardly rather disordered way that life is really lived. Empathy must be hoped for, cherished.

Whatever may follow in words is by no means a preconceived composition. Strung-together fragments depict, often vaguely, a life that to start with was not a willful composition. Yet it must have some organic consistency and some semblance to the lives of others, who thus can share its feeling. It has its peculiar linkage and unity over time, and over all the spaces and spots on earth where it plays.

All those varied constellations under which we live determine the individual life, and so that life is really inseparable from them. The "individual" himself is truly not divisible, and the very word stems from this insight. Yet he has no sharp barriers around him, but rather permeable membranes. He keeps absorbing through them. He has no existence in a vacuum or apart from an outer world; he is no lonely lamp post in empty darkness. The "myself" and the "yourself" fuse into one by mutual stimulation and, again, by working—yourself, myself—out to the fullest in this interplay.

Our life counts largely thanks to others. A full-fledged self-account would be the story of an individual, as everything life-descriptive is. But what the story tells is not of the individual as an independent. On the contrary, it brings before us the individual in his enmeshment—the individual as he is born into a context, influenced by it, effective in it only by prodigious give and take.

I have truly loved a host of very diversified people, have felt myself into them, and am given to an easy glow and flow of sympathy. I believe I have not been a picturesquely rebellious individual versus the group, or versus the world; on the contrary, I have rather enjoyed it and my indebtedness, my linkage, and my own gratitude. I not only find fairness and justice in it, but also delight and self-satisfaction that I have retained clear memory and an emotional afterglow from so many who have been so close, who have acted on me and for my inner growing up.

How many others—some dead, some still alive, some older, some younger—should rightly be credited as coworkers, or as having aided from start to finish by being wonderful catalysts and stimulators! There are a thousand "I-owe-yous." Giving names here would not be enough.

And it is not only the known names, it is the anonymous humans who often have helped immeasurably. The gifted collaborator, the expert technical adviser, deserve grateful credit; but also a young child smiling nearby may brighten the darkness, exhilarate the atmosphere in which one breathes, can create—or must stop creating. That atmosphere may most simply have become polluted and unbreathable by tedious trouble in the house, if not by tragedy.

The upshoot of anything biographical is, like a well-designed home, the vivid affirmation of biological individuality. It may be and must be an appraisal of the individual; yet, to say it again, never one in a void. The individual, and his story, lies embedded within a "biological assembly," but the "single and its singularity" shall not be lost in the shuffle of inorganic mass transactions. Especially in our time, this needs watching. *That seemingly narrow, short-lived individual has been spotted by science to have a momentous, even an ominous bearing on the continuous life of the big broad race.* And life, in the singular and the plural, must prevail if our short-lived "plans" should be even worth pondering and rendering. It surely *starts* in the singular and rather "unplanned," hardly ever wholesale.

The very beginnings of an individual in the mother body, those first nine months, have already a good deal of concealed but budding "specificity" and impenetrable linkage as well. Then, after the shock of being born, not into a wonderful natural nest, but into a man-made cradle, an artificial apartment and town, the fantastic receptivity of the impressionable young goes on. It is now linkage on a new plane. The daily experiences, and, later, if we strike out into the world, the more exotic ones, and, still later, the characteristic beginnings of a practice within that individual mission of ours—all become in turn "formative" to ourselves.

And finally it becomes formative again, and decisive, how such a mission, tiny or tall as it may be, is received by all those others who are exposed to it. They may or may not grant it fine or far-reaching validity. They may approve and applaud, or they may break the missionary's heart by sustained indifference. They do not need actually to crucify him.

An individual is by no means strong simply through independence. One should not say "free as a bird," because a bird is not free. Even a migratory bird, en route from Easter Island to Alaska, must not deviate. It is risky to be alone and out of bounds. A mile off his course, and that bird is dead. A human being, who can crisscross the map and seek out his companions, would seem much freer than a bird. That it so seems is part of our essential make-up. But our choices, anticipations, and plans are all really in proportion to *our vitality, which grants us context with beings and things.* We are strong by that linkage when it is most rich. We are vital by the force of this mutuality with others. When we are sickly and weakened, this grand gift withers and we are lonely; plans get short, they wane. And when we are dead, it's gone. That lively influencing of others, and of the future, and the capacity of being influenced by it all, have stopped and are still.

Age may close our portals one by one, and death closes them all. But a *living* soul has millions of portals; they festively stay open much throughout a lifetime.

EDITOR'S NOTE: The following series of brief sketches, fast from eye to hand, are a small selection from Mr. Neutra's beholding the world. They go back more than a century; mostly noted down by him on professional journeys, never as a tourist. They touch on what he relates in the essay on his two unequal eyes, which have meant so much in his life. (See pages 73-84.)

Hand Sketches

Glimpses into a Manifold World

LIVING THROUGH THE EYE does not mean that one is wholly "eye." A full soul collaborates. Trees—buildings—humans—animals—global scenery—drawn during a half-century.

Self-portrait, 1917.

Church spires and bells together remembered. The soul has many portals.
Tournay

Eternal Acropolis, over the cemetery of us short-lived ones. *Athens*

Spanish bullfight plaza with crucifix in the background. Noise, cruelty, and skill, and then again stillness and piety. *Chinchon.*

Quietly the river Tagus winds its way deep below sword-proud Toledo.

City of lagoons. Man's work static and enduring between water and clouds. *Venice*

Christmas snow many years ago—long thawed but not forgotten. *Austria*

North Nigerian desert city gate: from an outer into an interior world.

From the water pit, loam for a city. *South Sahara*

Winter-dry bush in deep snow.

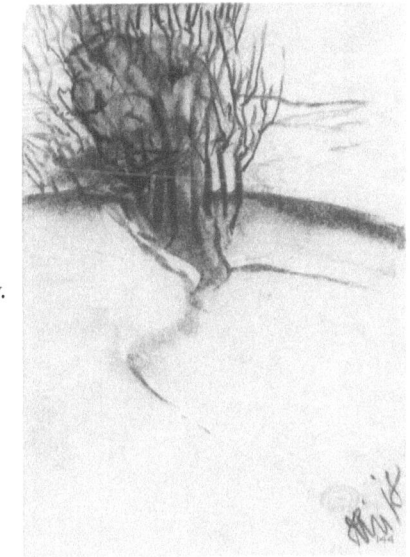

A ceiba tree looms above the Congo River.

Sunny slope in the Arctic. Will the northwest territory in this century be atom heated and teeming, perhaps?

Wind-shaded monastery court. *Lima*.

The Columbian Cartagena, once alert, now dreamy, peaceful

Two styles in religious fusion. The soul must compromise. *Ghent*

Mexican tramp before a modern mural. Amazement in humility.

Space and time measured more directly and intimately in dance than by measuring sticks and ticking clocks. *Sevilla*

An empire dedicated to heaven was at home in Vienna and Flanders, and expanded from Madrid to Manila. *Malines*

Human bodies drawn before the First World War;
much aged since. *Vienna*

Dione Neutra, musician, bride four decades ago, 1923.

Neutra's battle horse Tilly, saddled in 1914. *Montenegro*

Bourgeois houses in black Haiti, post-Napolionic era. *Tout comme chez nous.*

Canadian girl skiers rest after strenuous sport. *Alberta*

A universal faith such as Buddhism takes on different color from landscape to landscape. *Rangoon and Bangkok*

All around the globe, ceremonies at frontiers; yet separation is a sham. *Ahmedabad*

Anatolia, long drowsy, will wake again.

Mother and child before the ancestral shrine. Unending dependency through generations. *Ise*

Black sails before Shanghai.

Decay and growth—*anywhere*.

Battle becomes play. *Oaxaca*

Ancient but ever-green is nature. *Palomar*

Early Influences

From Floor to Clouds

WHERE could a child, some seventy years ago, learn to love a new sort of world, with warm, jointless floors, resilient, not too hard for a lightly dressed baby to sit on; with a free, clear, wide opening to look out on lovely grounds, water, trees—a world with all those things which I have later tried to put into what now seems a "contemporary feel"? In a way it was not new, but *always* good, even humanly needed. And, in fragments if not as a whole, some of it has existed—on the neat, tamped dobe-dung-mixed floors of a Nigerian or Zulu roundhouse, or in an open-front riverside hut in Malay or Thailand. But, how possibly did I, in a big city of tenements like Vienna, conceive of homes nature-bound, or a greenery shield against noisy, grimy, humdrum traffic; of houses where even small interiors hanging onto the mother landscape outside could offer living space for human beings, no longer cluttered or crowded out by their own bulky furniture and by pretentious, monumental trappings and curliques? How could a Victorian youngster later come to imagine a middle-class home brought down to bright harmonic essentials, uncomplicated to run, self-serviced by the family—without the ever more questionable institution of maids, imported into the household and, even then, ever changing after a week's notice before bewildered children's minds. For the very young, the family boat was rocked by every such strange newcomer. To a child, each new maid meant a new age in history.

Ever since, I have hung onto human beings close to me. The designed setting can badly interfere with that.

On the other hand, the waters were still, as for a sampan on the Pearl River. Houseboats, as their occupants, stay where they are, change very slowly. Grownups then had no "House Magnificent" magazines to get excited about, or Sunday "Home" supplements which they could drop on the floor so a little boy could study the pictures even if he could not read the suggestions in each issue about "seven new ways to arrange the furniture in front of the fireplace." There were no "new ways"—at least as far as I knew.

What started a feeling and thinking for my sort of career of trying to rearrange human setting must have been simply my old-fashioned surroundings themselves, without any television set to look into distance and into confused variety. Uneasy boredom and dull dislike were the only, the earliest, and probably the best guides toward a renewed, fresher world to long for and to develop ideas about. Quietly getting sick and tired of something is itself a stimulus.

For many people, childhood attachments begin early to color their memory of the physical place in which they grew up. Through human attachment, it becomes somehow an exemplary precedent for a whole life, hard to get rid of. I was, perhaps fortunately, able sometimes to fuse all these things traced into me, but, if need be, also to separate them. My parents, my sister, my older brothers, were good to me. I loved them, but that did not blind me or keep me from wondering about the tenement building in which we lived and the rather stale street upon which it stood. Thank heavens all these must somehow have developed my urge for a better human habitat, warmer, also wider, than the four walls.

Anything that is designed—a store counter over which a youngster tries to peep when he comes into a shop with his mother, a stair rail, an elevator cage with a miracle ceiling to gaze at for silent seconds of ascent—is remembered by him, and all becomes great experience and truly formative, especially in the plastic stage of infancy. Unsuspectingly, children's minds are molded by a million items in close sense-range. And most of these things, I am afraid, we have been putting there unwittingly.

The manifold life-encompassing feelings and trains of thought which later might help a man to become a compassionate and sensitively understanding architect of happiness are not to be learned in a few university courses. Learning comes much earlier, without talk, and seeps in much deeper. It starts when a baby is lifted up out of a cradle, changed to dry, warm diapers, and when its lips close to suck sweet mother's milk. Certainly one learns a lot before one gets up on one's legs and toddles through a room. And then it goes on and on. . . .

I remember the room I lived in when I was little. My mother did not especially introduce me into the routine of how to make a room in the morning, but I got interested. Many a day I intently watched the procedure of sweeping with a horsehair brush over ill-jointed parquetry flooring around me. Several "imitation" rugs and one "genuine Persian" were taken up. On occasions of special cleaning I heard these rugs being loudly pounded on the rack in the inner court, lower down. It was a four-story building we lived in, and our apartment was one widely winding, cold stairflight above the street floor. The windings and the cold draft are still with me in some dreams. What happens to one, *in* one, and around one while ascending a stair—and what of it sticks with us as a strangely lasting memory—is to me a master specimen for what architectural experience means. It's way beyond all that photography or motion pictures can convey.

When I was four, I thought I could see that the colors of the Persian rug seemed refreshed when they came back from the pounding in the yard. It must have been even earlier that I spent a great deal of my life directly grounded, baby fashion—"floored," often enough, but mostly just mildly amazed. I became a curious connoisseur of floors and flooring before I had any words to comment or met any of the many tract home floor-footage wizards and flooring salesmen who later in my life have come to educate me with their revenue computations and sample books. I remember to this day that we start our life with floor space. Also I recall our parquetry composed of a repetitive angular pattern of rosette-stars, both of yellowish-oak and purplish-brownish beech. I "studied" it all. My weak thumbnails, I found, did not penetrate those hardwoods, but were well capable of scraping off the dried-up wax film roughly polished on there months ago.

Then, of course, there was the interesting network pattern of flooring *joints*, the squarish and the diagonally throughgoing ones; some of them were wide open, or better, they were filled with a dry substance of dark but indefinite coloration. I tested this plastic material, plowing it out, and I used its yielding consistency a little later by squeezing paper-cut figures and seafaring boats into these cracks. I also made and footed in them diminutive architectural compositions and houses—whole villages of them. The parquetry network gave restrictive geometry and a grid, as do the streets decreed by a town-planning office. This rigidity troubled me in my incipient city plans, and I would have loved more freedom.

The material accumulated in the floor joints followed no rule; it was accidental and packed densely. In contrast, the rolls and balls of brownish-grayish fibrous dust fabrics which appeared, seemingly out of nowhere, during sweeping, were a little unearthly, unreal, lovely, like dandelion seed balls. Nevertheless, they were always more or less attached to the floorward ends of the broom hair. I was curious. The floor remained a big world to explore. The grownups tramped about, but I saw only big, shiny—sometimes dusty—shoes, or sometimes even ridiculously oversized bare feet. They lived on another level, high up above Lilliput.

Out of old habit sliding on my buttocks, even though I was already a toddler, I moved around while the women swept. Once or twice I applied the baby's tongue test to the floor-joint stuff. The taste was indifferent, unengaging. Grownups did not want me to try it. "Dirty, dirty," they said, showing me an ugly face. But bacteriologists are more like babies; they go into even more curious examinations of it all.

I was glad when the servant girl opened half a side of the double windows, because I did not like the smell of perspiration which accompanied sweeping and bending over the rug, to pull it here to the chest of drawers and there under the heavy upholstered armchair. My mother called it *fauteuil*. Later I learned that this was a French word. She herself, from her expression, did not seem to enjoy the cleaning at all. I must have got then the idea that housework is always with us, but is not a pleasure.

I don't know how often in fact there were scenes like this, how often I observed, but sometimes a split second of exposure suffices to set up echoes in the human brain for a lifetime.

While the maid rested, looking bored and bracing herself on the broom handle, I would sit on the lengthy cushion which had fallen from the window seat. It was snakelike, long and narrow, and fitted between the exterior and interior sash. In a way it interested me greatly. The whole jamb and window sill were, I recall, bristling with rebates and grooved details to keep the dreaded draft and rainwater out. But in addition to all those male carpentry tricks, there was the local feminine ritual of placing the white-linen-cased "window cushions" on the sill at the bottom of the intersash space. I took it all in at face value, as *forms*—puzzling or pleasing forms. That was all. I did not worry about functions then; such thoughts come much later, when the brain itself gets to function more intricately, with an emphasis on its frontal end, I guess. The window cushions, together with knitted glass curtains, supplemented by parapet drapes, which my mother, using another French word, called "lambrequins," were female touches added to the defense against the Viennese winter, and made an "ensemble." My mother, I gathered from the way she acted, was proud of it; it was "pretty" or "beautiful," she sometimes said. Here I heard that word for the first time—in my architect's life.

If the sashes were both swung in, one could lay the cushion on the rebated stool, place one's elbows comfortably on the cushion, one's head on one's hands, and look slantingly down to the corner of our borough's main artery. When the muffling snow was gone from the hard loud cobblestones, the varied sounds of heavy traffic incessantly rose; but I enjoyed that. Having the windows open meant that winter was over.

Our white terrier bitch, Hexl, often joined me at the window sill, and I teased her while she was trying to spot other dogs, busy with their noses or raising a hind leg, down at the gas-lantern post at the street corner. Hexl and I *liked windows*, and I have liked them ever since. But my inarticulate musings returned often to the puzzling details of these complicated, in-swinging French sashes at my side. Their glass was wavy, I noticed, and the fascinating brass hardware was movable, but it worked so stiffly that I could not operate it with my feeble three- or four-year-old muscles. I began hating things which were hard to operate. They troubled my inside feelings of the world outside.

Against the sharp corners of the window frames I had several times knocked my forehead, and it was awfully painful. I hate to think of it. My grandmother, Regina Glaser, who was seventy at the time, would take a tableknife and press the cool blade on the swelling, even if the skin was a little broken and a bit of blood was seeping out. I would look at myself in the mirror afterward, when the injured spot was turning purplish-blue. I began to like mirrors almost as much as did Louis XIV, who, I later learned, had built a mirror gallery. The mirrors made the space so wide that I forgot to look at myself. I loved them almost as much as windows. They were both a blessing in a small world, as our apartment was, to my eyes hungry for space.

I sat at my favored window and watched and listened. I heard the hooves of Percheron-like horses that slipped and clattered on the use-polished cobblestone pavement, raising a mixture of harmful granite dust and smelly powdered horse manure, as they pulled mammoth wooden trough-shaped coal trucks from the northwest depot to town. There was a double tram track, too, and every so often the trolley came from one side or the other, its belled horse trotting melodiously. Here was pleasure, as in watching the less periodical, the accidental, clouds or, through the glass when the double window was closed, the confused swirl of snowflakes, darkly silhouetted against the sky, and, when they came down, suddenly white as white can be in front of the building across the street. In all weathers were not windows and glass wonderful for a little boy in an apartment?

My neighborhood was not really one for getting much fun out of living, even if I leaned out of my hole in the wall as much as I dared. Down there were a few older boys playing in leftover puddles. But looking at other boys was not really much for myself.

The consumers' organization for employees of the Northwest Railways had a three-story building just opposite our own. The edifice was not old, not really new; it was yellowish, with a studied slight increase of gracile Victorian Renaissance ornament at window frames in the second story when you compared it with the first, and in the third story when you compared it with the second. I did the comparing a hundred times. I often scrutinized and pondered this subtlety of difference and upward progression in studied loveliness. Nondescript acanthus brackets supported an all-stucco dentil cornice at the top. I know now it was all awful, as Renaissance goes, or from any other angle. But then I knew no originals to doubt weak imitation. I was in a state of bliss and ignorance.

The young woman from the country, recently urbanized as our maid, got so bored by making the room that once, after having looked in a little round pocket mirror at her nose or gums, she for some reason or other did not slip the pink celluloid-backed reflector into her apron pocket again before giving me a diverting demonstration. She caught a few sun rays on the shiny surface and threw them back into the *Konsum's* otherwise shaded office windows. Like magic, the beams penetrated into the darkness behind the distant glass, lighting up some papers and an inkstand on a desk. The "official"—so I had heard the clerk titled—looked at us through his spectacles, raised his bald head, and angrily opened his window. Meanwhile our maid had closed ours, and we seemed to be ignoring his shaken fist. That was funny. Otherwise life was rather tiresome for a little boy—no playground or companions, no common activities, only loneliness. The situation made one become a philosophical observer of practically nothing. Maybe this was a benefit, too. Roots suck sustenance from unlikely sources. Now I like playgrounds for kids—probably because I had none handy.

The girl would usually leave the window ajar, opening it again from time to time to shake the rugs or dustcloth out over the sidewalk below. She would wipe polished furniture, plain surfaces of chest and table, curved and carved chair legs, rattan woven seats and backs of chairs, the conical glass shade of the cast-bronze kerosene lamp which, from the ceiling center, could be lowered and raised again by means of a shot-filled ball serving as a counterweight. Lots and lots of things to do. I would watch her until she had gone through all operations, quickly wiping the clear glass funnel of the lamp, suddenly noticing and catching with the broom a leftover spider web in one corner of the ceiling and finally applying the water vapors of her lungs to the brass door handle and escutcheon to shine them up. I loved the shining brass knobs of the lower cupboard doors, and tasted and licked them, too, because they were so appetizingly perfect and smooth.

No particular daily treatment was given to the wall, which a decorator re-covered with a new wallpaper when I was about six. He had introduced an exciting new color, blue-green, and new formal style into my life. The paper showed a sort of natural-size skeletonized horse-chestnut leaf; but I also have kept the earlier wallpaper clearly before my inner eye. It represents a pristine period of my life, but I could not describe in words its rhombic repeat pattern of white spot clusters on a steel-blue background. I still see the dark bespectacled head of my grandmother in front of it.

The furniture of the room consisted of a black fabrikoid-covered—visible tacking—sofa with stiff three-arched back, upholstered end rolls, and a pull-out drawer with a mattress in it, on which I slept at night. My older sister used the upper level. There was an oval walnut table with carved legs ending, at my close sight, in floor claws like those of a tiger in one of my picture books; a buffet, or credenza, as I was taught to call it, with two round-paneled walnut doors; in its lower section were drawers in which I kept my toys, and way above, two open shelves with knicknacks, and a pyramidically curved-up back to crown it all. Superb industrial products, bentwood Thonet chairs with rattan seats and backs, were later replaced, when I had kneeled them through, by entirely worthless models of current art design.

The room stove of white glazed Swedish tile stood catty-cornered, slender and door high. It carried on its top a life-size, equally snow-white bust of Ludwig van Beethoven. As at the end of his Ninth Symphony, Beethoven almost raised the roof, although, I judge, it—or the ceiling, I mean—must have been almost ten feet high. I studied and cherished his broad, sulking face. He was silent; you could only guess at the music my mother said he had made.

Finally, there was a rather dark grand piano, under which

I loved to lie on my stomach, wetting with saliva some old wrinkled kid gloves and stretching and smoothing them into their original shape. Here in this shelter, a quiet studio of my own, I developed an everlasting flair for perfection and endlessly perfecting a process. It was my first use of a piano.

Altogether, what kind of a room was it? Let me see. Three doors, two windows, with a worthless three-foot masonry pier between them, that catty-cornered white stove in which was kindled a little coal fire under the great composer; behind it was a dark, uncanny, inaccessible, uncontrollable space which frightened me in the evening darkness, and of which I still dream sometimes. There were a buffet; a center table with chairs and many, many chair legs around me, all waiting for the skirts of aunts and the trouser legs of uncles to keep them company when they came to visit my grandmother for supper.

The only possibly usable pieces were the sofa, on the end of which one could kneel with elbows on the window cushion, and that really grand piano, under whose belly there was a homelike cave, a "club," the very best place of all.

Otherwise, the tall walls and towering furniture—huge, immovable, oppressive—were given to me by fate, like prehistoric fossils towering around the crib of the human race.

It was good to get that young fox terrier she-dog as a companion in the lower stratum of the room. The grownups kept on living above table and piano height. With stretched arms they would probably, I thought, reach Beethoven's chin. At any rate, they easily lit the high-up kerosene lamp with a match. But under the piano it remained dim and cosy. I did love that place!

Careers may be started by early love for one sort of thing and disgust with another. These things I think of here were part of a powerful eternal constellation which, by a thousand imaginary levers and distant controls, have maneuvered the life of the person I was to become.

Parents and Siblings

To a babe, mother and all human beings are first just part of the surroundings. But soon they become specific, different from the wallpaper. They smile back, and we smile back again: in-feeling is a success. Empathy. We are not alone.

I was fortunate to be the youngest child of a happy marriage. My father and mother loved me, but not with a perilous, intense exclusiveness. I was not a first or single experience to them, although a little bit the "Joseph" (and this is actually my middle name, too). I had no dreams of sun, moon, and stars bowing before me, did not incense my brothers by telling such dreams, and was not sold into slavery.

It was some seventy years ago, in 1892, that good fairies surrounded my cradle. I have an inkling of it only now, rather late in the game. The luckiest thing, perhaps, was those older brothers and sister, and the non-neurotic, steady calmness of mature, good-looking, everywhere honored (as far as I could see) parents.

My father was the son of a physician, William Neutra, who died of typhoid when serving about the time of the Crimean War. Thus my father, to start his working life, was sent by his widowed mother to be an apprentice to a simple craftsman who made cowbells. When I was a little boy on his knee, he told me that the discriminating herdsmen who were the customers wanted the bells of the different lead cows to sound together harmoniously. The pitch and clarity of each bell was the outcome not only of its shape and size, but also of a little wizardry in alloying the metal before casting. *I pondered how sound would go with shape, color, weight—be linked with it all.* The wide, lovely world is so intimately fused, for us especially. I am still pondering!

Later my father walked down the gangplank of a Danube river-steamer and showed his journeyman's book to the Vienna Guild Office. He became employed in the big Austrian locomotive factory of Wiener Neustadt, and was soon absorbed in the early labor movement. Workers' adult-education courses made him a student after hours, and even a trustee of the informal school. Still later, he and a former colleague owned their own casting and turning shop, producing brass and bronze parts for the city's gas and water meters. As a little boy I felt happy visiting among their twenty-odd workers; my father treated them all like colleagues, and they adored him, from the apprentice boys to the old men.

When I knew him best—it was in the last third of his life—people said he looked like an apostle, with a much nobler shape of skull and nose, forehead, hand and foot, fingers, fingernails, and toes than I can boast. In his way he was as good-looking as my red-cheeked, doe-brown-eyed, black-haired mother, Elizabeth Glaser—everybody called her Betty—who, after my birth, suddenly appeared much younger and healthier than fifteen years earlier, when she had borne her first baby son. I remember that a salesman in a store—I was four at the time—told my mother, patting my then still-blondish head, how surprised he was that, young as she looked, she already had such a big boy. She laughed, admitting that she had three other, almost grown-up offspring, six to fifteen years my elders. But the salesman was not lying; she really looked young enough for his flattery.

My parents told me stories, each in his own way, and my mother read to me. I heard a little of *Uncle Tom's Cabin*, not dreaming that in time I would follow the footsteps of slavery from Senegal to Charleston, or worry for three years while building the Lincoln memorial museum on the Gettysburg battlefield. I listened to a great deal of Jules Verne, about underground and undersea travel, five weeks in a balloon over blackest unexplored Africa, and much later have seen myself Mount Kilimanjaro and the wake of our boat on the Congo. I learned of the battle to see the North Pole, and sixty years later got sick in Greenland between flights through the polar night. What I liked best was the wistful story of men letting themselves be shot to the moon, probably not to be heard of nor seen again. I did not weep, but I was awed by the great human brain—the sharp, calculating upper brain backed by the emotional middle brain—a combination which would drive men off the earth into the awfully magnetic unknown—the infinite. I always remember that the same writer's sequel, following those men *around* the moon and back down to earth, was a letdown.

But from the earliest memories, half subconscious and half conscious, the greatest influence was that of my older brothers. They were living in quarters which were highly respected by my unerudite parents. Their study bedroom was equipped with "*the* bookcase," a globe standing on it, and more books on a board; on the opposite wall were small white plaster busts of Mozart and Beethoven, again, as well as bronze-plated busts of Goethe and Schiller. I was not allowed to enter that room, but I liked to peep in whenever one leaf of the tall blond double door with its brass hardware and handles was left standing open. Without marble magnificence or curving stairway, this "big boys' room" was awe-inspiring; perhaps no one has ever been so awed by the Bibliotheca Laurentiana, as a place of study and a storehouse of the wisdom of the ages. Even a "lexicon," or world encyclopedia in many volumes, was in the glass-doored bookcase. I was told it held everything there was to be known in the world.

One of my brothers was studying mechanical engineering. Sometimes he would sing a miners' song, a chorus of the men who labored in the depths of the pit, ready to die far underground, where an endless technical pursuit had led them. Always the tears welled up in my eyes when my brother Siegfried sang this song, or even when he only whistled it—and he was a most admirable whistler. I was enthusiastic and sad about the miners. I identified them with all engineers and technical men, who represented to me man himself, with his restless brain of selfless nature-driven propulsion—like those Americans and the one Frenchman who let themselves be shot to the moon.

Siegfried was my idol, and, unobserved, I would listen to

every word he spoke to his schoolfellows. His best friends at the Vienna Tech were impressively sane and calm. To me, they all seemed ripe men. Capek, a Czech, talked with a sweet singsong accent. It is the foreign inflection I can remember as if I had listened to it a minute ago. From him I heard for the first time, and with emphasis, the names Frederick Nietzsche and Zarathustra. Taussig—they always called each other by their family names—had a steep tall head and was a well-balanced engineer; later he served as technical director for large concerns from Prague to Sidney.

Listening was a favorite pastime, and when disputes among my brother and his friends sounded through the study door, I would catch phrases and words—misunderstanding plenty.

When I was four, Siegfried would show off my ability to draw correctly a longitudinal section of a locomotive and graphically illustrate my explanation of a steam cylinder's plunger action, a daring mechanism; or he would boast that I could sketch all details of a steam whistle or bicycle transmission. While I drew scores of bicycles and locomotives on the blackboard, the idea of a *perpetuum mobile* machine suddenly hit me. I was wistful and awed at the consequences my invention would have for mankind. I was not exuberant, but humbly aware that I had a mission. I also invented track crossings, until my brother explained that these had long been known and in use. I invented things anyway, even though I had been preceded by Leonardo.

Everyone assumed that I would become an engineer. With a slight flutter of my heart, I looked at the old building adjacent to the Karlskirche, where I would study when I was big. In front of the entrance to the park stood a monument to Ressel, the great Austrian who had invented the ship propeller. Much later, when I actually was studying in that sour-smelling old building, contemporary to the Ecole Polytechnique of Napoleon I in Paris, another, much whiter, hero in stone was set on a pedestal—Johannes Brahms, sculpted by Helmer.

Wrapped in thought, the composer looked across the park toward the Imperial and Royal Music Conservatory and the Musikvereinssaal, where his symphonies had been premiered. Some critics had been fair to them, mostly to annoy Richard Wagner. Very early, I heard grownups talk about the clash of geniuses and the sufferings they were subjected to by the molders of public opinion.

My brother Siegfried, like my eldest brother, William, played the violin with gusto. They participated regularly in a friendly quartet, and mingled with Arnold Schönberg and his pupils. Like many Viennese homes, music belonged in our house. Listening to Haydn, Mozart, Beethoven, and Shubert was second nature to me, and I knew where to find their statues in the city. As a little boy, I would be slipped illicitly, without a ticket, into my parents' box when the "Friends of Music" Orchestra, in which my eldest brother played first violin, gave a concert in a beautiful hall of the city. Grinning, he would announce to little me: "We have Bach-Händel this evening," which, in Viennese, also means, or sounds like, "baked chicken."

William's influence upon me was entirely different from Siegfried's. A medical student, he often smelled of carbolic acid. He operated a terrifically valuable microscope, and had a large flat black case in which he placed scores of histological and pathological slides, some bloody, some pale, some colored to show up better when magnified. He also had vertebrae and other human bones lying around. I wondered where the rest of the people might be whose stray bones had been taken away from their total assemblage.

William became a passionate bicyclist and joined the Wienerwald Bicycling Club, proudly sporting a special pepper-and-salt outfit. It was called, in a strange English expression, "The Dress." He seemed particularly impressive at bicycle parades in the Prater, when the Wienerwald, wearing bulging gray knickers, followed the more famous Touring Club, with its deep-blue costumes. William, I noticed as I grew older, was also very impressive to girls, whether they bicycled or danced or just looked at him. He was so good-looking himself, with his little blond mustache, and so smart in all ways, that Siegfried, admiring and imitating him, developed quite an inferiority complex.

Ever since these early days, I have loved to listen to the discussions of educated men and elders and obvious experts. Ever since I have loved to listen to trios and quartets, and watch the fast understanding glances exchanged by the players. Ever since I have admired craftsmanship, whether it is in musical teamwork or in dialectic and constructive argument.

My two brothers' studying engineering and medicine and relaxing by playing orchestra and chamber music have linked professional and musical pursuits in my mind, as if they have a common denominator in artistic craftsmanship. William's *Ars Medica*, for example, and music as a classical art, both became enjoyable pursuits, although I preferred listening to my sister's piano lessons rather than having some myself. I would assume some crazy gymnastic posture in an easy chair, my legs up its back, when Mme. Leopold or Miss Hoenig, the first of a series of piano teachers, played at four hands with my sister, Josephine, and I would fall sweetly asleep. I may have been four or five.

Subsequently I studied piano for five years with fairly horrible languishing women teachers. My father could not play any instrument and had no educated taste, but ever since tuning cowbells in his youth, he had a fine ear, and he honored classical music. Both my parents seemed to take musical education as a natural requirement, although they had no such feeling about painting and literature. My father once worked his way through *The Count of Monte Cristo*, but after that he never read anything except the daily paper.

No one in the family had much knowledge of architecture,

although my older brothers were at least familiar with names and styles. On one occasion I overheard them debating whether our city hall was Romanesque or Gothic; finally the huge Meier Lexicon, which I have already mentioned as the treasure of the "boys' bookcase," was consulted.

"You see, I told you so, it *is* a Gothic building. It has pointed arches," said William or Siegfried—I do not remember which of the two won the wager.

This was the first time that I became *conscious* of architecture and of "style," at least as a topic of conversation. First I had learned about it, subconsciously, as a baby, sitting with a bare bottom on a splintery parquetry floor, digging dirt out of the cracks and licking the brass hardware of my toy cupboard. These, and my playing under the grand piano as well, had been preverbal experiences, but they were so deep as to deserve a most thorough analysis.

Can words ever define architectural experience, which operates on all senses at once—"stereognostically" and in our lowest association area, as well as in the higher ones—throughout our lives? It begins in the uterus and continues until we sink back onto our last pillow. Perhaps, as with love, which has so often been discussed, there is nothing really *to talk about*, nothing that can be grasped through words alone.

Putting things into words often requires us to pigeonhole our thoughts and emotions in a narrow, unnatural manner, separating them from all organic relationships. Similarly, ideas of architectural style which divide experience into "centuries" —into "dark" and "golden" ages—represent pigeonhole-ism of a very devastating kind.

Architecture, the man-made setting of life, has been an uncannily continuous problem to deal with ever since we came down from the trees.

We had no play space, really. My ancestors had come down from the trees, but I was an upstairs child, locked up high.

But at about ten o'clock my grandmother would amble with me to the Augarten, three or four blocks away. As a matter of fact, when I leaned out the window much farther than was good or than I was permitted, I could see the tall horse-chestnut trees way in the distance, behind a forbidding wall. Like the Viennese Prater, the Augarten had once been an imperial garden; its gates had been closed to everyone except the Habsburg family and their guests, who arrived in gilded carriages. But, a hundred years earlier, Joseph II, hero of the common man, had aroused the nobility by the vulgar act of opening these gardens to the people. For a hundred years thereafter serial pulp novels on Emperor Joseph's popular ways sold well. Our housemaid read to me from a story called, if I remember right, *Emperor Joseph and the Daughter of the Chauffeur*. Perhaps I am confusing it with a joke my brothers played on me, mixing up history. At any rate this tale could hardly have been based on fact, as Henry Ford was just then perfecting the automobile near a town called Detroit.

However, the profundities of life transcend literal realism. And the gates of the Augarten, through which my grandmother ushered me every morning except Sunday, were guarded against unreal dangers by unreal guardsmen, lame or blind veterans of the Austro-Prussian War of 1864.

Since these "invalids," as they were called, could not catch us youngsters when we drove our hoops onto the lawn, they would blow a shrill whistle to summon a policeman. The policeman, dressed in a simple black uniform, would soon show up sternly to remind our adult companions, such as my granny, of the rules governing the area between the tall geometrically trimmed hedges of the eighteenth-century park. Emperor Joseph II himself, in spite of his liberal enlightenment, wanted the populace to know its station.

This was my first experience of a neighborhood playground, and when I design one now—I am working on two such projects at present—I still respond to it. I recall the length of the walk from our home, and my anticipation as we approached the beloved tall trees behind the wall, and I compare the pebble-covered and lush grass areas underfoot—to play on or to kneel on to tie one's shoelaces—with what I design now. My memory has never grown too old for such tiny detail.

The entire plan of Vienna—the old medieval inner town around Stephansdom, St. Maria Above the Stairs, the Michaelerkirche, and that of the Minorite monks—is still in my blood when I talk of city planning. The baroque palaces, Karlskirche, and Peterskirche, and all those other witnesses to European grandeur which so impressed the first all-Russian czar to visit this capital, are in my blood, too, when I react to architecture and planning of the past. I love it, I may sketch it with a lusty pencil, but I always shrink from seeing it imitated: we live too late for that.

When I grew older, my sister's influence emerged. She painted; so I painted too—six years her junior as I was. When she and her girl friends began to giggle and moon after boys who looked like Greek youths, I wondered and watched. At twelve, I was already something of a mature but cautious counselor in love affairs. I was serene, so to speak, because in a pre-erotic-action period of life one can be as balanced as in a post-erotic-action period, if there really are such things. At any rate I was a steadying influence and chaperon to my impetuous, sometimes tempestuous sister, and I was anxious that she should not let those men go too far. Once I was present when my usually peaceful father decided to call her away from a moonlit lake beach in order to slap her face. I wondered, and he immediately wondered, and my mother wondered, whether he hadn't made a mistake by getting as drastic as that.

My seventeen-year-old sister was then in love with a geographer, physicist, and arctic explorer who was twenty years older than she. Dr. Q., good-looking in breeches, with his loose-jointed, sharp-witted talk, with his far-traveled knowledge of our good earth, made my brothers sound to me like beginners. He was but one of a long sequence of suitors—medical and engineering students, methodic sociologists and emotional nihilists, who were a little like the beatniks of half a century later. I came into all sorts of startling company as my sister's little companion. I remember how funny it was when I observed a young medical man trying to kiss her. He was not among the favored ones.

I began musing about love; with human beings it was so very amazing and long drawn out, because feelings were so much mixed up with thinking and talking about a lot of other things.

The German word for "sex" I heard only much later, and it is too flat-footed to help much where human brains are involved and play their fantastic complex role.

Later my sister was escorted by a Russian nihilist, Schvodransky, who wore a black shirt the way a peacock proudly displays his tail. He had heard *Tristan und Isolde*, orchestra score in hand, seventy-four times at the Imperial Opera in Vienna, fourth gallery, standing place. I have no idea why he still needed the score, the *partitur*. At 12:30 A.M., after the curtain had fallen on *Tristan*, he would walk with Josephine, my sister, into the Prater and other parks. I wondered, my parents wondered, my brothers wondered. But my family was now clever enough not to say a word, and nothing really happened. Schvodransky talked about God and the world in a somewhat vituperative, sneering way, exempting only *Tristan* from criticism. He looked at me with friendly condescension and wrote revolutionary plays, which he made Joseph Kainz, the great tragic actor, read. He became a young protégé in Kainz's house, and supported Kainz's widow at the funeral.

Thirty years later I saw Schvodransky again, in Hollywood this time. He had grown fat and no longer wore a black shirt.

"How is your sister?" he asked.

"Fine," I answered.

The next suitor of consequence was a young lawyer and economist, director of the labor school and a leader in the

Viennese workers' movement, which was quite different from anything now in existence. He was not good-looking, but he was very intelligent. His social consciousness spilled over onto my sister, who began to read Ferdinand Lassalle, the German socialist, and to attend courses. As a matter of fact, I remember being taken to a party celebrating Lassalle's birthday. The socialist congressman Dr. Friedrich Ellbogen stood under a red flag and eulogized the man around whom Friedrich Spielhagen had shaped his famous novel *Hammer und Amboss* (Hammer and Anvil). A century has passed since.

Siegfried, my second oldest brother, who was also a Wagner fan and operagoer, stayed at home for a while and then took a job with his friend Taussig in Prague at the great Ruston concern. I visited him with my parents and sister just before I came of school age. The railroad trip to Prague, the strange old city itself, the foreign language, the people—all were unforgettable. Young as I was, I tried to scribble a diary on the train; I could already write.

Half a year later, Siegfried returned, his health apparently broken, and suffered a hemorrhage of the lungs. This incident made a deep impression on me, and I should return to it later in a much broader context. I saw him recover, a little lonely, to follow his humane career. Never a ladies' man, he was liked by everyone, and displayed a good mind in discussion with educated people. Many years later, when I was fifteen, he bought me two books by the astrophysicist Svante Arrhenius, the Swedish Nobel Prizewinner, and with enthusiasm I rose early in the morning to read what often I could follow only by strictly applying myself, or not at all.

Meanwhile, my oldest brother William, whom I kept admiring for his good looks, had courted or had been courted by a woman painter (who laboriously portrayed me until, to her horror, my father suddenly had my hair practically shaved off by a horse-shear-armed barber), then by other girls, and even by a divorced woman in a red blouse. Finally, when I was eleven, he really fell in love with Louise Schmidl, and she with him. This was another stroke of luck which has reverberated throughout my life.

Louise was seventeen years old, the eldest of three girls in what looked like a completely bourgeois and rather wealthy family. I loved to see her with William; they made a good-looking couple. Sometimes I was permitted to accompany them when my rather bossy brother went with a heavy old-fashioned tripod on photography trips, hunting for "nature motifs" in the lowland woods of the Danube River or among the pine-tree hills and rocks of Vöslau-Gainfarn, where we regularly spent two and a half warm summer months. I surely learned something then about seeing the scene through a photo lens.

Louise proved to be anything but just middle class; indeed, she was a rare gem of a human being. She was womanly and motherly beyond her years, yet had a mind that could grasp higher mathematics and difficult original philosophical and science texts without appearing a bit bluestocking. While her youngest sister, Mimi, a year older than I, became my playmate and listener, and while I clearly saw the middle sister, Madeleine, a year younger than Louise, as the unusual beauty that she was, I definitely recognized a feminine ideal in Louise. My brother Siegfried, ever so often ailing, also loved her, and so did my parents. She simply became ours, though more specifically, of course, Willy's, under whose spiritual guidance she unfolded. I watched him and her, and felt with them.

When I was fifteen, Louise, like Siegfried, began to give me hard books to read: William Haeckel's *World's Riddles*; Schopenhauer, who became my favorite; Buechner, *Kraft und Stoff* (Power and Matter); Lange's *The History of Materialism*; or works by Wilhelm Ostwald, the German chemist, who had written something about the world as one grand phenomenon of "energetics."

I myself once heard with much awe Ostwald, a white-haired guest of honor from Germany—Leipzig, I believe—lecture at the Institute of Anatomy, and I began to frequent the university library. I decided to study chemistry, and Siegfried presented me with a book by Sir William Ramsey, whose writings led me to those of Sir Ernest Rutherford, also my brother's gift.

Eventually, Siegfried bought me Nietzsche—the complete works of Nietzsche! I am now startled that he had such an idea! I believe I began by reading *Birth of Tragedy* and went through all of it, reading all kinds of other things besides, and started regularly visiting the Burgtheater to admire Kainz and the old guard of classical actors. Shakespeare was played about twice a week.

A year after they were married, Louise and Willy had a baby girl. I would push the carriage over paths in the fields while I learned from a woman how to think. I felt that Louise's mind, while feminine and gentle, was also great. *Lange Haare-Kurzer Verstand* (Long hair, short mind), was a stupid current Teutonic proverb. I began to revere womanhood, and to be a little chivalrous.

I had very little self-consciousness. While my hair was as long as my black silk bow tie, which, I think, my sister had introduced on me, I was not aware of being a good-looking, bright boy. As to my erotic future, I was worried rather than attracted when I had to pass soliciting prostitutes on my way home nights, coming from the opera house or from meeting my cronies on the Praterstern for a walk in the park. I looked at these girls in wonder, almost with compassion. I never talked to my schoolfellows about it.

My friends then were Ludwig Neuman and Edmund Kalischer, who read Dickens; Felix Dahn; and the literary prodigy Robert Beer, whose taste ranged from Strindberg, Rimbaud, Dostoevski, Hofmannsthal, and lyrics from Anacreon and Sappho to Stefan George and Rainer Maria Rilke.

After the first two or three years in the humanist high school I turned into a student fairly pleasing to my teachers. Suddenly in the fifth year of the Gymnasium, I became Primus in mathematics as well as in history, and also did well in Latin, Greek, and physics. The combination was odd. My brother

Siegfried had the bother of helping me in literary composition. In this I was timid, and shrank back from speaking in public. I thought my brother was great at describing a walk through the autumn woods. In fact, he often roamed the Vienna countryside, lonely, without a girl, retracing the steps of Beethoven, whose every lodging he could point out in Heiligenstadt and Poetzleinsdorf, where the composer from the Rhine would spend his summer months in the vineyard hills. Going along with Siegfried was a treat, not always permitted. Through him, I began to love Vienna.

At this time my sister's final suitor entered my world. A wonderful man, he has meant immeasurably much to me ever since I was sixteen. Arpad Weixlgaertner was a high court official, an art historian of repute even then, director of the collection of arms and armor at the Imperial Museum, which is second only to that of the Prado. After heading the Albertina Graphic Collection, he changed to the famous department of small bronzes, with Benvenuto Cellini's saltcellar and other treasures which I learned to know. He also became custodian of the crown treasury of the former Holy Roman Empire, which is divided into two sections, secular and spiritual-religious. I had a chance to hold the crown of Charlemagne in my hands and to touch the spear which men of the Middle Ages thought had lacerated Christ on Golgotha. I remember the weight of these objects. Finally, Arpad was director of the gallery and the whole National Museum.

As I read this over, he has just died, almost ninety years of age, as a trusted authority in Sweden, honored by the king, in fact by all experts of historical art who know something of Dürer or Grünewald. I shall always love him; he gave me so much.

Arpad Weixlgaertner wrote several wonderful books, including his own strange family history. He was the natural son of a Hungarian count. The husband of an ailing countess, he never could marry the commoner by whom he had two children. Sometime after their birth he became mayor of

Budapest. Arpad's mother to me seemed wonderful. When I met her, she was a most dignified matron, trembling with palsy, but she could speak about her long-ago theatrical career in the loveliest Viennese. That she had had still another child by another man, a butterfly of an actor, we learned only from her bundled old letters, which Arpad read after her death.

My own beloved mother died at about the same time, after suffering for several years from a disastrous metastasis, at first a local carcinoma that later attacked her entire body. She was so very different from Arpad's mother, and not at all matronly.

I last saw my mother after a pain-filled night, under morphine, slumbering, as it seemed, with her face in the pillow, her still-black hair all spread out over the bed. When I came back from school that day, I found my father a broken man. She had not been sleeping; she had been dead for many hours. I thought life could hold no further fear for me; no worse loss was conceivable, all had turned drab and bleak.

But with Arpad, who was twenty years older than I, a new life began for me. An art-loving historian who could speak with a twinkle about the natural sciences and their monopoly on our age, he lived with original vitality and breadth. He enlarged my horizon by giving me a historical perspective of Austrian and European culture. He was familiar with all churches and monasteries, and had even met, often and intimately, and explained to me the character of, the heir apparent to the Habsburg throne, Francis Ferdinand, who only a few years later was to ride into the Sarajevo ambush that ended the Victorian age. Arpad understood the Austrian and Hungarian peasant as well as the thoroughbred aristocrats of the nations which made up that often-modified empire; he knew all the counts and noblemen, descendants of those who had been patrons of Beethoven and possessors of unique private art collections in their palaces in Vienna. He knew the city's liberal *bourgeoisie*, which vied with the cultural life and genuine aspirations of an old aristocracy. He knew the great men of our university, of the Imperial Opera, and the famous court theater which for a hundred years had overshadowed the best among the European stages, such as the Comédie Française and the Paris Opéra. At this time Vienna dominated the field of theater and musical culture; Berlin and even Moscow still seemed, to the Viennese, interesting upstarts. Arpad had known the composer Hugo Wolff before this genius was swallowed by an insane asylum, and he once took me along to Gustav Klimt's studio, where he and this bullish baldhead of an artist-hero talked on and on. Little could I or the two men guess that half a century later my town would confer the Gustav Klimt prize on that young fellow then standing by in silence.

The strange Hungarian name "Arpad" hardly fitted this arch Viennese, who belonged to a family of theater-lovers and artists. I preferred to call him Agathon, as his friends did. These men comprised a "Socratic circle"—"for the sake of the play," παιδιας χαριν as Socrates used to say—and greeted each other and signed their letters with that magic phrase. It was all very strange to me, having grown up in a family outside the humanistic tradition.

Not at all highbrow, Arpad flew kites like an overgrown boy, shot a Flaubert gun, threw a boomerang, and talked about life on the farms around Stoessing, his favored lovely alpine village which he knew inside and out. With his open-hearted love for my sister, he had no inhibitions whatever about kissing her ardently for a minute at a time while the janitor of our apartment—who had the beautiful name Heiland, "Saviour"—a candle in his hand, opened the door and waited patiently until it was over to let us in. It was an all around, most natural good-night kiss. My own family had been more bashful, but I learned not to blush when nature blessed a situation.

Being with an older friend who really knew classical, medieval, and Renaissance Italy, who could speak about Jacob Burckhard, the connoisseur of Hellas beyond all "classicism," about Theodor Mommsen, or Ranke, the historian of the

Popes, and so many, many other fascinating men and things, opened a new world to me.

Agathon was the great experience of my life after I was seventeen. My beloved Louise had turned blind under great pain and died of a brain tumor at twenty-six. It was a long agony, and my poor doctor brother had long known what was coming. I shall never forget the sight of him at the open grave.

William became a leading neurologist and psychiatrist, and years later he married again, this time an artist and an entirely different supplement to his nature. Siegfried turned into a prominent patent attorney, and dealt with and understood the soul of ingenious inventors; he should have written a book about it. He married a typical Viennese, a woman of great good humor. My brothers were very different from each other, but through character, vocation, and avocation, each was most exemplary to me. They are dead now, but I warmly remember them. The widows of both survive.

I owe more to all my family and in-laws than anyone I know. Perhaps, molded by this early benefit, my make-up brings me so close to other beings that I am indebted to them for happiness and wisdom, even if they seek my advice. And yet, while my life has come to grow in an intertwined fashion with the lives of others, I have had to oscillate on occasions between communion and abject loneliness.

Those who appreciate my work come often from far, from entirely different quarters. As to those nearby to me, our friendship is usually based on my empathy in their feelings and needs. Perhaps they cannot take the trouble to follow me when I become abstractly systematic, perhaps in what is the "frontal-lobe digestion" of my feelings. When I am lonely or hurt, I resort to pondering it on physiological terms. Physiologists tend to locate in the forward portion of the brain those nervous processes which take conscious form as conceptual thought, although naturally the brain, in the last analysis, will always operate as a whole.

It is easy to simplify formidable terminology once one has

everything mastered. But I am striving yet, and will never arrive in this short time allotted me. Even Einstein interpreted his grand theory later, though, also then, not very popularly. When he was originally at work, he had no time at all to do so, and was puzzling even to his brainy colleagues. But a practicing architect can never quite allow himself to be puzzling, and certainly not to those whose trust means creative work to him, his patients—I should say, patient-clients. Intellectual puzzlement must not harm the trust.

There is something strange about the spoken word which leads up to the long-lasting confidence that in turn leads to a building being born. That birth requires appeal to an audience. Whether or not people like or share a thought, they often respond to the attitude behind it, to the sound of the voice expressing it, and to the smile and the sincerity of the eye. They shrink away from raised eyebrows. No tape recording can quite make up for personal presence. Much in the uniquely human, creative relationship between the professional counselor and his client goes quite beyond words, and *both* parties actually advise each other, even though the greater training and experience enables one to take what he learns or has learned and fit it into a happy whole for the other.

The humans who surrounded me in my youth did not hurt or warp me; on the contrary, I have been happily conditioned to understand the feelings of others. This quality is exactly what an architect and planner of the good life needs if he is not merely a technician, but, by necessity and by passion, a coordinator of a multitude of man-born attitudes and actions. By desire, he is an artist of human interplay.

Designing our environment, which is the architect's task, requires more than a recipe for assembling physical items, or technical gadgetry. The architect must empathetically gauge a group, the potential impact on it and every individual within it, and of the present environment, as well as the potential surroundings of influence in an imagined and creatively conceived future. This can be ominous error and is more than social judgment; it requires a deep physiological knowledge and understanding to become of lasting aid.

Physician and Architect

My grandfather, William Neutra the elder, was a doctor. I never knew him except as looking down from a picture frame over my parents' bed. He had studied in Vienna, where the university had a great school of physicians. Perhaps grandfather's profession and the studies of my brother, Dr. William the younger, made me receptive to medical thinking. There is something strangely attractive to me in an art which is suffused with science. Too much these two have slowly become supposed opponents, but science is really only sporadically represented in medicine; it is not the whole story by any means.

As medicine is now being practiced, it is the domain of specialists. Some work in laboratories and many others collect colossal clinical statistics. To some Greeks and Arabs, medicine has been a combination of art and the science of sharp and collected observations rolled into one. But in the Asklepios temples another method advocated soul-searching diagnostic temple sleeps and group practice, preceding and preparing the path for the great night of self-diagnosis. The next morning a priest would interpret the *stimulated deep introspection*. These temples and other kinds of sanatoria, Old World research centers, which I visited more than sixty years later — traveling from Erzerum in Eastern Anatolia to the Kallinos Sanitarium at Hellenistic Pergamum and the Tiber Island health center — were impressive institutions which benefited from great physical and financial investment.

In contrast, Hippocrates took an oath to be good and make good by a simple stunning art. He was an enthusiastic observer and a practitioner of physiognomic diagnostic empathy, without any laboratories, which were then unknown, without the often swanky vacation hostelry or cuisine or ballet used by the more intricate and revenue-producing health resort. The singlehanded doctor is both applied scientist and artist. As the latter, he must appeal to the soul, so that hope carries people to him, ready to trust him with their life and future.

Such a situation, where profound confidence is justified, has greatly attracted me, and it influenced my attitude when I was about to select my life's work. At that time it seemed that a life of laboratory science might not be what I was born for. And yet, to me, art can never fully be removed from the curiosity of the scientist. As mentioned, such a separation has rather plagued our "age of science," but it was unknown in the Renaissance of Albrecht Dürer or Leon Battista Alberti.

An event which occurred in my youth and impressed me to no end may be related to indicate how applied science and the miraculous art of clinical intuition was demonstrated to me. It is strange that in the long run it helped to make me, not a physician, but an architect. Without fitting exactly into the mechanical chronology of a life story, it was one of the significant experiences that guided me early in this direction.

Impressive Clinician

My brother Siegfried was nineteen when, as I have related, he took his first job as a mechanical engineer in the distant city of Prague, in one of the leading machine-producing firms of Europe. He returned shortly before Christmas, after about a nine-month stay. We were appalled at his appearance—he was as pale as a corpse. That same night he had a hemorrhage. The volume of it is still quite clearly marked in my mind—I was perhaps six years old at the time—and I have retained the memory of that washbowl full of foaming blood. There was so much that it is hard to understand how the boy could have survived without any transfusion; but no such technique was known then. My oldest brother, William, a medical student, succeeded in approaching the most luminous star on Vienna's medical horizon—the internist Schrotter von Cristelli. Otherwise, it is doubtful whether this great man would ever have come to us—and he did so without even charging us for his visit. This professional largesse, of which Willy spoke before my young ears, impressed me profoundly and forever against any commercial attitude in professional performance.

We had to wait all Sunday morning for his arrival, expecting my brother's death any moment. Finally the appointed hour struck, and my parents, both half in tears and very much excited, stood at the window, watching the empty Sunday street, the cobblestones of which would resound from the trot of the horses bringing the carriage of the great physician. Suddenly my oldest brother said, "That is the carriage!"

A few minutes later Cristelli himself entered. He looked briefly, with a dry kindness, at my mother, nodded shortly toward my father, and addressed my brother as *Herr Kollege*, meaning that he treated young William as a fellow medico. He was shown the room in which my other brother, Siegfried, was lying, apparently in death agony. Bedside manners did not seem much in need here.

Cristelli entered empty-handed. There was neither diagnostic apparatus nor technicians, and no scientific paraphernalia. He was completely alone, dressed in striped trousers and a Prince Albert, and with his clipped, bristling white hair he gave the impression of an experienced man who knew what he was up to. He went inside and we remained outside.

We must have waited thirty to forty minutes. My brother William stayed with him, but I have never found out exactly what happened. The great doctor must have used his ear to auscultate Siegfried, who was clearly enough suffering from a hemorrhage of the lungs. But, with miraculous skill, he must have ascertained the scope and size of the lesion, small and out of proportion to the blood coughed out in streams. He employed physiognomic diagnostics, looking at the skin, looking at all the things the eye could possibly see, and supplementing this data by skillful auditory and tactile means, like a true primary clinician. He came out of the room, asked for a bowl, and I watched him wash his hands. As he was doing so, he glanced briefly at my mother, whose eyes were on that other terrible bowl with the blood, and said, "It's nothing to worry about. Looks worse than it is. Your boy is a bleeder. He's going to get out of it all right. With the lungs he has, he can live until seventy."

My brother died in a tuberculosis sanitarium just about fifty years later—six months before he was seventy. I have no idea what Dr. Cristelli's astonishingly accurate prognosis was based on. The performance was probably particularly impressive to me, never having seen such a great man before. It lives in me to this day because it was so truly extraordinary.

I tell this story to explain how impressed I became with clinical wisdom at that early a stage in my life. I had here almost personally met Hippocrates, the clinician who had pledged himself to unite observation and intuition for the good of humankind. To see *growth*, even in its deviations, in its swerving off into pathology, in its glory of self-help, and its possible losing battle against what man can do to mankind has colored my thinking ever after. It has colored my talking in earshot of my youngest son born almost half a century later, and innocently listening to my talk from childhood on. It seems he wants to carry this message, received by his father like a heart-moving revelation, to people when I am long dead.

Dr. Cristelli, who himself lacked today's resources for laboratory experimentation, has remained a consolation to me when, as an architect, I have little to fall back on except plain observation. Without instruments or tools, without technicians or laboratory supporting cast, a gallon of blood coughed up would have misled a lot of people—but not this man. He calmly comprehended and foretold.

An architect may also become a clinician of note—by finding in traces his own evidence, he may, and actually must, deliver the goods without the backing of a Rockefeller Foundation. His knowledge of human personalities and physiological processes, an empathic relationship with his clients and insight into their hidden depth, will enable him to make a more accurate architectural prediction for a life so hopefully and touchingly trusted into his hands. Thus he may be prophesying practically and preparing for a long and happier future. This requires more than a mere knowledge of wood, concrete, or vinyl tile.

I do not mean at all to imply that systematic research should be discarded or that its methods cannot possibly apply to architecture, in which an environment is designed for a long, forseeable biological situation—for man, woman, and child, and all their activities in the years of life to come. On the contrary, I am convinced that methodic and very detailed research is imperative. But I am also convinced that the intuitively gifted clinician—the medical artist as well as the one who deals with the biological individualities represented by clients of the "houser" of man—is often the best person to guide and introduce lines of experimentation to the researcher. The laboratory investigator needs the clinician's experience and opinion to indicate what lines of experimentation he should pursue, what to clarify by search.

Can the architectural profession take such a course from humble groping to influential systematics? Has any profession in a brief span of time been able to accomplish such a feat?

At the time Dr. Cristelli's performance engraved itself in my mind, it was quite customary for American doctors to come to Vienna for postgraduate study. They did this to gain prestige at home, for Vienna was acknowledged as the acropolis, or foremost city, of medical instruction and practice.

Those American students had no reputation for special gifts or fine preparation—in fact, my brother and his colleagues treated them rather condescendingly. The American medical profession had little standing before the year 1900; most European doctors seemed to be, or felt, superior.

But a truly amazing change took place within the next two generations, and at the present time the American Medical Association, as well as the College of Surgeons, is the recognized arbiter of medical matters in almost all parts of the globe. Officials building a hospital in Lima or Manila today will follow precisely all the rules of these medical organizations in North America, from numerical proportion of nurses to student nurses and interns, the size and number of patient beds, or what have you. Many countries offer no opposition whatever. Nobody would risk building a hospital which, if found "unqualified," would be unable to exchange personnel, and would find itself marooned with provincial talent only. A few attempts have been made to break this deadlock; in Buenos Aires, the new hospitals are deviating from the bondage of the American medical-supply industry, and the same is true for the cantonal hospitals in Zurich or Basel, the hospitals in Scandinavia, and, in a few cases, in Mexico City. But for the most part the American medical profession has reached the acme, the peak of prestige, dignity, and real dependability. Through decades it has represented practically by itself the present stage of the art.

It has proven that in a half-century—with concerted action and an education aware of social psychology and fully tied into contemporary research in related sciences—a professional group or organization can change its status in society and in the eyes of the world.

There is no reason why the architectural profession cannot do the same if there is a missionary attitude, built on objective criteria by which it can prove itself.

An architect, too, may be an intuitive artist, but he can secure and aid his intuition by learning certain things which are better known to other professions and better handled by other practitioners. As it is, the handling of engineering matters is what usually is expected from an architect, who nevertheless is considered only as a secondary, poor version of an engineer. Some people even think that he just "sells blueprints." There are very few men within the profession itself who can give a clear, generally accepted explanation or differential diagnosis of what their distinguishing specialty is. Perhaps specialty is altogether less needed than universality?

What might be developed into objective proofs for any valid

architectural decision? A vague uncertainty here is exactly what has badly hit and demoralized a profession which may carry the responsibility for the happiness not only of individual clients, not only for the well-being of people "over the amortization period," but for the survival of the race, now largely and very increasingly caged in complex artificial settings.

While a lonely great architect was later to impress me by his manifest works, I had first witnessed the precious performance of a famous physician. In my child's mind, I was soon to fuse the two pictures, and I still hold dear this fusion.

Reformer and His Community

In many a life one is conscious of the days of emergent vocational choice only much later than they actually occur. But when I was eight years old, without thinking clearly, I must have decided to become an architect. My unspoken decision was the result of a ride in the new, much-talked-about subway, the stations of which were designed by Otto Wagner. In a very short time I was enamored of him, his buildings, and his fights against strong opposition and public ridicule. He was Hercules, Achilles, Buffalo Bill, all rolled in one: he stood for all the heroes and pathfinders, punished Promethean victims chained to Mount Caucasus or Atlas, or to torture poles in the jungle of backwardness. Here was a missionary and one who was breaking with a worn-out past. As newly appointed maestro of the Imperial Academy of Arts, he opened his course with a manifesto on modern, contemporary architecture.

Recently, sixty years later, Otto Wagner's daughter sent me, with unearned eulogy for myself, a color reproduction of an oil painting of her father, and I saw how much more majestic he looked than Prince Albert, whose conventional coat he still wore when he designed those subway and elevated stations.

Wagner was a famous name in the second half of the century, though not through Otto, but Richard. Richard had found in Vienna, that music emporium of the world, only irony and derision. He had smarted under the devastating criticism of Edward Hanslick and the competition of great and burly Johannes Brahms, who drank a calm beer with the famous surgeon Albert Billroth and wore no velvet beret of showmanship. Otto was contemporary to this conspicuously musical Vienna. He did not have any competitors to speak of, but he soon had all the rollicking Viennese laughter on the other side, and hardly anyone sitting even on the fence.

By the time I was eight and ready to be an architect, Otto Wagner, the older, and Louis Sullivan, the younger genius, already were getting stymied by both amused and embittered opposition. But their energy was not spent; they battled on. The case of Wagner especially demonstrates that the best connections, all the worldly affluence, could not help a man over the socially crippling circumstance of being a genius.

Vienna had come under the domination of the great rabble-rousing demagogue Karl Lueger, a street-demonstration-directing prototype of the later Hitlers and Mussolinis. And we must remember that just then young Hitler had arrived in Vienna, and that with big eyes, although without mustache as yet, he watched those anti-parliamentarian, anti-liberal racial demonstrations and the breaking of shop windows. It was the end of the liberal "democratic" constitutional era, which had begun also in Vienna, as in the rest of Europe, with the second great revolution on the European continent in 1848, and had slowly led into smugness and a lethal torpor. The great demagogue himself had been a liberal representative in parliament and in the city council, and was also a successful lawyer. Karl became a name dear to a million hearts, especially to female hearts, since Karl, just like Adolf, the Austrian who duplicated his career later in Munich and Berlin, remained officially a celibate all his life—a seemingly successful formula for a strong man. Karl was a fiery orator, a wit, a finder of scapegoats, and a derider of Marxism, from which, however, like Adolf, he wisely borrowed the word "socialist" for his party label. "Christian socialism" it was, and in a later, similar wave it was to become, with absorption of a few other elements likewise being preformed in Vienna at the same time by Teutonic hundred percenters, "national socialism." This city was a wonderful training ground for young Hitler, whose postal-card art may have been precariously ridiculed by some art dealer, who thereby derailed him into the political field for more large-scale mischief.

Hitler remained a devoted artist at heart all his life. Lueger was nothing of the kind. But he was a close friend of Otto Wagner's, and had helped him to get the biggest teaching job and big commissions like the two dozen railway stations of the municipal transit lines. The Cardinal Archbishop of Vienna had amazingly approved his strange modern church, which with joy I saw rise on the foothills of the Vienna Woods, conspicuous far and wide to all the city, on those venerable verdant slopes where Beethoven had scribbled his sketches for the Pastoral Symphony. (Schubert must have passed that church site on an open cart with his gay friends on a weekend excursion to drink the new wine in October 1820 or so.) Yes, there was even a whole town on those gentle inclines, most visibly built by Otto Wagner, my ideal architect, and the cupola of his new church gleamed and floated over the flat roofs, which looked to me like the wonderful terraces I imagined on the Lipari Islands or in North Africa—or wherever ancient Latin orderliness had arranged communities on mountain slopes. Steel, glass, modern architecture—and yet above all a revival of essential human integrity of design. But that whole town was a public asylum for the mentally ill; it was built for the insane! Nevertheless, it had been built, and it stood there. Other city jobs were coming through for Wagner, but the "sane" people rejected him bitterly—and more and more. When I was fifteen years old, I watched breathlessly the ferocious fight over the city museum project.

The historical collection of the city of Vienna was in temporary quarters in the neo-Gothic city hall, with lots of crates in the basement, brimful of unexhibited items. Exhibited in a glass case, I remember, was the skull of the Grand Vizier and General of the Janizaries, the Ottoman Excellency Kara Mustafa, who failed to make the second Ottoman siege of Vienna a success while the German artillery of the Venetians shelled the Parthenon powder magazine of the Turks in Athens and William Penn got ready his plan for Philadelphia. The Viennese captured in the Turkish encampment a supply of coffee beans (some of them on display in that museum, too) and started the great *café*-house custom on which a good part of Vienna's cultural life still depended when I was coming of age. Cultures rise, others weaken, while venerable ruins get ruined still more. Finally come museums. There was not one but a series of competitions written out for a project to house that city museum. Otto Wagner, with his hard 4-H pencil designs, meticulous and functionally sound, always won first place with every international jury he had to put up with. The city council majority seemed serious in obtaining the best judgment of outsiders, to the dismay and disappointment of his ironical and teeth-gritting opponents. Each of Wagner's designs and all the stalling and alibis of the Board of Trustees, and other authorities mixed in, seemed only to fertilize and propel this cursed architectural movement which he had founded. And it began to spread over the provinces, especially to medieval Prague, which later became a hotbed of missionary modernism. It was then missionary, not modish.

Finally, it looked as if Wagner would win, and no further excuse and delay seemed possible. Dictator Lueger thought of congratulating his friend for having that museum job in the bag. But just before contracts were to be signed, before ground was broken for the commencement of the grand opus, the major achievement in the life of a genius, victorious at last—right then and there a most clever and insidious move was hatched out in the city council, directly under the eyes of the strongest mayor any city has ever had in my lifetime. He had perhaps one single weak spot, an unprotected heel. Lueger ruled by acclamation of the masses; his resounding superficial doctrines were supported by cheering throngs called into the streets on every occasion. Someone of the opposition decided to move quite cunningly, and proposed that a generous sum of money be allocated for the construction of a life-size mock-up of Wagner's prize-winning design on the actual site, next to the old Karlskirche, the pride of Vienna. Then the masses—men, women, and children—should be called for a grand show and a public appraisal.

The money was voted in a hasty roll call, and even the great demagogue could not prevent the council's summoning the people and their judgment, just as he did, calling out his masses onto the street. But what is perhaps more likely, he himself did not understand that it was a trap and that he would be up against it. Here were shown the real limits of his power, and the fox had been outwitted this time. No cliché-ridden oratory would help. This time people would face an unhabituated, unaccustomed visual shape standing free and quiet in front of them, a stark colossal mock-up. Lueger had to sell the work of a genius on display, not just shrewdly cooked up and shrilly shouted political slogans.

A four-story-high three-hundred-foot-long life-size model that stepped squarely on the toes of mediocrity stood on the familiar plaza of the conservative cultural center city of Europe—perhaps congenial, but right next to the celebrated Karlskirche, a great remnant of the past. And the bourgeois, the university professor, together with a vast street rabble, shouted it down in unison.

Not even a dictator, trained in all the tricky politics of the world, can support the sudden birth of a creative epoch or the work of a genius. It must be slow habituation that often takes one or two generations until perhaps slightly diluted copies can survive after the originator has died of a broken heart—or has resigned himself to the facts of life and tardy acceptance, such as sociologists have recognized. The usual time lag between the most ingenious inventions and their passage into reality has now been measured by psychologists as very typical; but then I saw, with a bleeding heart before me, only an individual tragedy of heroic proportions: man against a pitiless mob. A grand value of hope for a better future was snowed under in a tempest unleashed by clever and cold political intrigue, which looked to the people like righteous solicitousness for their noble heritage.

I am afraid I have seen, forty years later and in a similar way, values buried which I myself, with my friends, had produced in years of devoted labor and, quite literally speaking, with the blood and the waning energy of my heart. I only slowly recovered when it threatened to stop pulsing.

Unequal Eyes

What makes an individual evolve?

The extraordinary event and experience, the sudden sight of a vital individual in action, or his work, may be one guiding impact, whether one is conscious of it or not.

But small, continuous drops can erode even a rock! This kind of an impact is provided by daily environment and the human beings close by and present over long periods—family and home.

Still, a Chopin nocturne, often played on the piano by one's older sister, might be a great, long, sounding childhood experience—unless, of course, one were deaf, without ears to hear the music. Thus, congenital make-up and deficiencies are inextricably mixed into the phenomenon of becoming conditioned. The final human personality is very naturally a fusion and outcome of all these circumstances.

Life itself, observed and taken in by all means we have, is undoubtedly our basic over-all educator. It is the most remarkable molder of its own sequences. It writes its own, often unorthodox, study curriculum.

I began by recalling influences of the physical setting at work, from floor to ceiling—lookout windows very much included. Then there was the experience, towering over familiar human beings, of a great man, a clinician, standing before a bloody disaster and prognosticating calmly and correctly for fifty years to come. I also recalled the tragic struggle of a seer, this time an architect facing an entire community and meeting jocose and bitter rejection by his own people. These outer experiences of a young life undoubtedly exerted their power on it.

But, for contrast, we should perhaps now consider inborn sets of circumstances as coloring a man's evolving mission; say, the dexterity of his hand, the acuity of his eye. Often we shall find here also effective deficiencies which somehow may turn into benefits, and at any rate may contribute to that fascinating puzzle of biological individuality.

Others may have bravely defended the *individual* on religious grounds or for moral reasons: I have always liked to add, as a friendly architect of his setting, new defenses, those of the minutely observing physiologist, or even the pathologist, who hopes to become a therapist.

Who is a normal man? What makes an individual?

For example, I was born with eyes markedly unequal as to vision. This, as a boy, and later as a grownup, I have experienced as a very vital part of my make-up. It has brought a specific trend and character not only into my important double picture of the world, but has actually given different dimensions, different flavor, different creative consequences, to living in the world in which I, as a particular individual, have found myself as a youth, as an adult, and at a later age. Eyes change through life in many respects; only their color, after babyhood at least, seems permanent, almost as the pattern of one's fingerprints, which is constant even from birth to death.

When seen in a certain illumination, the irises of these eyes were of a clear blue and seemed to correspond to the fair hair of the infant. But the surrounding ensemble has changed. The hair—half a century before its whiteness of today—had turned a darker, even darkest, brown, although it never reached the jet black of my mother's hair. Her eyes had been of a beautiful, lively doe brown; those of my father, gray. As younger people, both parents had enjoyed normal eyesight, but after fifty they began to wear glasses for increasing farsightedness.

When I was about sixteen, my brother William, fifteen years my elder and already an experienced physician, suggested that an eye doctor should examine my vision. It seemed a fatal day when my mother walked down the stairs with me after this consultation in an old building on the Mariahilferstrasse in Vienna. I remember this anguished descent clearly. It happened to land us on the street near the statue of one of the great artists of the ear, Josef Haydn. I thought of how Beethoven had been Haydn's pupil, and slowly and miserably lost his hearing, with deafness painfully molding his life and art.

The doctor had shaken a finger at me. "Don't let him study architecture. It requires a lot of drawing. His eyes won't stand it in the long run. They are quite unequal, and don't work together."

My right eye had indeed a lens defect, and was shortsighted to boot; my left eye was then normal. Over the years, this one was to become farsighted as its lens shrank with age, while its companion got a little more normal. But the pair never cooperated to render me stereoscopic vision as other people enjoy it, and my visual world aged differently from theirs. That is the stuff by which an individual evolves.

From childhood my personality was influenced and molded by this trait of physiological individuality, or peculiar double deficiency, slowly changing in proportion. Correspondingly, my mental attitude of vision was twofold. Since most of the time I saw and worked with one eye, either the right one for minute sharp detail or the left for over-all composition, my mind similarly also swung back and forth—oscillated, so to speak, between an attempt at total comprehension, an integrated over-all view, and the minute perfectionism of near-sightedness. But I kept using each eye, one imaginatively and wholesale for over-all form, the other more observationally, for tiny, neat detail.

My drawings and sketches from 1906 on begin to show this neat detailing and sharp acuity of my right eye, unless—as still earlier—I worked on my toy blackboard, where I used to hold the chalk almost at arm's length, and drew "serial scenes" of the Boer War of 1899, with covered wagons forming fortress rings, and the lines of un-uniformed Afrikanders swarming out over the rolling country to meet the British, or peeping, just noticeably by their broad-rimmed Quaker hats, over the wavy line of the hill. Little as I was, I daily drew with cool method sequences of progress pictures of the battles. But my heart, before this chalk board, was for the courageous Boers, fighting for liberty. Two generations later I really saw South Africa, lectured before Africans, passed the architect's exam, and made friends and sketches from Stellenbosch, Cape Province, to the capital in Transvaal. Bloemfontain and Pretoria and President Kruger to me were still warm-sounding names, and the colored people from Asia and blacks whom fate had planted into this mix-up touched my heart when I sketched their huts.

But as a child I also admired the contemporaneity of industry and the current technology of the British, and their navy was the embodiment of these characteristics. I drew their intricately rigged, nobly shaped ships with relish.

I had from my engineer brother the idea that industrialization was the destiny of the age, and England was its instrument, a tool of it. I was six or seven when, during the Russo-Japanese war, not only the heroic but the technically up-to-date attitude of the Japanese won my childish approval, as opposed to the fossilized czarism of which the adults spoke in my earshot. My illustrative blackboard drawings were concerned with that Far East struggle only to the extent of a fantastic sketch of a torpedo boat sinking a man-of-war in the straits. I suffered anguish with the crew and despair with the admiral.

Aside from these instruments of war, bicycles, *perpetuum mobiles*, steam engines, and steam whistles, sharply detailed in cross and longitudinal sections as my brother had explained them to me, long dominated the blackboard. It all prepared me for detailing plumbing layouts on Chicago drafting boards later.

On the other hand, in the summertime I tried to draw trees as my right eye saw them, and foliage masses as cared for by my left eye. Ever so often my soul wondered which of my visions was the true one for me.

My memory jumps back and forth, as memories most naturally do.

I remember this indelibly; twelve years old, I tilted my head slightly and my breath stopped for seconds when a train in which I rode with my parents swiftly rolled around a wide curve—and there, below, lay the steel-blue broad sweep of water, the lake of Gmunden. I had never seen that much water stretching through the vision field of my far-reaching eye. Cool gray rocky heights towered over the foothills, densely studded in their lower reaches with erect green spruce trees. A darkly silhouetted hawk flew over the mountain skyline, with a sort of syncopated wingbeat. I still recall what I saw in a fraction of a second, between two unequal heartbeats. It had broken *my* rhythm, shaped it after the other, for a moment to remember.

But a month later I was on top of the mountains myself. I saw higher ones in eternal snow—the glaciers incredibly white against deep sky-blue, such as the Dachstein, looming there, seven thousand feet high, a twelve-hour climb.

Did the lake dwellers of prehistoric Hallstatt, of whom I had been told, climb that far up? What were their footsoles like? Did they see and behold with eyes like ours the beauty of the ice-cold lake, the green delight of the warmer Mondsee, or the lakeshore where later St. Wolfgang converted the heathens, only to be tortured cruelly and martyred by them? I stood before the medieval altar painting in the village church and thought: Did all these ancestral men have eyes like mine — eyes like men today? Eyes have not really changed in history.

In 1904 I had already spent five days riding gondolas and, with eyes wide open or squinted, walking through sunny Venice. By 1907 and 1908 my drawing hobby was well under way.

When, at the age of eighteen, I tramped indefatigably with a like-minded schoolfellow, Edmund Kalischer, through the Bohemian Forest for fourteen days, I carried a heavy pack-sack on my back—a sketchbook and a tiny "Schminke" water-color box plus a telescoping metal brush with lovely red hair which, when wetted with the tongue, formed a fine point. These were the best ever-present goods in my travel baggage.

With eyes wide open, we climbed and ambled through a prehistoric forest preserve of Europe, silent as this west end of Asia before its human story had begun to unroll or had begun being told. Finally we came down to flat Frankonia and Nuremberg. We found the cheap Inn of the Little Swan, *Zum Schwänlein*, near the old circumvallating masonry, where no self-respecting tourist had stayed, maybe, since the days when artists from Holland had come to pay a return visit to Albrecht Dürer.

I remember painting the city's old gates with deliberate brush strokes which were carefully kept from overlapping or flowing into each other; the sun really began to come out in my minutely brushed on and pristine water colors, with hardly any pencil "foredrawing."

It must have been about 1911 that I went to Trieste with Ernst, son of Sigmund Freud. We two young students, who liked each other so well, followed an itinerary which we had discussed, in the presence of the professor, with Sigmund's brother, Alexander, a lively traveler and man of affairs, who knew every inn on that then little-traveled East Adriatic coast. Mixing Slavic and Italian, we visited Pola, Split, Sebenico,

Trogir, Korčula, Lesina, Ragusa, Gravosa, and the rosebush-scented Lacroma, spending our nights in native inns, quaintly called *O Jelenu,* "to the Elk," or the like, and we met Catholic monsignori who were absorbed in archaeology and in festive pageants commemorating the pagan Emperor Diocletian. I guess he was a big Dalmatian, he built so much there—a palace large enough for a medieval town to settle in and too large to get into one vista. The many little church bells busily ringing in the morning air over the bay of Sebenico, the lonely islands of the Illyrian sea, were a wonderful springtime experience. My eyes opened to a crystal-clear dry mountain range over stunningly blue Adriatic bays. Fast sketching became a daily habit.

Once, coming from that picturesquely silhouetted mountainous peninsula of Peljesac—we called it Sabioncello—we were pacing the small deck of a minimum-size steamer, on the lookout for the tortoise back of the island of Korčula, which we were approaching over the choppy waters of an otherwise fine day. In broad outline, all the Dalmatian islands were very sketchable and, in detail, colonial Venetian in architecture, having once been dependencies of that grand seafaring republic. Trogir, or Trau, and Ragusa were pearls, but Korčula, with its *duomo* at the navel of the gentle convexity of its shield-shaped body, promised to be most lovely as it rose from the distance into the middle ground of vision.

As we approached, I carried a camera with roll film, and, most important, smooth Wattmann paper with a medium-hard pencil; I hardly ever used an eraser, which breaks the stimulation of line after line. How eyes, hands, and fingers work together in split seconds!

While we drew nearer, it became apparent that a crowd of people had gathered at the dock, or quay. Finally one could see—I still see it now, so sharp is visual memory—the glinting of brass instruments in the sun. As the boat, under half steam, passed beyond the breakwater into the harbor, the band had taken up its position. It seemed a grand reception, and hats were being swung through the air when the white-linen dressed figures of Freud and Neutra became distinguishable to the crowd on the shore; the brass, rebounding from the masonry of the medieval town, sounded over the now gentle waves. At the same time the bells from the rough gray stone campanile of the *duomo* on the crest of the island chimed in. We were all surprised; the captain, the first mate, and the deckhands of the crew mustered us, the only passengers on board, half with questioning suspicion, half with budding reverence, while we two looked at each other uneasily.

Then the boat was so close to its berthing place that one could distinguish individual faces. The band leader, staring at the two white passengers, slowed the rhythm of his orchestra, and suddenly I saw his baton halt in mid-air. The music faded out, one trombone and one trumpet after the other. Colorful silence. Then there were tumultuous inquiries in Croatian, and a pushing toward shipside and gangplank.

It developed that all these good people had expected that morning the bishop from Peljesac, and here were two young linen-dressed "Inglesi," as the crowd shoutingly referred to them. We, wrong recipients of a well-staged harmonious reception, walked meekly ashore, and finally it all broke up in general laughter and merriment. After that the town was open to us.

The late summer of the same year brought me, together with another fellow student, to Freud's family, vacationing in Bozen, Tyrol, an eye treat so different from Torbole on Lake Garda, where a week later I quickly fell in love with a young black-haired peasant girl, Giulietta Zeni by name, and from there to Verona, and to the tomb of the other Giulietta, to hill and valley Bergamo, Brescia, Milano, Firenze, Genoa, Livorno, Bastia, beyond the choppy waters of the Island of Corsica, Bologna, and Ferrara—and again to Venice in its lagoon. Pencil and water-color notations became faithful records of everything in sight, near and far. My speed at this recording became impressive to my friends. But I was not at all art ambitious and was fairly unconscious of both deficiencies and gifts.

In 1913 I was busy studying in the school of architecture of the Technical University in Vienna, and, in a casual way, I learned to draw nudes with great ease. Here, my pencil stroke was almost continuous when I followed the contours of a body—male, or, with particular preference, female. But the line changed in density and width, so that body surfaces, here softly, curvaceously flowing, there definitely turning around the variedly sharp outline—or the "horizon of the visible"—gave great plasticity to these unshaded nudes. Much later I saw sketches by Rodin to which these might be compared, at least as to attitude. I hardly followed any teaching, but I did listen to the anatomist, Dr. Heller, who gave us vehemently animated lectures about the morphology of the human form and even post-mortemed and dissected human bodies before the architectural students. Fat, perspiring Dr. Heller was a second- or third-rate artist himself, but a burly, breathless, dynamic talker. I always feel sorry and depressed when I remember seeing him in the anatomy hall cut off a breast from the body of a young girl which had been wheeled in from the morgue. What had she died of? Had she no relatives?

While drawing I have done much and sometimes my most worth-while thinking. Somehow it activates my brains and glands to this very day. Others drink coffee or vodka.

The year before World War I broke out, I participated in a students' excursion up the Danube River to the double river city Krems and Stein, while the fruit trees were in bloom. I sketched old courts, and craning my neck, stucco ceilings in *Bürger* houses: the inner-ear position sense acted intimately together with vision. Sketchbook in hand, I was delegated as the charmer-emissary to invite all the town's girls to a dance with the students from Vienna. I enjoyed the intrigue of persuading the mothers, and toward the morning of the great night, fell softly and elastically in love with two or more girls at the same time. Carlotta seems to have been the name of one who was older than I.

I was twenty then, and on workdays my architectural course with Professor Mayreder, back at the University, required me to draw Ionian and Corinthian temples as a whole, and in minute, shaded details as well, all in neatly measured and moduled proportions. It was only half a century later that I grasped, almost with a shock, how human was the dish these Greeks had slowly learned to offer. They had nuances refined, until all *had* to respond.

When eighteen or nineteen years old and in military service, I already had trained myself to sketch my riding teacher in motion. He was an aristocratic first lieutenant, Victor Imhoff von Reutlinghof, I suppose a descendant of the Nuremberg Imhoff portrayed by Albrecht Dürer. Monocled, he would stalk back and forth through the ring in wonderfully cobbled slender riding boots. I love that slightly bored, no-longer-young officer. I learned my way of rendering dynamic motion on paper. I drew horses, in trot, in gallop, in a jump. And I also began to draw sweet, tenderly milk-and-blood-faced Threska Sturm. I would meet her after working hours at Kroell's millinery shop in the Mariahilferstrasse, where years before, that fateful doctor had made his dire prediction that my eyes would fail. So far they were going strong.

Telling more about my drawing in soft Siberian charcoal, during nights in the Austrian countryside, the hills of Waidhofen an der Ybbs, or with Mona Lisa oil crayons, from Slovakia to Silesia, the Baltic Sea, from French Switzerland to New York, would parallel an entire autobiography.

In my life, loose leaves and sketchbooks have, in snatched moments, been filled, to review it only briefly, in Herzegovina, Montenegro, and Albania, during World War I. Later, but nowhere as a tourist or ever on vacation, I went bit by bit from Manhattan, over the Rockies into the desert and Death Valley, the Pacific South Seas, and the Caribbean islands, Canada and Japan, Manila, Thailand, Malaya, India, China, and Africa—from Egypt to Nairobi, the Cape, the Belgian Congo, Senegal—Mexico, Guatemala, Venezuela, Colombia,

Peru, Bolivia, Argentina, Brazil, Anatolia, and Greece. Everywhere I met with people concerned with the human scene in practical work. Constructive discussions would range from geology to traffic.

Mostly I had only minutes between duties and earnest professional assignments and while officials or clients were stopping the car, when I had won their hearts to do so, to give me the chance for a graphic note. My eyes guided my pencils through the interiors of steamers, busses, planes, exotic hotels, native huts and villages in Nigeria, Spain, and Sicily—quickly, just before meeting appointments or engaging in rush work en route. I drew men, women, and children, man fights, cockfights, and band concerts in Madras and French Switzerland; goats, llamas, birds, and giraffes, landscapes in moonlight and sunshine, or at sunrise, and "psychotopes," or soul-anchorage places, which animal behaviorists describe as attractive to prehuman creatures and often to ourselves. I, too, found such spots, and I, too, hung my soul on them for moments of vision and a lifetime of echoes. There were Burmese temples and Belgian medieval churches, bits of Scandinavia, Baltic shorelines with scraggly pine, and Hungarian grassland—the *puszta*—with hardly a trace of man's artificiality.

A sheer endless row of lifetime experiences has been visually recorded in those snatches. The University of California at Los Angeles hospitably has dedicated a little section of its huge library as an archive of these endeavors, my many dream plans in blueprints, my less frequent realizations in photographs, my attempts to write, in manuscripts. Especially, then, rest there in peace those sketches done on the way while crisscrossing the world as a consultant—really less counseling than learning about humanity in its early and later settings, and falling in love with the "mystery and realities" of sites, on which I wrote, drew, and photographed a book.

It would be fallacious to see this output of lines, colored or black and white, as a colossal time investment. Measured by mechanical clocks, only small brain-exposure times were necessary. Such important nervous play takes only hundredths of seconds of a lifetime. The human eye is speedier than a camera, the retina is a fast-working film, and the fingers holding a black pencil or colored crayons become trained to be quick. While each line is drawn or a dot is made on paper, inner glands busily discharge molecules of biochemicals. In the consciousness, or half-consciously, it spells slightly egged-on emotions—one line, I feel, stimulates the next, one color spot, the one to follow in juxtaposition, contrast, or harmony. Art teachers might have an easy time, were they connoisseurs of those brain dynamics. At least they could cautiously sound a note of warning before a stimulative white paper is messed up with the first dull, defeating timid line. (It is hard to overcome a false and deadening start. How many human and individuality-expressing organs are in on such a beginning—from a good start through sequels to the "stop in time"?)

My two eyes, one shortsighted and the other of long range, have done their faithful, if not normally co-ordinated, work. Perhaps the world I have seen was an unreal one. At any rate, physiologically speaking, it was not quite orthodox. Such is destiny. One simply can't escape one's individual world. One must and can and shall get along in it.

If the recording of my world ever bordered on art, it was in the most casual manner, but a real human experience kept on oozing, dribbling, sprinkling, and sometimes freely flowing onto all kinds of accidental paper, whatever happened to be at hand. No spoken or slowly written word can quite express in the same way this past life, as lived in tiny fractions of time.

Teacher and Apprentice

Apart from the realization of one's own deficiencies and endowments, witnessing a great master at work has always seemed to me the strongest sort of influence. And many others besides our masters become exemplary performers before our eyes.

My time in high school and the university was an important

and influential stage in the never-ending venture of meeting fellow beings in new situations. Although I enjoyed this period very much, and consider it invaluable, I must confess that once my father had told me of his own training as a caster and turner of bronze and brass, apprenticeship seemed to me more than a substitute for a good school. And, fundamentally, I still hold this belief.

Schools have been the training places of mankind only for a comparatively short time, and are very recent in relation to the total course of human culture conveyed from generation to generation. People have learned things and acquired technical, corporeal, and mental skills—if one may justly separate these three—long before the wholesale official enrollment of students synchronized as to age and learning hours, and before formal schools began to function and to dispense paper certificates.

Much later, I have taken on many apprentices in my office, studio, or drafting room; some have had formal training and some did not. Some are well-known architects today and some will be. If we take stock in their testimony and their often almost bitter recollections of their schooling, it was often not worth while and failed to live up to their expectations. But generalizations are unreliable, and schools *can* give much, too.

I myself am grateful to my teachers, and some have greatly influenced me, at least those I encountered in high school. Some time ago I visited a friend and schoolfellow who lived in Oregon. He had left Vienna under Nazi rule, as his convictions and law practice became unfeasible; in Portland he had tried to sell the *Britannica*, and had later pressed pants, finally developing two small cleaning establishments. We spoke of our high-school days, and I proposed that we each name the teacher we remembered as the most influential. I was now an architect, and he had originally been a lawyer. To our surprise, we both promptly named the same unlikely man.

He was Dr. Regen, a young, tall, blond-bearded and blue-eyed Croatian, who held a Ph.D. in zoology. He spoke with a funny, heavy accent and hated boys and teaching in high school—or anywhere, for that matter. He also taught botany, without enthusiasm, and to get over the general boredom of it all, he engaged in bombast and bellowing; his questions were never completely comprehensible, and he flunked the intimidated boys right and left. With a quick movement he would put a pinned beetle under a student's eye, frightening him so that for precious seconds no sign of recognition came; Dr. Regen would enjoy this stupefaction.

Why did we nominate him, and what did we get from him? We remembered no data, no information his teachings had yielded. Was there anything we had retained after so many years, something that may have looked like a product of education?

We recollected that on various occasions Dr. Regen had talked of what evidently was his specific research interest. When he spoke of the physiology of Arthropoda, he became so fully absorbed that he forgot the boys in front of him, the misery of teaching mischievous, uninterested youngsters. The classroom dissolved, and he was either in the bush or in the meadow, collecting specimens, or in the laboratory, microdissecting them for their secrets of life and death. On such occasions his language was way over our heads, even more so than usually. Forgetting the base reality of a high school, he somehow seemed to exude the atmosphere of a whole congress of congenial biologists, to whom he might have happily, and with burning ears, submitted his latest paper, imaginative and cautiously systematic, ready to be printed in the science journal. My friend and I used to sit spellbound. It was like looking through the plate-glass window of a restaurant and seeing someone eating with a most remarkable relish. One cannot taste, smell, or recognize the dish itself, but the consumer's relish and gusto is physiognomically so exciting that one decides at once to enter and enjoy the menu.

For years my friend wanted to become a natural scientist, reading E. H. Haeckel, Weissmann, Hugo De Vries, and all the literature of the post-Darwinian controversy. I never learned much about Arthropoda, and became a designer of buildings, but one with an ever-intensified physiological-biological bias. The unorthodox educational impact of red-blond bearded Dr. Regen, who was more a terror than a teacher, is proven by nothing so much as by our independent, spontaneous acknowledgment of our debt to him.

The shock of his excitement over detailed natural-science research, and our empathic reaction to it, was so profound that even forty years could not lessen it. Psychologists in their terminology may say that emotions are older than reason and reverberate longer. The lifetime influence of this man was—speaking the language of Regen's science of physiology—more of an endocrinic than a rational cortical affair. Although it is a very ramified root system from which we and our organic fate grow; perhaps Dr. Regen's effect on us reveals the core of all lasting educational impact.

Or is it too much of a liberty of words to call fate "grown"? Perhaps growth is the most fateful thing that can be thought of! Nothing is, everything becomes. Learning and teaching are of biophysical and biochemical fastness. The upper brain actions we have long heard called intellectual; the under brain processes, emotional. But they melt together every moment.

They certainly do mysteriously melt—observational curiosity and lyrical penchant. I remember Hugo von Hofmannsthal, whom I admired as a writer, saying somewhere: Books do not speak, they answer; this makes demons of them. Perhaps a teacher, too, answers; particularly one who guides us through the natural scene and history is, in spite of threatening red hair, a good and long-wished-for demon. His greatest effect may be in replying to unasked questions and half conscious, half unconscious, individual trends, primevally rooted.

Recently my sister, Josephine, sent me diaries of mine, out of a forgotten box she had in Goteborg, Sweden. In them I have found the things that occupied my mind in Vienna almost half a century earlier, before and after Dr. Regen, and later William Wundt, impressed me so much with the need to understand organic nature. It was many years before I should build a Health House or endlessly and laboriously write on *Survival Through Design*.

Those diaries are a little like and halfway between the late James Joyce and the Codice Atlantico of Leonardo's free associations, intermixed with physiological sketches, also quotations from many scientists, antique and modern philosophers, and descriptions of waitresses and other human beings in all detail of anatomy, as related to gait and physiognomic expressiveness.

It appears I was in a way of my own prepared to apply nature study before reading any scientific "papers" or drawing plans, as I did forty years later, for an interpretative nature science museum, on a greening hilltop in Dayton, Ohio.

Evidently on a long nature-bound course of viewing the world as to fitness for organic survival, I find on June 3, 1917, this notation made in Vienna: "As I walked this morning through the Weyringer Gasse, quite suddenly an indescribable, nameless tedium, i.e. hatred, grasped me for this bumpy, hard pavement. How can we human beings only live and exist on such a surface? The most horribly arid ground of the Karst, chalky waste mountainland in Dalmatia, is a refreshing promenade patch by comparison and satisfies the eye by a hundred little and large shadow castings. A husky rhino put on this surface would dry up and wither. Man has fostered, pushed it under himself, and now drags himself on it back and forth! Whenever once I happened to ride on horseback down a paved city street, it seemed to me more chilling and worse than a bitterly frozen lake. City dwellers hardly grasp what troubles them and why each of them feels like a fish back in the water when his footsoles walk at least over a gravel path through a green town park."

To see man thus out of reach of his original ecology made me both respectful to the study of the prehuman scene, and later a "naturalist" architect. But architecture, of course, has evolved also through a lot of man-made historical scenery, for which he alone is responsible.

Dr. Friedrich Blank taught us Latin, and put emphasis on the military prowess of Caesar's subtechnicians and legionaries. He brought a Roman lance into the classroom, and recalled visibly that Dr. Blank himself was an officer, at least of the reserve.

He, too, had sarcastic tendencies which devastated his pupils. Just before being expelled, a desperate fellow student wrote, in revenge, and submitted in lieu of a required test paper, a long-prepared Latin poem about Dr. Blank, likening him to the commander of the cavalry of peasant women who then used to ride to Vienna with milk cans in the early morning. But small, pock-marked Doctor Blank had a knack of relating the peace treaties between Punic wars to contemporary news stories of diplomatic moves. Besides, Latin syntax became a school of mental orderliness, if not logic, when, broad-chested, he strode heroically onto the stage. He, too, was more feared than loved, as supposedly a good teacher is. This manlike Professor Heinrich Saliger of my university experience, expert in reinforced concrete and later, under the Nazis, tough as nails, rector, or president, of the institution—all, whatever their specialty, had sarcastic traits, and their cortical appeal was not pure and simple nor rational by any means. There was "diencephalic" emotional tension in the air between givers and takers of education.

The history teachers, who engaged my lasting interest in the subject, like Doctor Franz Ruthe and later the principal of the Sophiengymnasium in Vienna, were good storytellers, and offered rounded-out shapes—as raconteurs do—where fuzzy, puzzling events, merely enumerated, might have become drowned in chaotic confusion. At the same time, by reaction, they planted in me a healthy skepticism against the clichés of historiography, and sometimes I have shown some eagerness tentatively to substitute another quite possible good story, to see whether it sounds less probable than the orthodox one!

On the whole, whether it was physics, Greek epics, or German literature, I do not doubt that I received a much more durable, workable education in high school than on the university level. Very unfortunately, no one taught me English.

I have already mentioned how stimulation to read and to listen to articulate discussion at home supplemented my formal studies. But there were other places, apart from home and school. In the University library I had run into the first and basic researches on experimental physiological psychology, because Wilhelm Wundt's book title attracted me greatly. It interested me even more than the work of Sigmund Freud and his now well-known early disciples, many of whom, just as a friend of Freud's sons, I glimpsed in his house.

Many faulty and productive human relations had been discussed within my earshot. The psychological conditioning of a person, alone and in society, began to interest me deeply. Perhaps, I came to think, no professor, no formal school, can assimilate a young man and his mind into a team, a creative trio, quartet, sextet, or orchestra of workers. And ours is not the era for solo play. Later, I myself have tried to raise such a team within the walls of my office. There, work done close by—say, sketches drawn on neighboring drafting boards—sets off inductive currents. Also it is examined and conversations in bitter earnest are overheard and become instruments of learning.

The organic interplay of individuals to attain mutually stimulated group creativity has since become an endlessly intriguing subject to me. Taking my later professional field as an example: What happens when a client, a bank appraiser, a building inspector, by resistance or by concurrence, influences that creative process? *How are newcomers absorbed into the sanctum of a harmoniously functioning group?* The human issues always seem important, how people make others feel and think.

One apprenticing must not only imbibe technicalities, but above all *attitude* and *working habits*, a sacrificial, cheerfully co-operative mode of thinking which general schools cannot easily teach concretely. In a creative, productive place of work he learns to become a contributive member of a crew. He does not sit passively in a classroom listening to a man who knows all without ever a setback. He does not sink into feelings of inferiority.

An apprentice must be himself an active sharer. He must, I think, do more than empty the wastepaper baskets—although the volume and variety of their contents should be an eye opener to any who believe that trial and error can largely be omitted in a creative effort. He must see and observe at close range how the principal and his older assistants labor to fill that paper basket, and, doing so, slow down slightly in speed as they arrive at more tenable solutions.

As a doer himself, he must watch the psychological give and take which permits them to function as a team, and *by empathy he must respect their honoring each others' accrued feelings*. Once even slight antagonisms are allowed to break out, cortical action is blurred. On the other hand, it is lubricated by favorable emotive events in the group. Then that pattern of many billions of firing brain cells seems to become attuned from skull to skull, and faces smile at each other or they easily share depressive moods.

Whatever the work in hand, the apprentice must talk and telephone to many human beings involved and he must be forewarned that every word he says, every inflection of his voice, may either add to or detract from the productive effort, because every minute action of such nature affects mutual confidence, lets it grow in continued service as it should, or lets it be whittled away. Slow and slight gains, made earlier, may evaporate through any wrong move. An orchestra, a dance group, a football team, may in a sour second suffer from a single bungler. No mere onlooker will ever gauge that.

There is nothing more wrong than calling the gaining and holding of confidence an instruction in "salesmanship." Salesmanship may be a most respectable skill, but it deals purely with a packaged offering. The salesman handles the goods but never thinks of producing or creating them. A car or a TV set stands finished and brightly illuminated on the sales floor before he enters the picture.

But in creating man's accommodations an architect, for instance, offers no fixed merchandise; it all slowly emerges out of darkness. His product develops very slowly, or sometimes may jump into or out of his mind by leaps and bounds, while he acts as an explorer of circumstances, as a diagnostician fitting symptoms into a comprehensive picture, as a therapist, prognosticator, and consultant to his client on matters which may affect a whole lifetime.

Since Hippocrates took his wonderful oath, no physician has openly and "ex cathedra" recommended salesmanship to his students. But, reluctantly, I have perhaps to admit that architecture cannot yet be taught like medicine. Some professionals allude to the importance of sales skill and to the cursed interference of other parties, especially of the client, who is pictured as hampering the aspirations and inspirations of the artist, a self-expressionist practitioner! Yet for the designer of human settings a fascination with the wealth and variety of other individualities, rather than overindulgence of one's own, is the greatest blessing. Perhaps one can be conditioned to such a selfless attitude from kindergarten on. Maybe this is too late, and nursery school is the place! Because such an attitude leads to the acquisition of confidence. It is a natural instrument toward possible creation, an intrinsic and passionately desired support of an individual's contribution to social benefit. If it is allowed to degenerate into a commercial device, confidence-holding shows itself to be perishable.

I have long told young people, who come to me from many quarters and lands, that it is a wonderful experience to be "understood." It is a feeling for which any human being longs, and is connected with our particular type of brain development.

Animals may not long for understanding, do not feel isolated in the midst of a crowd, do not seek or give advice. These are all human traits. To be helped by an experienced professional, a therapist, a minister, a psychiatrist, an architect, in bringing to realization and fruition our innermost motives and aspirations—this is a strictly human performance, full of tension, a human drama and sometimes a tragedy.

Professional confidence-holding is a glorification of these very human nonanimal relationships which no beings except us have to each other. A doctor gains almost magical powers if we trust him fully. Should anyone have the suspicion that his doctor wants to "sell" him a cardiogram or an operation, the doctor's powers are lost.

A "designer for happiness ever after" is here an extreme case. Provided we can gain and hold trust and confidence, our creative powers of integration grow and grow while we work on and continue to create. Without it, the most liberal budget may not mean success, but, on the contrary, tantalizing, embittering frustration and resentment.

School can't very well teach all this, but one given in apprenticeship sees daily, hourly, how the psychological processes of getting together, of welding and fusing motivations, evolve: and whenever the "boss" has time, while driving to the premises and dodging metropolitan traffic, brain-physiological interpretations of all that has recently happened—more than far-reaching "psychology," have often and most practically been discussed by us clearly but in short order. Aristotle taught while walking around in the Lyceum at Athens; Zeno, while promenading in the Painted Stoa; Plato, in the Academia; and the learned friends of Lorenzo de Medici, in a convent in Fiesole. We had often to solve our profound and exhilarating problems, as well as we can, behind the steering wheel of an automobile. There is often no time to seek the shadow of cypress or olive trees, or to sit beneath the mango boughs which Buddha found so inspirational.

I was soon to see similar things happen fast in military service and in hectic war action. Here, naturally, results must come as fast as measures are being taken, in contrast to academic peace.

But observing the architect's perennial rush to produce in a brief time values for a long amortization period—or even for the endless transition into what man imagines to be eternity—is significant for the pulse of our day. Our rush is one of an apprentice's great experiences. He can observe all, not only from nearby, but from a position in the middle of the fray. Seeing the old man jump from task to task in fast succession, seeing his endless patience exercised on so many persons and all personnel, but above all on clients, who cause the creative doing, is an eye opener to the young man. He does not simply learn a few technical tricks; in the midst of it all he soon can become assimilated.

Most desirably, he learns to note each person's faculties, say, each client's capacity to read drawings and to grasp ideas in conversation. Always people are entitled to be addressed in the *language they understand*. I do not mean only Portuguese or Danish or Urdu, but on their level of speech, precisely in the idiomatic vocabulary they use. The sketching as well as the explaining will be different with the learned president of a junior college, a sophisticated art lover, or the owner of a second-class millinery store on Hollywood Boulevard, nervous about whether he still can get his share of the Christmas sale after completion of the building.

All are human. Slowly, slowly I came to value more than to deplore this circumstance. And I have endeavored to transmit my feeling later to younger collaborators and apprentices.

Presence of mind, continuity, and steadiness, which are equally necessary, are here in life demonstrated differently than in the classroom or seminary of this or next term. Contract promises run over long years, and the best specimens of design, like the cathedral of Chartres, have been executed with patience over vast periods. Moreover, an artist's work, or *oeuvre*, as the French say, consisting of many hundreds of paintings or productions over a lifetime, is an entity, to be understood as ONE, with expansion and holdovers from one task into the next. All solutions are, in a way, only temporary, abatements and fulfillments as life goes on. Technical and spiritual experiences are the most significant by-products of each episode, to be stored and treasured for the benefit of coming performance.

In this way the career of a workshop goes on beyond individual jobs. An endless overlapping and continuity prevails over and above completion dates, beyond individual clients and contracts. The team of coworkers must feel and understand this perpetual fertile sedimentation; recalling and utilizing past experiences as base for ever newly structured performance.

The concomitant long-span emotional investment must not be chopped up nor lost. Needed is order, neatness of thought, recording, filing, and *treasuring* of all, even of small detailed achievements. Once realized, they play their role in the creative effort to come. They are not a momentary glitter, there is never a start from scratch. The whole methodic operation is far removed from old-maidish pedantry, and perhaps also from the best-directed short course of a few months or even a few years. Neither could encompass the entire long-drawn-out process.

The growth of a unique, distinctive whole from the layering of its parts, of course, occurs with many kinds of sustained efforts. But my own most authentic experience simply happened to occur in planning and architecture. Still, much of this is indeed a case of far-reaching and more general import.

Here, to convey design ideas, with gentle friendliness and yet with sharp definition, to all collaborators and to the construction crew, on windswept or sun-drenched premises, is the creative duty, need, and cherished prerogative of a design team. *Communication under trying circumstances fills a life.* Drawings and written directives may be almost as warmly sonorous, amicably exhortative, and stimulating as the spoken word. They can also disrupt the friendly formation of creative collaborative human and group relationships on which any building up has depended from time immemorial. And now we surely are—on both sides of the famous political drapery—in the midst of the mass-transaction age.

It is hard for a student of theory to learn as concretely as can an apprentice. The latter has the chance to observe the older, responsible men in their worries or working with glowing eyes and visible relish. He need not faintly *simulate* the real flesh-and-blood experience, nor settle for viewing finished specimens on slides or in books and magazines. Physiology, biology, are studied less well from frozen specimens than from observation of live functional processes. In the "profession of empathy" which I have chosen, it is done, if possible, by sharing in those processes from moment to moment.

The sorcerer is said to have apprentices to whom he does not disclose the last inner secrets. I, on the other hand, have loved to disclose the organic growth of my career, and I learned from disclosing it. It was one of offering humanitarian and much to-the-point biological understanding.

Later, I have often had all my apprentices, as my collaborators, present at face to face, heart to heart meetings with those who trusted to us a task, although this might be very unorthodox. And yet, with all that openness, I am afraid sorcerers have to take a lot of last secrets into their graves, even if they most willingly try to give them away.

Each of us, locked into his mysteriously complex individuality, and into the world as he alone takes it in or experiences it, can never spell out or truly quite describe his inner workings and the characteristic intimacy of his own human chances. Yet perhaps the older man can feel himself better into the apprentice than vice versa.

I should say one thing before turning from education, especially also where it touches on building design and lastly aims to give house and town to human beings for years to come.

Our civilization is by no means, as often assumed, uniformly geared to quick turnover. Picasso's periods, or even yearly car models, easily traded in, have little in common with new three-door-two-tone-wall-hung refrigerators. Once built in, these are hard to remove every spring and fall, quite unlike mobile lighter-weight ladies' hats or other modish apparel. Some things are not easily turned in or given up.

Above all, optimistic human beings must still scratch together lifetime savings (or strain all credits to pay off—again during a lifetime) before they put their funds into hands which for them will draw lines of lasting decision. There *are* quite lasting decisions also these days. We must surely learn to recognize them in the midst of all our rush.

Our main theme and subject in creative and critical building philosophy, however, is not *economic time*. It is not least the problem of *physiological time*, short range and long range, profoundly interwoven. This has been on my mind for many years.

During a "space age" in which time is so often mentioned in connection with colossal velocities, we must be doubly careful to guard against subtle organic experiences, sudden— or again of reverberating endurance. True enough, nervous propagation velocities are themselves very high, and have been so with us for almost a biological eternity. On the other hand, in human tissue and receptors, fatigue phenomena are creeping up at slower, lower speeds, but nevertheless once more, with very decisive significance for our life. After a while they begin to emerge gloomily, when we try to translate fast-entertaining jazz irregularities and syncopation into concrete and stainless steel, into architecture and building bric-a-brac. Left for those long amortization periods, they burden our system and clutter up the street.

The nice and essential thing about fashion talk and jazz is that they pass—even if you should hear them over the ether for a whole night. Matters architectural stay with us much more lastingly.

Our apprentices—the men who will build on the moon of tomorrow, or deal over the planetary spaces, will have to solve their problems, not from a corner of Madison Avenue, but by a deep penetration into human organic make-up, of which we know more and more every year. Our metabolism, circulation, heartbeat, respiration rhythm does not, must not, change while we orbit or travel into the farthest distance—or else there is utter failure. For that matter, little has changed in us during the last million years. Let us use this fact as the basis for combating fashions which might easily become a bore for the duration.

Architecture can turn tiresome, like a joke repeated for thirty years. But we know that some buildings have had a tremendous time run; somehow they must be organically safe and, more than others, *right* for reception.

The classical field of grandest, fastest progress—and decay— is not architecture, cautiously paid for, but our mushrooming spendthrift weaponry. The proud fighter bombers of last year become heaps of abandoned sheet metal this year. It is a bit crazy to cover acres of ground with this inventive debris in that growing Air Force museum and try to keep the old-fashioned pigeons from nesting in the hollows of yesterday's jets. The next oncoming war will be much more "progressive," will differ greatly from what history has had to offer so far and from the kind of lessons it supposedly can teach. Still, in peace and war, a human common denominator persistently remains, or else there is and will be nothing at all to talk about.

Perhaps it is best to continue by remembering what happened to me and others in that old-fashioned World War I. For a student of wholesome human setting, experience was then way off in a darkly clouded future. For years to come, there was no school, only some apprenticeship in resourceful presence of mind.

Exotic Training

It is instructive to ponder the comparative powers of the routine and, again, of the extraordinary event—a brief festival like Christmas Eve among the three hundred and sixty-five days of a long year; the sliding open of a door on a first freshly scented spring day; a period of sudden mourning, sudden disaster, revolution, and war. *Short emotive shocks are at least equally as momentous as long-lasting habit.*

A designer of human setting must comprehend that life molds man by both the usual and the extraordinary. Even a house does not make one happy by the month, but often in fractions of a second. Our organic system responds this fast, and it keeps reverberating. The out-of-the-ordinary becomes a significant life event. A world war breaking loose after storm clouds have gathered for a long, anxious time is a striking example of what I mean, and such it was to a young man like me. A future architect learned here to be less parochial, more cosmopolitan, and even to feel himself into exotic situations.

In a Far-Distant Fortress

A month before the war began, Archduke Franz Ferdinand was murdered in Sarajevo. I knew him not only from the newspapers but through my brother-in-law's personal acquaintance and narratives. As custodian of the crown treasure of the Holy Roman Empire and director of the national art collection in Vienna, Agathon was often ordered to see Franz Ferdinand. Now, as the summer of 1914 was getting under way, the heir apparent and his morganatic wife, Countess Chotek, were first bombed and then, a few hours later, shot to death in their automobile as they crossed an ominous bridge. That meant war, some people said.

It was an exciting Sunday. Strangely, I remember the horse-chestnut tree under which I happened to hear the news. But life seemed to go on, and I prepared for a peacetime call into the armed forces, in which I had a tour of duty every second year. I was a field-artillery cadet, horse-mounted, but this time I was to go to some mountainous place at the southernmost tip of the Empire, to a fortress called Trebinje in Herzogovina. I hardly bothered to study the map, but I thought that after the anticipated four weeks in uniform I could get passage across the Adriatic and start a vacation trek from Brindisi through Italy.

I bought a Baedecker of southern Italy and tried to find out whether the military "distinctions" could easily be torn off my linen summer tunic. I would then more or less look like a civilian tourist and pass the border to our southern neighbors, whom I pictured peacefully growing lemons.

My relatives—father, one of my brothers, sister, brother-in-law, and sister-in-law—had dinner with me and saw me off at the Southern railway station. That tunic of mine was tight, very tight around the neck, and the July evening was as hot as the dickens, so that I almost fainted before I boarded the fateful train. Then it began, an endless rumble south, veering east, through Hungary and Croatia. It changed to a narrow track and chuck-chucked through Bosnia for another day, then paused for a few hours' stopover in Sarajevo. With some new traveling acquaintances I hired a taxicab, passed some Moslem mosques for the first time in my life, and went to look at the spot where the archducal pair had spilled their blood as Gavrilo Princip fired his Serbian army pistol. Now a silly sentry was positioned on the bridge to prevent, I suppose, a recurrence of the historic incident.

I noticed some people standing around telephone poles,

reading a printed proclamation: it was a copy of the Austro-Hungarian Empire's famous ultimatum to the kingdom of Serbia. Somebody told me, grinning, that I would not get to Brindisi or anywhere else for the next six months. For the last five years there had been constant mobilizations against Serbia. Once caught in uniformed service, people had stayed on for nine or twelve months; but I, far away, had had no idea of such things. When I was on the train again, I peacefully read a section in my Italian travel guide. For the next two years I carried that little red book through all the mountains of the Balkans, until finally I threw this useless ballast out of a now bearded warrior's baggage, to lighten the saddlebags of my pack mule.

I would not see the architecture of southern Italy until a quarter of a century later, when a Japanese (*Nippon Yusen Kaisha*) liner landed me briefly in Naples, having come from California, after passing the South Seas, Asia, and Egypt.

But in those distant days of July, 1914, the narrow-track train continued south, winding its way through the green-bottomed craterlike or bowl-shaped valleys, the *Poljes* of the chalky limestone mountains, which for two thousand years had been denuded by the Roman shipbuilders, Venetians, and Turks. Often the scenery looked like a weird moonscape. A short stop brought me into the ancient provincial Turkish town of Moztar, in front of a bridge which might have incorporated a Roman arch centuries ago; it was most picturesque, as were the prayer towers of the near-by Moslem tabernacles. I found, provincial as metropolitans are, that I knew little of my far-flung imperial native land and its physical or ethnic geography.

After several days spent traveling through strange stretches of the world, I was informed that we were approaching Trebinje, the old, now modernized, fortress which was my destination. (Night had fallen when the train stopped at the track's end. A crowd of people had gathered at the simple station, sleeping beside their baggage—women and children waiting for a train to take them north. Evacuation!) The fortress had just been alerted, put on war footing. Still, I was only mildly interested; probably it was one of those routine mobilizations, one of those false alarms which, as I just had been told, happened every year on this southern frontier—because I now understood that I must be close to the border. Some travel companions and I squeezed through the crowd and managed to grab a *Droschke*, which took us "to town." Pretty soon we saw a few dim lights and the old Turkish city walls of heavy stone masonry, dominated by minarets reaching into the starry sky or sometimes silhouetted whitely against the tall mountain scenery. It was hellishly hot, even by night. I was landed at the "White House," an old-fashioned edifice housing a third-rate hotel. Lots of people were on the street, and many officers in the dim lobby; everywhere excitement dominated the noyau, to use the classical military word for the inner core of a fortress. It happened to be a sleepy, hot fortress, "alerted" only a couple of hours ago.

I went upstairs to a primitive empty room with a rickety metal pipe bedstead on the wood floor and a few wall hooks on which I hung tunic and pants. I crumpled a newspaper and a copy of the ultimatum to Serbia and looked for a wastepaper basket; finding none, I threw them under the table. There was a glass and, beside the table, a water faucet like those in old-fashioned kitchens. Troubled by thirst, I turned and turned the faucet—no water. I cursed, and dropped naked on the bed.

My sleep was fitful. I was bumping along on some tracks, as I had done these last days. I dreamed of bombs being thrown by anarchist nationalists. War was on, but I was at Niagara Falls, of which I had seen a photo as a child. It was a big waterfall, refreshing and cooling in this damned heat. It rushed and thundered. Suddenly I was awake. It was dark—in fact, pitch-dark—and I was close to a rushing waterfall, trying to remember where. I saw some white, light object hurrying under me in fast circles. I found my matches and lighted one. Water was pouring from the faucet and swirling round and round on the floor; the crumpled newspaper and ultimatum to Serbia, and to the world, was in the vortex, speeding without end. Later I learned that there was a great water shortage in the fortress. Water was released by the pumping station at 4:00 a.m. and turned off in the early afternoon. Two days later the Montenegrins took over the pumping station somewhere near the village of Lastva, a few kilometers from the frontier, and had to be driven off by a fairly frightened garrison.

That was the beginning of World War I, and occurred some time before the official declaration of war. In Paris, St. Petersburg, Berlin, and London diplomatic wires were burning up. In Rome, our Italian allies of the Triple Alliance were sitting on the fence, from which they—much later—jumped in the wrong direction as far as we were concerned. I knew nothing of all this European excitement. It was just Trebinje for me, a name I had only recently learned to pronounce. I washed my face and shaved, girded myself with my sword, and had a cup of coffee. It had been a little cooler before the sun rose.

In spite of my youth—I was twenty-two—I had done some thinking on the future of the world and of myself in particular. I recapitulated whatever cosmopolitan views I could muster while drinking coffee of Turkish aroma from the stores of a fortified town, and thought of the long talks I had had with my brother-in-law, Agathon, about the imminent downfall of our world. For here was the ponderous reality of a thousand-year-old empire going on the last lethal warpath. Inevitably, I also remembered our discussions about our Viennese heritage and our visits to the foremost artistic and intellectual personalities of that cultural metropolis to which we belonged with our hearts.

My thoughts led me further, to the physical silhouette, profile, and architecture of Vienna. I had once pictured myself as a peaceful architect in that city. She had the leading men: Otto Wagner, spiritual father to Joseph Olbrich, Josef

Hoffmann, Fabiani and, in a niche for himself, Adolf Loos, a revolutionary of another brand. Before I recognized Frank Lloyd Wright and Louis H. Sullivan in far-distant America, Otto Wagner had been my idol. (Loos was enamored of America's warm humanity crossed with matter-of-factness, and he had become my most influential personal friend.) Recently I had changed my plans, and had decided to make the United States, which had been the unrequited love of Loos, my home—perhaps going to California, where, as I had vaguely heard, Frank Lloyd Wright was at that time. Spiritually by then I was second generation to another continent beyond the seas.

I stopped the wanderings of my mind and said good-by to other projects. For the moment I seemed to have a European war on my hands, specifically an alert of the South Herzogovinian fortress Trebinje, surrounded by the high Karst Mountains, with faintly visible outlying forts on their backs.

I had never been in a fortress before. I finished breakfast and walked out into the excited, busily scurrying crowd. At once I was spotted by a messenger from fortress headquarters, who escorted me, the newest newcomer, right to the commanding general. Major General Braun, an old-timer with a drooping gray mustache, told me with scarcely subdued excitement in his voice that every man, especially every officer or officer's aspirant, such as myself, was welcome at this crucial moment. "You know, young man, the fortress has been alerted since yesterday night. I am busy. This is Captain von Tharnay, my artillery staff officer."

Fortyish Captain Tharnay, with short-cropped black hair, at once arranged that eleven privates and one private first class were subordinated to me—the latter being the only one who could speak a few half-intelligible words in my language. All were Serbian country yokels, of course Serbians under the Empire flag, and supposedly loyal. They goose-stepped behind me as the private first class led us to a group of horse-drawn wagons. We requisitioned three or four, with my guide handing out the proper order and written receipt. Then we went to munition dumps, where we loaded cases of old-fashioned projectiles, grenades, and shrapnels of venerably ancient model and vintage. I had never seen a machine gun close by before, or its cartridge belts. This was all thoroughly unknown and startling to me, the commander of a dozen men, whom I was to lead to an equally unbeknown outlying fort. I understood its name was Kravica; much later I picked up the Serbian language and was able to equate the word *Kravica* with "little cow."

War started laboriously, as it probably did for a million other people as well.

Before we were ready to leave the fortress core, the sun had risen high and perspiration was dripping from me and my twelve men. We had one more chore. We went to the sanitary warehouse and reported to the commanding staff surgeon, a bespectacled, bearded, and, as it turned out, stupidly circumstantial elderly officer. He had been through many such alerts and mobilizations, and always was troubled by one or the other loss when the rumpus was over. While giving out the sanitary *Tornisters*, puzzling cases and packages of sanitary material, he was most bureaucratically anxious that piece by piece the contents—bone scissors, scalpels, gauze roll after gauze roll—be checked off from an inventory as per army rules and transferred in an orderly fashion to my "responsibility in full." At the end I was directed to sign the list of transmitted medical treasures and a receipt for same.

I almost fainted in the heat. Finally I pulled myself together and jumped on the first of my wagons, loaded with a cargo of two machine guns, ammunition for some 1875-model field cannon, which I was to find emplaced on the mountain, and bone scissors and bandages, all of which, to my perfect ignorance, then seemed useless. We began to move, passing the old buildings and the dark-gray stone masonry of the circumvallations and minarets of the old Turkish town which may have dated from the time of Suleiman II, whose armies were turned back at Vienna in the last quarter of the seventeenth century.

Indeed, it was awfully hot in July at 11:00 a.m. as we passed the bordello, with the girls, after a long night and as yet without renewed hairdo, already up and looking out the open windows. We passed through the old Bielicer city gate of the fortress and started our march first along the valley of the Trebinschica River toward Lastva. Some peasants sitting at the roadside were selling watermelons. I did not know then that cholera was endemic and the sellers and their wares out of bounds and medically contraindicated. With the private first class as an interpreter, I bought some melons, and we began munching them. He claimed to know the way to Kravica, where he had been on shooting maneuvers, and pointed out other high mountain forts with lovely Serbian names—Gliva and Gličanje. Kravica was the farthest south, halfway to Zaslab, Bilica, and the border of Crna Gora, as Montenegro is called in the Serbian language. I started to learn the attractive southern Slavic tongue on this wagon trek, as I have learned so many other languages, later around the globe, without any schoolbook.

We began to climb into the mountains to the left of the valley, and at last reached a desolate, neglected spot, a building with four ancient 70-mm. field guns standing, forlorn and out of order, at the side of an emplacement under construction. We were on an exposed point opposite a savage guerrilla-trained enemy. The night had fallen overhead before we reached the mountaintop, and down in the dark valleys we saw the frontier hamlets go up in fires laid by our Montenegrin adversaries. I would soon learn that matches played an important role in Balkan wars.

War is impressive to hear of only from a distance. Our daily effort to entrench and defend ourselves was an exhausting as it was petty. For two weeks we worked like madmen surrounding our machine guns and cannon with barbed wire. We laid a phone to distant Fort Gliva and started to speak with a

Captain Endlicher, who had also been there the year before. He was our commander and supposedly knew the place and purpose of our command. In civil life he commanded a fire brigade from a desk in Vienna.

After a week or two a platoon of sappers arrived to lay wired dynamite charges around our barbed-wire fence, which we duplicated, triplicated, and supplemented with desperate diligence—twelve men from Bosnia and a young officer aspirant from our distant metropolis, facing the mountains and mountaineers of Montenegro, who had knives with which to cut our throats, pistols, guns, and matches.

At night, while I lay gazing at the incredibly bright stars, dynamite charges would suddenly go off a hundred feet outside our barbed-wire fence. Had a fox, a weasel, or a rabbit run into the trigger wires, or were prowling spies behind the dark rocks? Finally a Polish first lieutenant arrived with a few men and a big searchlight, gasoline powered, to light our forefield in surrounding valleys. Its motor would rattle along all night, and make the shrubs glow in the distance. Then a platoon of third-draft infantrymen came, elderly men from German-speaking Bohemia. It was a motley of nations and a babel of languages, just as it was throughout the Austro-Hungarian army.

Duty four hours, off duty four hours, the clock around. And we started to shoot—the war was on.

Meanwhile the Russians took Lemberg, the greatest Austrian fortress in the north; the Hohenzollern Empire went "shoulder to shoulder" into the fray. Clemenceau and a million other Frenchmen, Englishmen, and other human beings got excited all around the globe. I turned the searchlight at Kravica, saw no newsprint, knew nothing of the world.

Within the international "tale told by an idiot, full of sound and fury," life went on for eighteen months in both Kravica and, later, in and around Trebinje. I learned to talk to men, and also to girls, in Serbian; a hardened soldier can be a confidant of young femininity, pregnant by other officers who had meanwhile fallen in mountain ambushes and skirmishes.

We began to prepare for an offensive into Montenegro, and I was ordered back into the noyau. There I lived under the shadow of an old minaret in a Turkish house, adjacent to its harem but, of course, well separated from it. The young children, boys and girls, were my friends.

One day as I cleaned my army pistol—having first emptied it, I thought, of all projectiles—it suddenly went off while pointed out the window. The last of a round had been in the barrel. A group of kids was playing out there, and I watched them anxiously. Would any one of them fall, face down? None did; I breathed deeply. Fortunately the shot had gone a little over their heads. A captain, visiting my landlord's daughter in the neighboring room, cleared his throat. I heard him tiptoe to my door. He knocked, vaguely supposing that I had committed suicide. But no, I was all right. Yet the thought of suicide had come to me and others under the load of the questions: How long will this war last? How will it all end for our country, an empire subtly balanced upon eleven quarreling nations?

Nevertheless, life within this heterogeneous empire and its army provided a good preparation for a later cosmopolitan constructive consulting career on a still-diversified globe, a career almost always in the midst of disunified groups of human beings.

I did a lot of thinking during these endless four years of war, in the fortress, in the wintry mountain campaign, often alone on horseback through pathless solitudes in sultry Albania, a country almost as shut off as Tibet. Its natives may have been the first Europeans, thousands of years before Greeks, Romans, Germans, and Slavs pushed into this fateful, smallish west-end peninsula of Asia. My thoughts dwelt on the relativity of living customs; I became kindly impartial to "natives," existing around the planet and getting innocently enmeshed in world civilization and now industrialized technology. Often, in the midst of rocks and gunfire, or on the top of Albanian hills, looking over the primeval landscape of mosquito-infested marshlands, I thought of another country, as yet unembroiled in this, America.

The first year it was a war without Italy or Africa in it. The other great militaristic powers were engaged in a terrific display of peace-accumulated energy and armament. My life's destination was construction, but there and then all aimed at destruction on an unprecedented scale.

Sea Power in Silhouette

August 18, 1914, was the eighty-fourth birthday of Franz Josef, the Austrian emperor of endless reign. As a boy of eighteen he had been seated on the uneasy throne of Austria during the "liberal revolution" of 1848.

In the town of Trebinje a milling crowd of soldiers on furlough, Serbian peasants, and lots of girls had got together for the celebration, and preparations had been started for fireworks in the evening. I looked forward to a good time, all dressed up in my best linen uniform, with my cavalry saber clanking and clattering on the pavement at every step. (I was one of the few mounted warriors in town, a horseback hero.) Suddenly I was accosted by an orderly, a messenger from fortress headquarters, who summoned me to the general. I was received personally and told what I proudly knew so well, that I was commanding the only horse-drawn field gun, a "movable unit." Then, like a bombshell, the general said with a flare: "The combined English-French Mediterranean fleet is steering up the Adriatic Sea at full force." They might use the Emperor's birthday as the occasion for a show of strength, or they might take advantage of the festivities to attempt a landing.

The artillery staff officer placed a map before me on the table and showed me a route from our position in the fortress toward the coastal mountains. "Assemble your crew at once," he ordered. "Leave the fortress in thirty minutes. You must find and alert your men wherever they are in the festive crowd. Understood, cadet?"

"Yes, sir!"

"You will proceed at a trot-gallop on this route west. Sweat the horses as much as you need; never fall in step—like the fire department, understood? "

"Yes, sir!"

"At five-thirty p.m. you will be approaching an old *kula*, or Turkish fortress point, at three thousand feet, overlooking the sea. Do not expose cannon or horses to view, of course. Dismount and find a suitable emplacement, invisible even to sharp naval binoculars. I know, you have no spare horse for the ammunition cart. All you can have are the twenty-seven shrapnels you carry in the nine ammunition cases under the front seat of your field cannon. Correct?"

"Correct, sir!"

"You have a seventy-millimeter gun and you may face thousands and ten thousands of naval-artillery caliber. Your job will be to delay action in case they should try to land detachments around the small port of Gravosa. You know, it nestles between green peninsulas, far below where you'll be."

"I know, sir!"

"Be judicious in using your twenty-seven rounds of shrapnel," said the commanding general. "Yes, Excellency, I understand."

A boy ready for holiday fireworks a few minutes ago, I suddenly felt myself growing up to a task of historic dimensions, of perhaps lasting significance, possibly a tomb of honor as that of Leonidas at Thermopylae.

Small people, small things, suddenly can count as colossal. A shoestring budget ingeniously managed may mean more for the world of tomorrow than ponderous investments handled without inspiration. How often have I later, as an architect, relived this feeling, sparked by an important moment and suddenly realized, with all its potential consequences. As trifles can become very big, a single moment can ruin an eternity.

The captain of the artillery staff placed a thick brochure in my hands. "These are silhouettes," he explained. I vaguely remembered that in the eighteenth century such black profile silhouettes eternalized the loveliness of a French king's mistress, and that a Swiss psychologist and writer of that time, Johann Kaspar Lavater, had tried to base a science of human character upon them. A great deal can be seen from a little black profile. It implies life or death. Briefly I had to think again that I was a student of architecture from Vienna who knew nothing much of battleships or landing gear—French, British, or otherwise. My mind swirled, my heart palpitated.

Flipping quickly through the brochure of silhouettes, the captain said, "We have no time to go through this, but here is the *Waldeck-Rousseau*. Four funnels, you see ... watch the number of gun turrets, it is easy to recognize. This is the *Gambetta*." It dawned most practically on me then how important shape details may be to the whole, and I have tried to follow this insight through a lifetime.

The captain paged rapidly through the French Mediterranean fleet and turned to the British dreadnoughts and superdreadnoughts; Winston Churchill had been advising their employment to force the Dardanelles, and now, suddenly, they were steaming up the Adriatic. "Their armor is naturally far too heavy," he remarked. "Especially don't waste shrapnels, but you may scatter lead over the decks of the landing detachments. Normally your range is too short to reach this bay here, but, of course, you can take into your calculations that you are three thousand feet above it; this lengthens your range appreciably."

I learned fast that a man in a strategic position might make his mark. But at the moment my head was turning; the afternoon heat was stifling. On such occasions I felt a little like fainting, but I looked at the general and my instructing superior, and suddenly I felt smartly animated by the latter's confidence. *He became my client.* I replied almost professionally: "Yes, Captain, I shall remember my own elevation. The main thing, I guess, is to shoot judiciously and sparingly; some unexpected exploding shrapnel here and there might delay action until they investigate. Of course, we must keep the detachment behind the rocks, invisible, especially the horses."

"You've got it," said the captain. "Dismissed! Good luck! Remember, two battalions of infantry are marching up the coast from Castelnuovo (Ercegnovi), but they can't fly. You are the only artillery. Delaying action. Everything is confidential, keep your mouth shut. Dismissed!"

Thirty minutes later the holiday crowds near the southwest gate of the fortress gasped, seeing me on horseback, with my only gun pulled by six galloping horses, the crew holding on to their hats. I wondered whether all the inland fireworks were off this evening. Gallop five to ten minutes, trot ten to fifteen minutes. The road was poor. The horses turned white with sweat, but the afternoon sun was slowly sinking into evening. Rocks, distant mountains, scrub oak. I thought of my father, my brothers, architecture, the guidebook through Italy; my saber clanked against my saddle as I galloped to fend off "the Allies." The British Navy had been the object of my admiration from boyhood on, although I knew little more about it than the fact that it was big. Their salty language I knew only from translations of boys' fiction. I wondered how the English admirals would signal to the French counteradmirals.

"Trot!" I commanded, to catch my breath. I caught a grateful look from the cannoneers, the gunners, whose bones rattled on their springless perch above the ammunition compartment. But soon, in devotion to my commanders in the fortress and my duty to the Habsburg Empire, which had stood so many hundred years, and in defiance of Churchill's British Navy, I gave the command, "Gallop!" The water canteens, already emptied in the hot afternoon, flew about hips and chests of the crew, my saber rattled again, the saddle squeaked, and my brain worked feverishly amid all this shaking, planning to bring this battle off right and be victorious. Toward six we approached the high rocky ridge, and I perceived the old Turkish *kula*. The round rock-built guardhouse stood out against the sky like an orientation point, and the thought crossed my mind that the British admiral might see it, too, and use it as an auxiliary aim to train his gun turrets—let us hope, elsewhere—by using a specified angle.

I shouted, "Halt!" and after cautiously dismounting, began with stiff legs to climb up the rocky path to the ridge. Here— I reached it—I raised my head between two stones—and saw, far below, the sea in the evening light—enlivened by a huge crowd of ships. They were there all right—in plain view: the British and the French! I recognized those four funnels of *Waldeck Rousseau*, and the characteristics of *Gambetta* and the dreadnoughts and superdreadnoughts from Malta, Gibraltar, and the other British Mediterranean bases. Through my binoculars I surveyed my old friends from the silhouette book. The whole fleet was lying still, smoke rising slowly into the western sky. Maybe they were cooking dinner.

No landing detachments were embarking for the moment, and I remembered that I was to spare my powder but keep it dry. I crawled back and explored a suitable emplacement. I corralled the horses behind a big rock, and the memory of an Indian story which I had read six or seven years earlier flitted through my mind. Now I was no boy, but a commander of imperial forces, locked in combat, so to speak, with France and England. I wondered how I, an apprentice in architecture, would come out of an engagement with experienced admirals. The situation seemed more static than dynamic.

As night descended, lively signaling started between the anchored ships out in the bay; we built a concealed fire—after having carefully blanketed and covered our sweaty horses— and heated some cans of Irish stew, which we used to call Hungarian goulash. My Serbian was still very scanty, and I just listened to the singing of my men under the stars, as I had done so often. During those war years I listened to the unison of Hungarians; the six-part harmonizing of Slovene voices; Rumanian clarinets doing pirouettes, or their imitation of human vocal color, Italian *canzones*, Swabian-

German sentimental songs; Czech and Polish songs—songs of all the eleven nations which then made up the Austrian melting pot. I became a cosmopolitan in the army of a far-flung empire, marching and camping in strange lands, where I learned to like the civilians, male and female, boys, girls, and infants—even learned to tell jokes in their language and harvest their laughter and a little good will. All my life long I have benefited from this exercise.

In the morning came the anticlimactic moment of the story which had started so heroically in both camps. Every account of war ought to end in a fizzle; it would greatly help pacifism through the ages. Fear must have crept into the hearts of the admirals; they might have dreamed through the nightmare of a clever ambush; by no possible espionage could they have availed themselves of the glorious knowledge that all their many turrets and guns fronted only against a 70-mm gun with twenty-seven projectiles, to be aimed by a civilian student-architect in a temporary artillery uniform. The British admiral and the French counteradmiral stopped their signaling. They had agreed to weigh anchor. Properly arranged in a cautious formation, the ships began steaming north for a demonstration offshore at Pola (Pulj), the biggest imperial sea base at the Istrian end of the Adriatic.

I cannot claim that I frightened them away, although my heart was stout and I was desperately determined at least to hold up their sinister strategic designs. At any rate, I had bravely faced the assembled might, the pride and display of Allied martial diplomacy. Mine, too, had been one of the last and remarkable displays of Habsburg dauntlessness, even though historians have not made as spectacular a report of it as of the Battle of Lepanto, where Don Juan of Austria was so magnificently dressed in red tights, or of Charles V's colorful march *en grande masse* into Brussels—or was it Antwerp? Lonely courage, even unsung, is a greater gain for life, I have found, than even conspicuous victories, which in the end prove inconsequential.

Well, later I heard that the French had landed, indeed, practically under my nose. They had sent a torpedo boat straight into Ragusa, where it lay by the pier, to the terror of the patriotic bystanders. A young French naval officer, with two men, disembarked and slowly strutted along the Stradone, the lovely old palace-studded main street. For medieval centuries Ragusa had been a dependency of Venice, and its principal pedestrian avenue of the Stradone peacefully displays architectural imitations of the dignified Palazzo Ducale at the Piazzetta and the Riva degli Schiavoni. The Frenchmen walked into a tobacco store, courteously paid French money for a few packages of Bosnian cigarettes, which are famous for their flavor and their slender conical instead of cylindrical shape, smiled "Oh, la la" at the curious girls at open windows, and reluctantly embarked again on their torpedo boat.

A year later, having passed through many experiences, both most personal and military, I was again in those naked chalk mountains, from which yellow-blooming bushes of broom cascaded down to a subtropical coast and a deep-blue sea. By then it had become clear to me that life and history can seesaw. The long-revered "Iron Chancellor" Bismarck, monumented in so many German city squares, suddenly had become a blunderer, a colossus with feet of clay. His whole idea of German friendship with Russia and later with Italy had woefully collapsed, and now Italy, our former peacetime ally, had entered the war against us.

This time I was acting as first officer of a more regular field battery when the entire Italian fleet showed up before me about three miles offshore. At sunrise it started to shell a curve in the one-track railway along the coastal mountains. I watched behind our guns, which now numbered twelve. Compensation for rolling and pitching had not yet been perfected, and after the first shots from those formidable turrets, the shells started to miss their aim most amazingly as we looked on. Projectiles in their flat and slightly swayed trajectories flew five miles farther inland, and only a few hit the substructure and bed of the strategic railroad. At 8:00 a.m., as we watched, something most spectacular happened almost only a jump offshore. Within ten minutes after what looked like a diminutive explosion, the Italian flagship *Garibaldi* heeled over and disappeared second by second, and then altogether, into the sea. Simultaneously, as if upon a signal—probably, indeed, upon a signal—all the rest of the fleet dispersed quickly in all directions without any attempt whatever to salvage or save lives. And hardly anyone could swim some five kilometers to shore.

That afternoon, after several thousand men had tragically drowned and a hundred million lira of a still-hard currency had sunk to the bottom of the bitter blue Adriatic, the railroad was fixed, and I set off on a mission to Castelnuovo. As the little locomotive began to wind along the curved coast of the bays, the Bocche di Cattaro (Kotor), I saw from the car window quite a commotion on shore. A brass band was playing, and a small Austrian submarine emerged and slowly moved to base. It was the one which that morning had torpedoed and sunk the huge battleship *Garibaldi* in the midst of its guardian torpedo boats and companions. The submarine commander and the heroic crew stood on the deck of their tiny vessel behind the periscope and listened to the ovational music of a brass band on shore while newspaper presses began printing the story in Vienna, London, Berlin, and New York. The Roman papers, I am sure, reported: All men saved.

I thought of all the schools and hospitals and community centers and housing which had not been built in order to finance the Goliath battleship and its David killer: the submarine had not done the job with a simple shepherd's sling and a cheap fieldstone. I pondered our famous technological and budgetary progress since the Philistines were routed and figured out the cost for two hours' naval shelling of a railroad curve which was fixed the same afternoon. I am still figuring how much less peace costs when architects are employed in civilian clothes, which I yearned for.

This budgetary and revenue discrepancy between war and

peace, between investment and yield, has become much more extreme while I have aged and lost control of the figures.

During those decisive years of and after the First World War, which also were decisively molding my own life and that of my generation, I was breathlessly engaged, and there was little time to jot down a diary. Half a century later, I found confused notes puzzling even to myself, who once hastily penciled them down in little books. Some may have been fever dreams. Some seem like Ulysses, scribbling himself, amidst a tempest, far-slung brainstormy associations of his own. I never really was committed to an asylum. But I might be; the story is not yet over. Or, again, I might reach Ithaca and put things right, even though they are at sixes and sevens.

Unknown Europe

I have an idea that an architect without much of an Odyssey, who is living in a metropolitan area and does not know much more than his own provincial surroundings, is really not capable of service to mankind as it now exists on a very shrunken globe.

Lands that need development and could avoid our confusion and perversion of natural assets, our "civilization damages," are plentiful. I think that even in periods when I was completely deprived of the possibility of working at my own profession, I have acquired a great deal which has helped me in this production later. The First World War, in which I spent four years, was one of these periods.

The area to which the war brought me in southeastern Europe is one which was as remote from civilized centers as any place I have ever seen. As a matter of fact, I believe that there are very few spots in South America, or Africa, or in Asia, which are as remote and forsaken by cultural progress as were countries like Albania and the eastern portion of the rugged country called Montenegro at that time.

Montenegro is a very mountainous region indeed. Once

upon a time it was covered with woods, which were recklessly depleted by the Romans—I suppose to build vessels to match the fleet of Carthage—and later by the Venetians, for the piles which serve to underpin the greatness of Venice. This area has never recovered its topsoil, and is now just a chalky, rocky, arid mountain country. Only a few oaks and shrubs growing out of the crevices between the huge limestone boulders save it from being as barren as the moon. On horseback or afoot the terrain is extremely difficult to negotiate unless one has shoes with soles of woven rope like those of the Montenegrins. With this kind of shoe the natives can run like mountain goats over the dry bones of their geology. Their speed is amazing; it was very hard for soldiers wearing leather shoes with spiked soles to follow them. And, of course, the traveler in this country must be able to jump the crevices. The ground over which beast and men move shapes them psychosomatically.

Our march from Trebinje, Montenegro, started first against strongly defended high mountains which, I remember, were called Glumina. The Russian guns which the Montenegrins used were old-fashioned, but our march forward was restricted to very narrow mountain paths which could only be passed at very slow speed. It was really very difficult to carry our cannon over these passes while being continuously shelled from much higher positions. I recall how exciting it was when I came under fire for the first time, but after a few moments I strangely became the least excited and the calmest of the group—every time giving the order to get under cover when, long before the detonation reached our ears, I saw the flash of the guns going off across the valley. At that time almost all human abodes were already burned down, matches being what we humans employed before fusion bombs. At any rate, anything which was possibly edible or could be used as a shelter went up in flames. Occasional night attacks brought hand grenades from the cliffs above down upon Austrian heads, some, those of close friends of mine.

The first great city which we occupied was Podgorica, second in size only to Cetinje, the capital of Montenegro, and had not one quasi-contemporary building except the palace of King Nikita, who had already fled. I took my first tub bath in many months in the palace of this king, who owned the only bathtub in the place now called Titograd. Even the hospital, which was a very temporary affair, did not have one. By that time I had acquired quite a command of the Serbian language and could participate in civilian life. I ate with a local family and also arranged for them to cook for my fellow officers. I fell in love with the daughter, learned to play the balalaika a little, as well as an instrument with only about three strings which are all tuned to the same pitch and are only fingered to different tones. I believe it was called a gusla. I recall a celebration in the house of these people, who were very dignified—as are all Montenegrins, especially those who have always lived in the country as opposed to those who have returned from Manhattan. In the very small house, a two-story affair, a wedding took place with the accompanying festivities. The chain dance through various rooms, through all the doors, with hands always interlocked, appealed very much to me. So did the music, which moved in quarter tones. Without a piano, I tried to write down these tunes by ear. I recall a Serbian girl telling me, with a hardness in her face and voice: "You victors play, and we must dance."

I had varied adventures with civilians of both sexes. Slowly I became more acquainted with the countryside. When I was sent to Kotor, an Italian-speaking seaport, I rode in a truck which took me through the whole country in something like two days. We traveled on a fantastic zigzag mountain road which led down over the Lovćen mountain into the Bocche di Cattaro, or Gulf of Kotor. This fiordlike inlet contained the greatest outlying naval fortress of the Austro-Hungarian Empire. I recall that when I first made this trip, it seemed extremely adventurous.

My journey took me to Cetinje, and I was highly interested

in seeing for the first time the capital of Montenegro, which in peacetime had been a little more open to tourist traffic coming up from the sea. It even had a hotel of some sort, as well as a legislative building and a Victorian palace for the king. From Cetinje we went down the winding highway, one of the most precipitous ever built. Coming over a crest, I suddenly experienced the fantastic view over the blue Adriatic sea and the mountain-girdled bay.

This road was a life line, and was continually reconstructed, improved, and reimproved during the campaign. It had to be kept open, regardless of cost and casualties. The wreckage of at least a hundred trucks could be seen strewn over the canyons and gorges. I saw steamships being towed up this road—in parts—to go into service on the faraway and inaccessible Lake Scutari. Much later, in the Peruvian Andes, I learned that the same feat of steamship transport had been accomplished, and vessels had been carried up to Lake Titicaca, 12,500 feet high. Here, three hours of maneuvering were needed at each hairpin turn, and during this process many trucks had ended up at the bottom of some deep precipice.

I particularly remember one of my many truck rides over the Lovćen which took me from Niš and Podgorica through starry nights, heat, cold, and danger. I was riding in the back of a truck with several men in ragged, dirty uniforms and two big barrels of gasoline when we approached one of the endlessly busy pioneer, or repair, companies. They were under the command of an "engineer" officer, who in civilian life probably had been a dentist or a high-school history teacher. They were trying to carry out their instructions to rebuild the road, which was always being destroyed by the wheels of the army supply trucks. As our vehicle tried to pass the "engineers" on the valley side, the ground beneath suddenly gave way. Our left rear end began to sink gently, hanging over the rocky steepness. We held our breath: it could be no more than two or three seconds till our truck would tip over and plummet into the gorge. It is an indelible experience to feel life so thickly condensed and to become so clearly conscious of it in a fraction of a moment.

Yet, almost imperceptibly, the sinking stopped. We still did not breathe or utter a word, but gently, gently, we began shifting to the hill side of the inclined truck platform, where fortunately the gasoline barrels counterweighted our fate. One after the other, gingerly and in silent prayer, we jumped out, and started breathing again only when we could look at our slanting truck from outside.

Several months later, after the surrender of all the Serbian and the far-flung Montenegrin troops, I was sent out with an orderly and two horses to travel over a huge portion of the country for which there existed no maps at all, or, where they existed, had only large white spots marked "moderately high mountains." This part of our earth had never really been cartographed, and we journeyed thus through the whole of northeastern Montenegro, always asking our way. I could speak sufficient Serbian now, but we rarely met anyone. The area is very sparsely populated, and one can travel for half a day without seeing any human habitation or human beings.

My orderly and I were a lonely pair of strange bedfellows. We would occasionally find someone, a boy or a girl, tending some goats amongst the rocks. From them we would try to find the next named place—I wouldn't say "town." There really were no towns and hardly any villages. We would usually get the answer *Po ura*, "half an hour or so," but then it might take something like three or four hours. We would find these places, but frequently slept outdoors in our sleeping bags. It was bitter cold, and most of the mountains were under snow. The upper portions of the mountain paths were continually so covered up that we couldn't find any trace of them, nor were there signs of any other travelers. Sometimes we would get directions such as: "Well, you go up this way and then to the left and then you go down the valley and you will come to another very steep climb. On top you will find a horse, a white horse, which is lying there and still has its eyes open, and then you turn sharp to the right and . . ." But when we arrived, that white horse wouldn't have eyes any more, because some birds had gouged them out. Frequently cadavers of beasts and corpses of soldiers or civilians were given as landmarks.

We had our own meat and other provisions in our baggage, and we carried preserve cans and paper packages of so-called coffee, a very vile sort of powder mixed with sugar which the army used to issue. The Montenegrins, who are used to that wonderful Turkish coffee, were ready to sell their souls for such a package containing something which tasted only very remotely like coffee. We would sometimes use this brew as an entrance gift when we wanted to make the people's acquaintance. They were also quite anxious to get some salt, which they hadn't had for two years. A pinch of salt was worth quite a bit. We could practically buy a whole chicken for it, together with a package of the horrible "coffee" powder.

Houses, if any, were grouped only very loosely and were built of local rocks and stones, so that they blended with the surrounding mountains to the point of being invisible. The only way to distinguish them was by the smoke coming out of the crevices along the joints of the roofing rocks—for the roofs were also made of flat rock slabs, and they did not join neatly and hermetically. There were no chimneys; the smoke just came out of every crack.

Inside these cavelike structures the people lived together with their goats. When one entered such a house, it was almost impossible to keep one's eyes open because of the stinging smoke. All the inhabitants looked quite pale-faced and poisoned from it, especially the children. This returned to my mind almost half a century later when I saw similar primitivism in the round huts of Zululand, South Africa. But this was Europe! From a wooden rafter, which was made out of a scrub-oak trunk, a kettle would hang over the fire, and the cooking was done in the middle of the room.

There was very little to be cooked: the entire country had been reduced to starvation by the surrounding enemy for something like two years. The people had practically nothing to eat. The men, of course, had all been in the army, and only the women produced anything that served as foodstuff. The goats, mules, and whatever they had in the way of small, shaggy horses had been more or less stolen—"requisitioned"—by our own army and, I suppose, by the Serbians, too. The inhabitants were in a terrible state, but they kept a stiff upper lip extremely well.

These people are born for warfare. Tall, aristocratically built, very tough and proud, they have a history of at least five to six hundred years of constant fighting against the Turks. They had some right to be violent warriors, because they were not at all given to self-pity when mistreated. They did not expect any quarter to be given; they could be absolutely sure that they would be killed and robbed and that their women would be raped. They just expected this and took it as natural. The Montenegrins are even more remarkable in this respect than the Serbians, although the latter, too, are capable of stoically taking it as well as of dishing it out. Both are very much in contrast to the Italians, who cannot get used to being mistreated by an invading enemy, although they have had plenty of experience. On the whole, I have found that most people and races today are not well adapted for war because they are so sensitive to being conquered.

A place that really struck me was Shavnik, one of the most important settlements. We came upon it suddenly, in a very deep valley which had the character of a steep-rimmed bowl, like a moon crater. The water came in on one side under the mountains and made its exit on the opposite side, also under the mountains. Since the rock strata were very porous, the water easily formed a tunnel and flowed out without eroding a long valley, but instead just irrigating a green plain. Such round bowl-shaped valleys are quite frequent in southern Bosnia and especially in Herzegovina. They are called *poljes*, or "fields," which their flat bottoms actually are. It was quite a climb downward for our heavily laden, cautious horses.

The picture of this valley, so surprisingly deep to have human habitation on its floor, has stuck firmly in my memory. It emerged in my mind again, many years later, when I saw La Paz in South America. At the boundary line between Peru and Bolivia I had been received by a whole delegation of friendly architects and planners, who traveled with me to La Paz. As I left the train, I wondered where the city actually was. We were almost 12,000 feet high up on the Altiplano, and all we could see were the 26,000-foot-high glaciers—nothing in the way of a city. But then I walked approximately ten steps toward the train shed, and there it was below me: a breath-taking sight. I looked down a terrific precipice, which descended something like 1,500 feet. The whole city of La Paz was packed far down in this deep hole. The chasm was not really a round valley, nor did it have a crater-shaped opening. It descended steeply, and at the deepest point there was, faintly visible, tropical vegetation. The sight was more spectacular than the Grand Canyon.

Throughout my life I have had similar amazing experiences: one landscape or townscape ringing a strange, faint bell of another memory from far away. Such is the remarkable switchboard of the brain, and it all works with an emotional cargo—with endocrine discharges in which an artist-architect must be justly interested. He himself is a master who can arrange for changes in our sensitive body chemistry by what he does to our room and our surroundings.

Animal behaviorists give sites credit as psychotopes, or "soul spots." Long before a church spire or the Empire State Building was built, organic life at the higher levels, and human life also, has tended to cling to conspicuous turns, twists, and towerings of the landscape.

Whenever we entered a village, we found everyone carrying a gun or two, although these people supposedly had been disarmed immediately, according to the armistice regulations made somewhere far, far away. But nobody did us any harm, and we certainly made no remarks to our friendly armed hosts that would have antagonized them. I was quite humorous and could tell jokes in Serbian. Also, I was considered a news-bringer, a person from the strange outside world who had many things to tell. Word would spread quickly through the whole village, through all the little mountain caves out of which the smoke was rising, and people would gather in one place, a house, in which we would sit with tears dripping from our red smoked-out eyes. I would hand out some salt and "coffee," and then discuss what I had seen. The people were very chivalrous, as they could have done away with us very easily. In a way they had every reason to do so, since they had never been treated at all well and had been so terribly ravaged by war.

But evidently I was capable of making friends, and besides, I had a rather moronic orderly, who was not obnoxious in any way. He didn't step on anybody's toes, or kiss any girls, or do anything else that might have caused trouble. His slow talk was like that of his Saxon ancestors. He came from Transylvania, the southeastern section of Hungary near the mountainous Rumanian border. His home village was so underdeveloped that he had never seen a stairway. When he first beheld stairs, later on in a "hinterland" hotel, he climbed them on his hands and feet: he only knew how to use a ladder. Being a primitive of another kind, the Montenegrins looked at him less strangely than they looked at me.

The journey offered much practical instruction in anthropology. Montenegrins in the country, as I have already mentioned, give the impression of being probably the most noble and dignified peasants one can find, perhaps more so even than the Spaniards. In a city such as Cetinje one can find a few people who have spent a couple of years in America and are engaged in selling liquor or running brothels. But most of the population are wonderful replicas of the noble savage as described at the end of the eighteenth century by Chateaubriand, who idolized the red Indians. But when one entered a cavelike dwelling and unexpectedly saw the wall covered with post cards and photographs of relatives in America, it looked most incongruous and spoiled the scale and character of this primitive environment. The cultural consistency of human beings and animals living together in a smoke-filled room, which is so wondrous to behold for an architect and designer of the human setting, can easily be destroyed. It is like a New Mexican Indian village where one can suddenly find a piece of linoleum in front of a built-in kitchen sink, all in an adobe hut of neolithic origin, or a framed flat Madonna color print on the curved wall of a circular Mau Mau house of packed East African dirt.

Tropical Malaria

Many months later we marched again through Montenegro, this time to the lake port of Rieka, which means river, and crossed Lake Scutari, which separates Albania from Montenegro. We landed at Shkodër (Scutari), which was a very important commercial center in Roman times, and still is. Its population is predominantly Catholic, quite different from the Greek Orthodox Montenegrins. Nevertheless, since the city was under Turkish rule for four or five hundred years, it is studded with the minarets of mosques. Shkodër had been "internationalized" approximately ten years before World War I. The four great powers of that time each had military detachments there to maintain a sort of political balance over all the Balkans. One street was called Napoleon, another, Bismarck, and so forth. Every Sunday a different military band played in the central square, impartially rotating the Italian, French, German, and Austrian uniforms on display. This occupation by so many soldiers from different nations had, of course, a corresponding deteriorating effect on the civilian population, especially on the female contingent.

It was difficult to find one's way around Scutari. Its many large, high garden walls blocked everything except the tops of the trees, and the minarets and mosques were confusing, too. The city represented another world, with another past and another present. Once as I was walking through the winding streets, I climbed on top of one of the minarets. Suddenly I could see that the high stone walls hid many other parts of town and especially the homes of the rich merchants. The houses in which the women lived were built to one side and somewhat withdrawn. Even the Catholic women lived in very much the same way as their Moslem sisters. When they walked on the streets, with a sort of rocking gait, wearing bulky dresses and trousers, they gave the impression of being very heavily overdressed and overloaded. But they were picturesque, and I made many sketches.

We left Shkodër to continue the march into Albania, but there soon ceased to be any trace of a road. We marched through the marshlands of western Albania, our route roughly paralleling the Adriatic Sea. To the east of these lowlands are mountain ranges whose inhabitants are even more primitive than the Montenegrins. I have never been in the Malcija itself, a forbidding territory which is almost impossible to enter. The Turks occupied Albania for five hundred years, but were never able to collect taxes in this part of the country, so effective were the guerrilla tactics of the mountaineers. Altogether, there are some sixty different tribes living in the Malcija. I saw these people only when they came down to the valley and the coastal towns. They had shaved heads and wore conical hats, so that they resembled Tibetans. The tribes are distinguishable by the pattern in the hand-woven ribbons or borders sewn onto their dresses and by the curlicues of these decorative trimmings on their white, mostly woolen trousers, but they were difficult for a foreigner to discern.

These tribesmen perpetuated blood feuds for generations; according to their moral code, every member is obligated to kill any person who is guilty of some offense against the clan or family. This tradition extends also to the protection of travelers and foreigners who enter the country. The tribesmen have a very deep conviction that hospitality is sacred and must be maintained and enforced at all costs, even if it means the life of the host. When an outsider travels from one village to another, he commends himself to a certain clan or family. One of its members accompanies him on his journey until he reaches the next host, who is, of course, in some amicable relationship to the first. If anything should happen on the way— if, for instance, the traveler is killed, or even if he is only robbed—it would be another reason for the feud to continue through the centuries. For every life another life has to be taken, somewhat like in the Corsican vendetta. Therefore, this business of having a guest is a bitterly serious one. In some of the tribes only 60 per cent of the male population, I was told at that time, die a natural death.

One would not readily risk such a blood feud; one would rather do anything to keep one's host from engaging in an endless warfare following an unwanted accident or offense. I have been told that if one has started with the proper host, it was safer to travel in the Malcija than it used to be to pass through certain parts of Chicago at night, where the police were very much less dependable.

In Lesh (Alessio), on the coast of Albania, some of the townspeople looked like ghosts. The country had been malaria-ridden for many centuries, and no knowledgeable attempt had been made to combat it. At least 99 per cent of the population suffered from the disease, and were exhausted and degenerate. Lesh was surrounded by mountains up to 1,100 feet high, and our battery was in place on one of them for quite some time. Here all its members—some three hundred and forty-five men and about six officers, including myself, accompanied by something like a hundred pack horses—contracted malaria, cholera, or typhoid; toward the end, only about sixty-five men remained, with me as their last officer. We were unable to make any move or to pack the horses, which also had to be fed; we could not lift our baggage or fire one shot. This gives an idea of the efficiency of this sort of warfare.

The sixty-five men who stayed were not well by any means, but they refused to go to the hospital because if they did, their blankets would be taken away for delousing and they would be laid on a mountain slope, practically naked in the streaming rains which had started the wet season. The hospital was a field unit with three hundred beds, but there were twenty-five hundred soldiers on the mountain. The men preferred to stay with our provisions, "at home," so that they at least had something to eat. Of course they still had to suffer through the chills and sweats of their malaria.

When I finally succumbed to my infection, a tropica plus a tertiana, I was taken away in a horse-drawn cart. We traveled through marshlands which were completely covered with water, and constantly plunged into invisible holes. In the hospital I, being an officer, came under a roof. As a matter of fact, I recall with great relish that I was given some stewed pears and some canned milk. I traveled to the next hospital, not by car or horseback, but sitting on a board some twelve by sixteen inches, which was hooked to the rope of a suspension railway, a sort of primitive monocord, that swayed and moved a hundred feet above the endless sunny marshland, and sometimes hung in mid-air, motionless, for an hour or two in the heat.

This was the beginning of my long journey through hospitals—something like eighteen in as many months—slowly inching my way north until I arrived in a tuberculosis sanitarium in Styria. I was brought there to get good food because nobody really knew what to do with a malaria patient. They gave him so-called *Nocht* cures, which consisted of systematic doses of quinine over a twelve-week period. But the treatments usually ended with a new attack and a chill. Every time I got such a chill, the bedstead and the whole floor began to vibrate with my trembling. Afterward, when my temperature had reached its peak and I started to sweat, the water actually dripped from under the mattress. This went on for a long time, and the attacks always returned again.

Finding a Companion

It is strange to think that from the gibberish of half-conscious confusion, out of a period of kaleidoscopic sequences of nonsense, slowly sense should accrue and momentous consequences should grow. It is not easy to see the point of departure for a truly "causative" story. From the source to the mouth of the river, the narrative winds along its sinuous, amazing route.

There are people who seek all their lives and never find. They seek a wife, have many of them, and keep seeking. They seek steady companions, chiefs, or crews, or places and positions to work in. They move and zigzag over the map and through an endless, senseless series of situations, and fail to find. Others find morsels every day. The latter are of biological individuality, with great capacity for absorption, assimilation, adjustment, adaptation, accommodation. One of their capacities is empathic observation, falling in love and successfully remaining in love with the concrete instead of courting abstractions of a never-never land.

Architecture, properly gauged and satisfying, is the least abstract art. Twenty-four hours a day are spent in closest contact with concrete response—responses naturally grown and acquired over a lifetime, everything pulsatingly real: biological realism.

From Albania and Slovakia to Switzerland

At the beginning of this devious story I was solitary and naked. To let my tanned skin catch a cooling breeze, I was sitting on a mountain, nine hundred feet high, overlooking the bay of the natural little harbor of Shinjin on the Albanian coast. Under the water lay five or six small freighters, torpedoed and sunk with cargoes of grain and flour which the Italians had tried to ship into Albania. After many months the salvaging crews of divers had brought up black, salt-encrusted sacks of flour from the water-filled holds. A gluelike mess of somehow waterproof quality was found to have jelled inside the sacks, lining them, as it were, and protecting the humid but still powdery flour. There it was, spread out to dry on the beach in the hot sun, and it stank to heaven and my mountaintop.

Sometimes I rode on horseback, naked, down to the bay, and took a swim, or at least a cooling dip. But it was too hot and exhausting to go back up the mountain. On this day I was sitting and thinking of architecture and what my future life might be like, chasing the flies away, and observing the free shapes of clouds over the Adriatic horizon. I had not even a sketchbook to exercise a draftsman's hand. Then I saw two near-nude figures in heavy boots stalking up the sunny trail between the bushes. The ascent took them a long time, and often they would wipe the sweat off their faces. They were young fellows, and they recognized me as an officer by the paraphernalia—the clothes, the cap, and the saber—lying around me on the ground. They snapped to attention and reported their arrival at the battery. They introduced themselves as two ensigns, Baron de Erlanger, a thin fair-haired boy, and Ensign Herzka, dark, a bit ugly on first glance, but with strangely beautiful, sad light-brown eyes.

The encounter with Herzka, who soon fell sick like everybody else, proved to be momentous for me. More than a year later I met him again in the hinterland, in Trenčín, Slovakia. He was a lieutenant then, and we both were sick with recurrent malaria. It was near the end of the war, and also of the Austro-Hungarian Empire. Herzka knew Trenčín already, and much better than I. He found me a room outside the hospital with the lame but lively Hungarian Baroness Zahoransky, whose husband had been in England and America and had built his villa in "Anglo-Saxon style," with bathtub and everything.

Meanwhile the war came to its disastrous end, the Czech war of secession started, and the Hungarian officers took the last train to Budapest. Herzka also fled, but no train left for Vienna, and I stayed on with another family he had recommended. The husband was a merchant, and his wife made my heart heavy by cumbersomely falling in love with honest me—the poor stranded stowaway, or relic of a wrecked army. She gave me a civilian overcoat of her husband's to cover my uniform, and his hat when I ventured into town or strolled up to the medieval castle to while away the time, now with a sketchbook on my lap. There I would also meet Kate, a very young girl—very dirty, unkempt, and something like a shepherdess. I have often wondered what happened with all these people later—who died, who lived.

During this time the Czech military had marched into the once Hungarian-held Slovakian town. All the officers and hospital nurses I knew had left, except for a blonde civilian technician from Munich, with whom I walked in the evenings, speculating about the future. Ever so often I was discovered by the Czech military police and marched off to jail or to a hearing with the commander. There was peril and drama in this to interrupt the humdrum. On one such occasion a girl I did not know, but who was evidently warmly attached to me, just from seeing me at a distance, threw herself, wailing and with tears streaming, right in front of the two soldiers who were escorting me with fixed bayonets to the straw mats of the jail. I was both perplexed and deeply touched. It was a heart-rending scene, like one that might have taken place before the execution of her beloved. But I was not executed and never learned who the heartbroken girl was.

I was then going into my twenty-sixth year of life, and during that period I expressed myself hectically in Mona Lisa oil crayons and even in oil paints. The castle, the town, the church, and the synagogue-vaults of Trenčín were my architectural meat; also an uncanny catacomb aisle through the dark interior of a mountain, with lonely life-size saints standing in its darkness—remnants of an abandoned monastery on the other side of the Trenčín River.

The late autumn of 1918 was a significant time in world history, but I knew little of what had happened except that actually the Hohenzollerns and the Habsburgs were out. I began to think more and more of escaping to Vienna, or perhaps abroad, to the world outside. But how?

When the Czech military commander had granted me leave and passage through his newly "liberated" country, my landlady gave me a letter of introduction to her cousin, a nurse in Switzerland, who ran a rest home someplace at the Lake of Zurich. On the train which took me to Brno my Austrian officer's insignia were torn off my tunic by a stern Czech patrol. As an old soldier, I felt funny about it, but my mind was already in Switzerland—if only I could get there. Maybe, I thought, they would have building-up there instead of ruin and destruction—architecture in the making. Half a year earlier, on a three months' leave, I had finished my studies in Vienna and captured a university degree while Gabriele D'Annunzio was dropping Italian leaflets over Vienna, inviting us to surrender. In 1918 we all got warmed up to revolution rather than to surrender. A little wistful revolution against a crumbling thousand-year empire on the brink. (Or did it date even further back, to Roman Emperor Probus, perhaps to Julius Caesar, Kaesar, Kaiser?) At any rate, I chafed to see Central Europe's fortress a little from the outside, if possible, from where the Habsburgs had come eight hundreds years earlier. It seemed amazing that I ever accomplished it, but, visa in hand, I passed that border of Switzerland.

I had changed a good deal of wrecked Austrian currency into a few francs, and when the train stopped for baggage inspection and all had been scrutinized, I raised my eyes gratefully toward the Swiss mountains: I had escaped the prison of a four-year war. The mountain air was wonderful. I walked to the little railway depot restaurant, and, with unbelieving eyes, saw people eat ham and eggs. I ordered some and consumed them with reverence. I paid with almost my last coin. Next I crowded into a Swiss coach for smokers, where I recognized a small man as Mr. Steinhoff, architect from Vienna, but a *habitué* of Switzerland. He offered me a Stumpen, a light Swiss cigarillo, or cigarlike cigarette.

I felt that I was in paradise as the train rolled along the south bank of the Lake of Zurich, and finally landed in the little Hotel Simplon, near the railroad station, which the great Gottfried Semper had designed two generations earlier. (Semper was the same Victorian visionary architect and philosopher who had created my beloved Court Theater in Vienna.) I introduced myself to Mr. Immer-Schneider, a patent attorney to whom my brother Siegfried had given me a letter. The handsome white-bearded old patriarch, like many an elderly man in Switzerland, looked to me like Gottfried Keller, the wonderful Swiss romantic realist writer whom I loved.

I was enchanted by this peaceful, balanced country, but there was no job to be had. I walked all streets, climbed all stairs, rang all bells, met all hesitant architects. They must have seen me as a strange bird; besides, a not-unjustified daily newsprint propaganda campaign was directed against the damned foreigners (*chaibe uslanders*) who were crowding in.

But I had not yet lost all hope. I looked at the beautiful lake from the Uto Kai, and saw the gleaming reflection of the little ice garden of Verena, which sits as a glacier crown on the distant mountains of the Zurich upland. Then I took the train through the wintry landscape along the north coast of the lake, to Staefa. There I would deliver the letter from Slovakia and the heartsick landlady to whom Herzka had introduced me, and meet her cousin, the nurse, who ran the rest home.

From the village depot I lugged my suitcase up the hill to a gabled chalet, neatly painted and towering over the snowy skeletons of fruit trees. I was received by Sister Elsa, a strange creature, most conscious of her ugliness. An abortive early X-ray cure of a goiter had ruined her face and human features. She wore the Red Cross habit, and spoke with a slightly assumed Swiss accent intermixed with her native Viennese. She ushered me into the comfortably heated living room, lit up in the early winter evening. To my surprise, two young girls began talking down from the top of the big green tile stove, which served them as a comfortable resting place right under the ceiling. One was Anita, and the other girl, I understood, was her half sister. They were orphans, I was told, the daughters of a charming Russian newspaperman, a capital fellow who had died in Switzerland not long ago. Augusta, the cook, and a true foursquare Swiss, was summoned to bring me a big pitcher of milk and a few slices of bread from the kitchen.

I felt very happy when I saw my clean little room under the rafters, looking out over the nocturnal lake. Down again, I engaged in a sparkling conversation with Anita, a lively, precocious high-school girl who had looked forward to my arrival with curiosity, and who now did her Latin lessons in my presence.

It was Saturday, and after the two girls had gone to bed, I had my first of many long evening conversations with Sister Elsa, over a cigarette, in her "office." This Swiss peasant house struck me as neat, homelike, and silvery, like the entire Canton of Zurich.

The next morning, Sunday, the sun shone over the now steel-colored lake, surrounded by snowed-in land. During the breakfast I ate belatedly, Sister Elsa and Anita briefed me that lunch would be at noon sharp. At it would be a habitual Sunday-lunch-guest, old Alfred Niedermann, a remarkable Swiss artist and writer, gruff, tough, and a bit of a misanthrope.

From Albania I had been moving slowly but surely toward this Sunday luncheon table in the *Erholungsheim* at Staefa. But I had no inkling of how momentously close I was coming to the most significant turn of my career.

At noon sharp Alfred Niedermann the elder, the great-grandfather of my children to be, entered with his once good-looking spinster daughter. He was suspicious and glad at the same time to have me as an audience; because he was a most earnest and a good philosophical talker, my listening pleased him more than my talking. Occasionally Anita giggled about my *faux pas* at the other end of the table. It was a sunny midday, with a blue sky over the lake.

Alfred Niedermann, son of a master in Zurich's glaziers' guild, had traveled far, even to Russia, as a young man. He had written excellent poems and novels. (One of them, *Dione Peutinger, the Physician of Ingolstadt*—or is it "the Witch"?—was set in the Thirty Years' War and has given my wife her un-Christian name.) Alfred Niedermann was a classical heathen or atheist or post-Goethean freethinker. He, a bit boisterously, hated the Vatican, but had to put up with a Catholic daughter-in-law. At first this had made him tremble with fury, although she herself gave up her allegiance to Rome most readily for her allegiance to the Swiss engineer and ever-loving admirer she had found in his son, Alfred Niedermann the younger.

"They are an interesting family," Sister Elsa informed me after the meal and the discussion on Goethe and the Greeks. They *are* an interesting family; I think so still, forty years later. My parents-in-law, while I note this down, both well over eighty years of age, are vivacious and good to look at; they now live on this side of the ocean, west of the Rockies. Unchangingly I think so after having been married for the span of more than a generation to one and the same girl, and indeed, to her people.

First, I had met her grandfather. Then I was told that Alfred Niedermann's son was coming for a visit and would bring the youngest of his four daughters along. He came, looking well groomed, *à quatre épingles*, and impressive. His cute ten-year-old daughter was named Regula, after the Zurich patron saint, and we liked each other at once. Soon I drew her portrait. It now hangs under glass in her parents' interesting one-room garden apartment, which I built thirty years later in Westwood, California.

Regula has gone many ways, and we got around and through the world on different paths. She has joined me repeatedly; so when she followed me to California after World War II, in order to learn my ways, she became a great help in my work of giving people satisfaction in the architectural pursuit of happiness.

It was Regula who alerted the other girls in her family to the presence of the newly arrived Viennese ex-officer still wearing the tunic and leather gamashes of the beaten Habsburg army. The four girls were under the radiant leadership of forty-year-young Lilly Antoinette Niedermann, born in Leer, Ostfriesland, from where she had married into this Swiss family which then resided in Munich.

The girls were brunette Dione, then eighteen; very blonde Verena, sixteen; Doris, slightly curly-haired, fourteen; and, of course, Regula. In addition there was Trude Eckstein, tall, with black hair and a small narrow forehead. Her mother was a businesslike beautiful worldly divorcée who ran a motion-picture house in Vienna—later Trude was the first furtively to put a piece of chocolate on my bed when I came as a boarding visitor to the Niedermann house on the Schmelzberg, that overlooked stretches of the lake below. It was she who, with a sort of ironical ambiguity, whispered to me that the Niedermanns had established a "provincial paradise." She came from the high life and urbanity of the metropolis, and I suppose the kind of culture that goes with it. In war and peregrinations I had learned to love solitudes and to wonder about megalopolises, which seemed so restricted to one used to his sleeping bag in the wide open spaces of primitivity.

I thought Zurich provided a great deal of architectural satisfaction, except perhaps for its pride, the Bahnhofstrasse, its metropolitan thoroughfare, which stretched from the railroad depot to the lake vista. The city was like an old coin, neatly cleaned and, the thought recurred to me, distinctly solid and silvery, in spite of all and everything that had accumulated in the post-Victorian age. The train on which I commuted passed the five or six familiar suburban villages of the lake's north shore; mornings and evenings it provided a view across the water and over the gables of typical old Zurich houses, a style preserved and prevalent in the *oberland*.

I had found a microscopically paid apprentice job—not with an architect but with a landscape nursery, Otto Froebel's Erben (the heirs of Otto Froebel). I generally commuted both ways with vivacious, intelligent Anita, and she introduced me to one of the "alcohol-free" fast-feeding places, which the Swiss abstinence movement maintained throughout Zurich. I suppose many Swiss, like Mason Lienhard, Gertrud's husband in Johann Heinrich Pestalozzi's famous eighteenth-century story on the native mind, may have lost their bearings in front of wine or beer glasses in the regular inns.

I became deeply interested in this glacier-studded country over whose mountain passes more foreigners had wandered than over those of Kashmir, which I was to see many years later—again with memories reverberating in many ways. Switzerland, even Zurich, in spite of its cosmopolitan hostelry and university, remains foreign to many foreigners. It became close to me.

Anita began to take a young, girlish interest in our get-togethers, which I very honestly kept within bounds. She spoke with the animation of a sixteen-year-old, and with flashing eyes. I had learned chaperoning with my own sister when I was twelve and she eighteen. Sometimes Anita expressed the isolation she felt at not being understood by the people around, although to me she seemed to have made an excellent adjustment to the country she lived in and spoke the Swiss-German language or dialect as fluently as a native. She became a bit uneasy when she found out that all the Niedermann girls, too, had taken me close to their hearts. Instinctively she worried less about the advances which might be made by sophisticated

Trude, who was chronologically her age, but, compared with her, mature as the serpent in paradise—that paradise which she had termed provincial.

Work at the nursery was under the supervision of Gustav Ammann, a diligent and methodical Swiss pupil of Jacob Ochs and the great Carl Foerster of Hamburg. To my amazement I met Foerster forty years later as a very old but enthusiastic leader and lover of landscape art, and became friends with him when the University in West Berlin so kindly honored me with a doctorate.

The small drafting office of Mr. Ammann, the nursery grounds with blooming perennials and small trees in cans and boxes, and the basement, where I made cuttings under the guidance of foreman Brauchli and the upright head nurseryman, Rusterholz, pronounced *Rushterholz*—a wonderful, woodsy name for a gardener, I thought—all became true eye openers for me. I learned in brief and quiet conversations with Gustav Ammann something of Foerster's ideas about our being socially conditioned to garden plants; we in turn attribute to them secondary "character," while they express their own primary natural biology, and thus color the landscape by their "physiognomy." The landscape designer can play up both cultural "character" and natural "physiognomy" to support his site creation and its allegiance to the surrounding of natural and cultural landscape.

This perhaps reflects more the way I myself began to abstract these thoughts than the way Gustav Ammann briefly related them to me, wrapped in technical discussions on perennial beds blooming in sequence, for which I made very detailed space-time drawings. I learned to arrange plants as to growth, size, color, and season of bloom. I recognized the associations which may link their character to peasant or castle gardens, or on the other hand, their physiognomy, seemingly indicating to everyone, not only to the botanist, say, a moisture-laden habitat, or a dry sandy spot, or a wind-swept hilltop, or a deeply eroded ravine, bravely reclaimed by "native" vegetation. It all became a never-ending inspiration. I especially cherished watching the natural equilibria of the plant ecology and the generative microclimate of a site. Why not care equally for humans in their growth and biodynamics, I began to think. Why care less for *their* roots and bloom?

Mr. Ammann spoke a friendly High German to me, as he had studied it especially in Hamburg. But I began to love the Swiss tongue. The idiomatics kept reminding me of Gottfried Keller, his stories of Seldwyla and Zurich and his autobiographical *Der Grüne Heinrich*. This wonderful book may even quite unwittingly influence me at this very moment, as I jot down something of my own life.

The others in the nursery, the middle-aged telephone girl, the gray-haired bookkeeper, and young Mr. Froebel, who was perhaps forty, all smiled at me a little when I passed the office. All must have seen through my strange attire and appearance and recognized my determination and my willingness. I drew some hundred francs a month, and began building garden models. The concentration on this sort of site study influences me still, way beyond the mere mechanics of it.

As I remember it, my first morning at the nursery I began pounding long nails into a wooden, perhaps plywood, base, driving them in to a varying extent so that their heads would coincide with the elevations of a contour map. I pounded and pounded, and at lunchtime I almost fainted: To my terror I noticed that I had pounded the nails through into the desk top on which I worked. Pale, I approached Mr. Ammann with this discovery, expecting to be chased from the premises. He must have liked me already, since he did not fire me in a rage.

Later, when Professor Karl Moser charitably invited me to join him on a university students' sketching excursion to Neuchatel, Mr. Ammann gave me leave. Much later he loaned me $150 when I went to America, so that I should not be completely without funds and partly to defray the fare on the Cunard liner *Laconia*. Within three months I had repaid the debt. Much later, he sat, aged, through a talk I gave in Zurich, and only a few years ago he and I agreed that I should write the preface to his book on landscaping and gardening. Gustav Ammann died before his lovely work appeared, complete with my eulogy to my master in landscaping.

During lunch hour all hands used to leave the nursery. I would have a few pieces of dry bread I had brought from Sister Elsa's breakfast table. Sneaking behind the tomato shrubs and into a patch of green corn, a cunning "food gatherer" spied anything which bore fruit and other edibles, either roots or leaves. I do not know whether Mr. Rusterholz ever speculated why, although the tomato shrubs had bloomed properly that year, they bore less lasting fruit than could have been anticipated, or how many ears of green maize disappeared mysteriously. I surely lived on the country, and ravenously, as I often worked hard in the dirt, bent to the ground, with a good deal of perspiration on my tanned forehead.

Occasionally Mr. Rusterholz would take the more grasping intelligentsia among his nursery hands, the organized garden workers and myself, to the Arboretum, where he would name for us and explain the trees and shrubs, their habits and soil requirements. It was a quaint instruction, reminiscent of a medieval builder's guild crew listening to an elder craftsman. Mr. Rusterholz's Swiss sounded to me like the forgotten German of the Middle Ages.

I was delighted with what I learned, and I discussed it and literature, God and the world, with Anita when we hungrily traveled back in the evening to the *Erholungsheim* in Staefa, where Sister Elsa and Augusta and a paying guest, Mrs. Scharlach from Seattle, expected us to push our chairs to the dinner table.

Seattle, Seattle ... little did I know that one day the Arboretum Society there would invite me to lecture to a huge audience and appear on television, or that I would eventually have many friends in that city. Then, at the Lake of Zurich, when the American lady spoke to me of her home, I innocently thought

Seattle was a sort of suburb just north of Los Angeles.

After dinner I would regularly follow Sister Elsa to her office, smoke her cigarettes, and tell her of my work, ideas, aspirations, hopes. She called me *Herr Ingenieur*, an Austrian honorary title for an architect, and maintained her slightly Viennese, slightly Swiss accent. In her friendliness she concealed from me the fact that some people in the village spoke bitterly against the foreigner, who still wore shreds of a foreign uniform and evidently worked in Zurich, thus depriving some native of his bread. A few urchins shouted *Gamascha Chaib* when I passed them on my way to the morning train—a foul curse word, aimed at the leggings which I still wore with my field-gray artillery riding breeches. But I did not gather the ringing of a little unfriendliness in the abundance of friendliness that came to me.

Meanwhile the Niedermann family had decided to invite me for lunch, and, when they did, the great day in my life arrived. I plundered the blooming perennials of Otto Froebel's Erben to have an impressive colorful bunch to take along, shaved, and walked the hilly streets from the nursery to the Schmelzberg to spend a short lunch hour opposite Mrs. Niedermann, who at once won my heart. Mr. Niedermann was indeed a very trim-looking, respected paterfamilias—he still is now, at eighty-seven—and finished a classical piece on the piano before we sat down with all the girls in attendance. Dione wore blue stockings, and I tried to ignore her and all the other girls, for I thought this was proper. Lovely Mrs. Antoinette Niedermann, who spoke with her North German accent from Friesland, commanded my most sympathetic interest.

Later I learned that they thought it strange that I had not had a haircut for a long while. Of course, they did not know that I was long of hair because short of cash, and by lively and interesting conversation I diverted their attention from the fact that I was hungrily eating more than a well-behaved guest should.

From then on I was invited for lunch once a week, and that was my eating day. But I loved the people, especially the youngish mother. The girls made a sporty arrangement among themselves to take turns picking me up from the nursery and accompanying me back.

I was invited to spend the night on the Schmelzberg, and began to find furtive little gifts on my bed pillow. Trude's dark eyes glanced at me ambiguously, and in spite of her apparent attachement to Mrs. Niedermann, she proved a disruptive influence and fence-sitting critic. She cleverly competed with Dione, Vrene, and Anita, but by calculation seemed as reserved as the smiling milk-and-blood-complexioned fourteen-year-old Doris was by nature. Regula remained childlike, frank, and attached. The whole house, to me wonderful, bristled with feminine tenderness.

We all became close, and I was adopted as a brother by a unanimous girls' vote when we walked the greater part of a day over hills, valleys, and mountains—from Staefa over the Pfannenstiel to Zurich.

Vrene, who had straight, deep-blue eyes, recited Latin poetry, and was the most educated. She went to the girls' humanist high school, the "Gymnasium." The three older sisters sang German and Swiss folk songs beautifully and with artfully divided voices, *"Vom Berg ins Tal"* and an endless, remarkable repertoire, fondly listened to by me and Regula, who did not sing. But Dione was undoubtedly the musician of the young generation; with her father she played Beethoven at four hands, and on cello, which she studied at Geneva, she was practicing several Bach suites and dances by Franz Lachner. Wearing a gaily printed cotton dress and a ribbon around her hair, this slender girl would handle her cello with professional confidence. Fortunately, I was of a "classical" musical family, but my own singing and guitar playing did not impress the girls. Dione found it too sentimental for her.

Gradually but boldly she ventured ahead of her younger sisters and became recognizable as something of an informal sweetheart. She used a ruse to come to Staefa as a boarding guest for a short vacation, and although an early bedtime was prescribed by stern Sister Elsa, we found time together; on her part there was no trace of female design. Natural as she was born she has wonderfully remained through all her life. Our attachment meant a little grief to Anita, some worrying and uneasiness to Sister Elsa, but the empathic tact and compassion of the sincere young man I really was kept the others from becoming truly unhappy. I was deeply grateful to all for the warmth I found in this foreign land when my little niece and nephew, my sister's children, six and seven perhaps—strange, lovely little birds—arrived with a Viennese vacation-and-welfare train to board with me for a month. The entire idyl was even more firmly cemented by their charm and their friendship with Regula and Dione.

After Dione's return home I again visited there, and the intimacies continued and were partly noticed, so that the parents decided to ship their eldest and her cello out of town. It was a melancholy and anxious daybreak following a night of mixed feelings when we, still in the winterly dark, together boarded the train which was to bring Dione to the Austrian border on her way to my home town, Vienna. There she was to study the cello and live with friends of the Niedermanns', a family of Viennese intellectuals who belonged to the upper middle class; they owned a house designed by Adolf Loos, my master and my fountain of ideas on architecture.

I myself disembarked sadly at Wädenswil, on the south shore of the lake of Zurich, where, some time before, I had begun working in the diminutive half-basement office of Wernli and Staeger, architects. I stood looking after the train rolling out of Wädenswil on that winter morning, as it thundered east, carrying Dione and her cello away. When it had disappeared into the dark—it may have been seven o'clock—I swallowed and walked, heavyhearted, to my office, to do the same chores as every morning: light a wood fire in the little cast-iron stove, sweep the floor, and dust the drafting boards. Other mornings I arrived at six, after taking the tiny ferry *Die Schwalbe* (Swallow) across the dark, wind-swept lake.

Without any experience, I worked on a fairly extensive competitive housing development and on various less important projects, filling the time as well as I could. Mr. Staeger, the younger partner, kindly gave me a pea-green suit which he no longer wanted to wear. He wielded a pencil with facility and liked me, with his twinkle of understanding, better than the older, more businesslike Mr. Wernli. To both of them and to their firm my 150 francs must have been a net loss. But at least the office was heated when they arrived.

Meanwhile I began to receive letters from Dione, who reported in wide-eyed wonder about fabulous Vienna and its society life, of her hosts and of masculine advances toward her. She also visited my sister and brother-in-law, where her old friends of last summer, the two children, glowed with pleasure, showing her off to their parents. At one glance my sister saw what the situation was with this frank and naïve girl from Switzerland, who could talk Frisian North German and whose eyes shone when she told how her sisters and she had voted Richard as their "brother."

Being alone and separated made me realize how dangerous this situation at the Danube was. I was anxiously jealous. I knew the charm Viennese gentlemen could exercise on Swiss girls just emerged from a provincial paradise. And Dione was now moving in the best social and musical circles, in which even well-groomed counts were to be found. But also on the streetcar, her sincere and amazed letters reported, she was skillfully accosted by university students and wolves in sheep's clothing. However, her imperturbable straightforward humanity was her cosmopolitan armament. In a deeper sense, she proved to be no provincial whatever, and she continued to prove it through the next forty years, while I dragged her from Lima or Rio to Boston or Copenhagen, from Tokyo and Thailand to Istanbul, Cape Town, and Caracas. With her wonderful human common denominator applied to every place and any earthly situation, she has remained the truest blessing. Besides being my dedicated helper in all needs, she has mothered three boys, without, in the midst of so many tasks, ever losing herself or abandoning her own art and creative gift. I have no idea how, as young people, she or I could have guessed that such a linkage was thinkable or could hold so fast over four decades. Destiny is not designed.

Once—many years later—she accompanied me to a little town in Texas, adjacent to Texas A & M, where I was to lecture for a week. She took her cello along, hoping for an extended period of practicing. A & M, noncoeducational, became, with a lot of male youngsters around, quite disturbing to a female on the campus trying to be dedicated to music only. In competition with me she soon gave a course on "How to pick your wife to become a good architect!" Inasmuch as the college offered no such course, it proved immensely attractive to the students—so much so that she added another for those more advanced, "How to train your wife after you have selected her!" They thronged the lecture hall, and later checked with me on certain details of Dione's talks. Since then many young architects have read an article she wrote, which was translated into three or four languages, to their brides, and these in turn formed Dione Neutra clubs to stand by their husbands.

Nevertheless, it is not true that anyone prophetically "picks" a mate, or trains his companion. This idea is little more than an innocent joke, and such blessings simply drop on one's humble head. No such training would have made Dione a cosmopolitan or given her adaptability; it was an inherent quality. She proved to be a human being of the wide world by birth. That is a profoundly subtle endowment. A natural linguist, she sings, writes, reads and pronounces many languages without having "studied" them. With devotion she penetrates almost silently into the essence of creative problems and human relationships, without losing herself, although never at all being on her guard. All this is done with naïveté, without any kind of calculation, like her artless winning of hearts in Puerto Rico, Guam, Vancouver, Cuzco, Karachi, Oslo, or Vienna. And her capacity of assimilation is as great across social as across geographic distances. In Santo Domingo she would very successfully sing to Negro street urchins—or in Stockholm, Kyoto, or in the houses of old-aristocratic New England ladies, or to traditional intellectuals of pronouncedly different and seemingly fixed stripe. Always she would be accepted and produce a flash and steady glow of warmheartedness. She has been gifted with an amazing attraction for women as well as for men—simply the Sunday-child character never to meet resentment or adversaries. She has never been possessive of anything, not even of her three boys, or grandchildren, or her daughter-in-law, whom she treats as her equal. I could not have known or foreseen any of these things to save my life, although as a planner I am supposed to be a professional "anticipator" and wizard at prognosis. It is amazing what funds and hopes are trusted to an architect, to know and shape the future, while he must admit he is an ignoramus.

Human individualistic and cohesion issues and their cognizance are at the bottom of design for living. I have often thought that great and small architects' matrimonial and love relations are profoundly informative; far apart from any gossip. It may not be equally so for civil engineers.

Encounter and Renewal in Vienna

I decided to go to Vienna before Dione turned nineteen on April 14, 1920. With this in mind, I called her mother from the Wädenswil basement office, and she promptly dropped housekeeping and cooking, and took the next train up the lake to join me. I think she even brought sandwiches and appies along, and during my lunch hour we walked hand in hand, a little like lovers, up the hill, and sat on a bench overlooking the lake in the sunny pre-spring landscape.

I proposed nothing, but I said I was going to Vienna soon. Unprepared, Dione was wonderfully surprised at my arrival. I met her by "accident," prearranged by my sister in the wonderful Park of the Imperial Rococo Summer Palace at Schönbrunn. Dione, unknowing, turned around when I tapped her on the shoulder; she could not say a word because she had just put a piece of imported Swiss chocolate in her mouth, which she now desperately tried to swallow.

Shortly thereafter we both fell sick with influenza, which killed so many, including the young, gifted artist Egon Schiele, whom I, as many in Vienna, admired: he and his wife both died on the same day. Influenza also took my father, who never saw Dione. He followed my mother after a dozen years of half-life as a widower. I suppose the safest base for marriage is having happily married parents. Only now can I see fully this unearned blessing.

Dione moved to my sister's, where, in fact, we both were through our sickness. Then, much weakened, we began to walk feebly through Schonbrunn again, through the Wiener Wald, the pinewoods of Moedling, the low marshlike meadows of the Danube to the winter harbor surrounded by groves of trees. We were weak, convalescent, and happy. Our uncertain future hung like a dark cloudbank beyond the blue stretches of a paradisiac sky. We did not talk about the future and I did not propose to Dione. She is a girl of the present, and has never worried much about bridges not yet to be crossed.

It must have been June when she left from the Western railway station. I made desperate attempts to find a job, and finally landed in the American-British Friends (Quaker) Mission, which had quarters in old Viennese palaces in the

Singerstrasse and Herrengasse. I was determined to learn English and get a favorable "affidavit" from a United States citizen, necessary for entering America. Unfortunately, I loved the Quakers more that the U.S.A. did, as the Friends had hesitated using arms. But they were good to us.

Getting permission to enter America took an endless time. I accepted a telegraphed invitation from my friend Ernst Freud, architect son of Sigmund, who had just visited me with his Berlin bride, and had started a practice in that northern metropolis. He was out of town, on an island near Rügen, when I arrived in the many-faced city. I began working with two society architects, Pinner and Neumann, but my soul was vacant. Evenings I sat on a bench in the Tiergarten or took the subway and walked about on the Kurfürstendamm and listened to Edwin Fischer or some organist in the phony Romanesque Kaiser Wilhelm-Gedächtniskirche—later, in the Second World War, to become a picturesque ruin.

I was in wonderment about that great city. It was full of questionable architecture, except the department stores and some subway sations. Impressive, though, was its matter-of-fact bigness and its museums.

Now I was twenty-eight, and still a rank beginner. I began to design gardens in Dahlem, where Freud designed houses. I resided in a dark half room in the Gleditschstrasse; Mrs. Mamroth was my typical Berlinese landlady. I ate at a "family table" nearby with the old Prawitzens, to save the greater expense of restaurants, and heard the old man tell cavalry stories of the Franco-Prussian War, and of the time when the famous Wintergarten variety theater was a new institution and Berlin began turning from a Prussian town into a world city.

Dione came with her mother while en route to Friesland and her grandmother's in Mannheim. She had persuaded, her mother to make this side excursion to Berlin. She visited the museums with me, and both she and her mother went with me to see *Julius Caesar*, with Alexander Moissi as Marc Antony.

I sat glumly and distractedly through the performance in the Grosse Schauspielhaus, which looked like a stalactite circus and had been designed by Hans Poelzig for the great theater-director Max Reinhardt. I was distracted from Poelzig, Reinhardt, and Shakespeare because I had lost my job that day. And now what was I to do next in Berlin, the big full vacuum?

Mrs. Niedermann had introduced me to her friend and admirer of twenty years earlier, Otto Krueger, now married, living in Berlin, and owner of a big lighting-fixture firm. Krueger, ruddy faced and bald-headed, seemed still in love with her. And I could understand it, although for me she was Antoinette Niedermann and might one day be my mother-in-law. I started to make wonderful illustrations and advertising drawings of desk lamps. They looked real, and Krueger, an engineer with aesthetic leanings, was delighted, talking in his snappy Berlin idiom, with his blue eyes expressing increasing confidence in his young architect protégé from Vienna, friend of a slender young thing, "Lilly's daughter."

Otto Krueger gave me another job. About to leave on a business trip for western Germany, he lodged me as sort of chief eunuch in his household, a tiptop Berlin upper-class apartment. The only other occupant was his somewhat timid, dark-haired, and dominated wife, who was fearful of staying alone. She was from Trier, which I remembered mostly from a photograph of the Porta Nigra, so prominent in colonial Roman archaeology. I loved her accent, which was ever so exotic to me, and I lived with her in her husband's somewhat *nouveau riche* apartment, with her feeding me beer and salami sandwiches between breakfast and lunch. I had a wonderful time, watching over lovely soft-spoken Mrs. Krueger so that no evil might befall her, not even a little too much sympathy for a conscientious young man attending her. After all, since my teens I had been trained and pledged as chaperon, and it has been a recurrent role in my life.

Again, my deep sympathy was with my friendly hosts. I wished them well and enjoyed my own wishfulness. It was grand to be related to human beings in such a strange place as big Berlin was then.

Then I walked the streets again, with addresses of architects noted down from the telephone directory. I fell in with Professor R. a topnotch architect high up in society, a protagonist of cozy *"heimat"* style, and nervous tyrant of a sabotaging staff and of his girl friend, with whom he housed in the rear part of his office. Nobody really worked except for the young, ambitious chief draftsman and young, ambitious me. Everybody would talk and smoke until the chief would explode into the drafting room, raving and ranting against loose-jointed, sneering indifference. Then again, his youngish girl friend would come into the drafting room wearing her bathrobe, looking for and receiving moral support against the common boss. One of the crew, a tall and arrogant youngster, had just quit a job, under Baurat Bischof, with the municipal building office of the Brandenburgian sandbox town of Luckenwalde, and he told me that there might be an opening.

I took the Leipzig train, headed toward Bischof, landed the job, and by this step regretfully depressed Professor R., who took me into his room and wanted to hold me by means of a raise. But we had to part, although I felt for him.

Brandenburg, a Wedding, a Household

Then, always an empathic stranger, I entered the life of a small German town and joined the male glee club. At the weekly song meetings—where divided and sweetly harmonized voices performed something sentimental about a rabbit in the meadow, I worked hard while drinking a goodly number of steins around the long table in the inn.

I learned to bicycle to a housing project pretty far out, which was semirustically conceived around a duck pond reflecting birch trees. There I lived with a family whose stolid head, a part-time printer, indifferently mistreated his young but very deaf wife. They lived downstairs with their nine-year-old daughter, who sang, in the full soprano and vibrato of a grown-up woman, songs which she had learned from her musical father. From my attic room I would listen to the parents' quarreling when the husband came bicycling home from his part-time town employment and found his wife hard to talk to, her agricultural accomplishments not living up to his expectations. A Prussian woman, she worked like a horse in the housing colony on whose extensions I, for my part, labored with my bespectacled colleague Mr. Kuras (brother of a Protestant minister of Spartakist-Communist leanings) in the drafting office of this industrial city of fifty thousand. A socioeconomic revolution was spreading simultaneously and along with the Berlin metropolitan area.

I worked for the resettlement of industrial workers who, for dearth of dwellings after the war and during the depression after the defeat, had been living in urban basements. Now, while working on semirural housing plans, I watched from all too close by as a town family transplanted into rustic circumstances went to pieces, with each member following a different pamphlet on how to raise potatoes, how to fertilize and water the vegetable patch, and what to feed the ducks. The human issues behind the "hard economic facts" fascinated me, to reverberate through all my life as a "houser." They sprinkled their savings into the soil, rabbit husbandry, and the raising of chickens which were expected to lay eggs, and violent disputes arose around the common duck pond we had designed in such an artlessly charming country shape. Settlers from Matanuska, Alaska, to Luckenwalde, Brandenburg, or Dyas, Tennessee, have, as I found out, a tendency to get irate and quarrelsome when their savings dwindle into the pit of slowly tested experiences in a new-fangled sort of life. It is just the reverse of what happens to the *Andinos* who become semirural squatters in the hills of Caracas, then are smoked out of their shacks, their chickens scattering, and marched by a police squad to fifteen-story housing projects designed by the Banco Obrero government agency for as yet scarcely assimilated country yokels. Resettlement of families by well-meaning but stern housing officials is a risky act one way or the other, and strains and stresses develop, as in all transplantations. This observation has followed and haunted me.

I believe my landlord hit my young, deaf, and diligent landlady before they got divorced, and the upper-floor insulation was not dense enough to prevent me from hearing her cry. From my attic window I saw the settlers gather at the duck pond. They had found out that I was one of those civil-service white-collar housing experts, and a foreigner to boot. (In a way every planner and architect is a foreigner in the family.) Murmurs arose and fists were shaken in the direction of the house I lived in. Meanwhile, the German women, like others I have seen—the black African girls of Haiti, or the Hindu girls from Agra to Madras—were carrying water, although not as picturesquely, and singing other songs, and finally falling into sullen silence should householding chores become too unfamiliar and too hard to bear. I was a doctor prescribing housing, and by living with my patients, I took my own medicine down to the bitter end, and watched the breaking up of family life. Structurally and formally all the architecture was in lovely shape, but humans were not fully understood; design did not fully serve survival.

Meanwhile, the civil servants went on with their songs and steins every Wednesday evening at the inn. There too I was a strange bird, but I was accepted, as I have been in so many out-of-the-way human situations and groups, because, I believe, I love people of all kinds. Again, love is a pleasure, quite unsanctimonious.

I subordinated myself to Prussian small-townism and to Baurat Bischof, who began to respect me and did not notice my inexperience. Young, thin Kuras, a head taller than I, took walks with me, bicycled with me, and, on his part, fell in love with a young girl in my presence, drawing me excitedly into the confidence of his affair of the heart. From youth on I was trained as a *confident*, as I have already mentioned. It molded my usefulness in the social group, I guess.

During that time I switched from housing the live and quarreling to housing the peaceful and dead. I became the official designer of the Luckenwalde Forest Cemetery, a socialist municipal scheme which upset the various local churches. In the council chamber I listened for the first time to a most skillful oppositional harangue by Alderman Bauchwitz, which in literal English translation means "belly joke," attacking a scheme and project I had elaborated on. Bourgeois Bauchwitz was a master of clean and convincing attack; he showed the forest cemetery project up as folly and nonsense from the budgetary, political, moral, and civil-engineering points of view. For me it was a wonderful demonstration of politics in civic architecture. But with the socialist majority support and the city forester and the whole city building office on my side, I succeeded in getting my plans accepted. While discussing my system of clearings in the municipal woods, designing and promulgating regulations about permissible tombstones, and relating all aesthetic and landscaping features to chapel and gatehouse, I underpinned my comprehensive full-bodied brain child with an equally comprehensive well-arranged brochure, bulging with research and design wisdom.

The undertaking was a tremendous experience in the realm of silence; the result looked—and probably was—the epitome of philosophical and engineering thought on serving the departed, or the bereft and remembering. Many thoughts came to the young man I was as I bicycled in the Luckenwalde woods or walked through them on autumn evenings. When my work was published in some of the magazines, Baurat Bischof graciously volunteered to grant me official credit. This was highly uncommon, and it meant that for the first time I saw my name in print and connected with a subject which I had insistently mastered as a self-taught enthusiast. I have ever since spontaneously spoken and written of those who have stood by me, and have been quick to acknowledge their help.

Berliner Tageblatt

One day my coworkers in the building department showed me some wild color sketches of a hat factory, submitted by a man called Erich Mendelsohn. To me they looked like expressionistic art, and strange to put before the eyes of a municipal building inspector in Luckenwalde.

On holiday I had been to Leipzig during the fair, but the greater metropolis again beckoned. The following weekend I took the fifty-minute train ride to Berlin, where I visited Mendelsohn. He seemed at once drawn to me, and warmly invited me to join him. It was the last of the month, and I had a cancellation period; I could not decide. I had mental reservations, but I liked Mendelsohn, too, and especially the fact that he entirely overlooked my inexperience and seemed to notice only the "timber" that was me. He persuasively showed me all he did and planned to do, until I said I had to leave to catch my train.

"But can't you come?" he said, following me into the stair hall. "Come," he repeated.

"Tomorrow is the cancellation day according to my contract," I answered, "but I don't know what to do."

Erich Mendelsohn was charming. He talked and acted boyishly. "Come on," he repeated as I stepped into the elevator.

"Phone me tomorrow in Luckenwalde," I said as the doors closed. Was I going down or was I going up?

In the morning I talked with Bischof, who was bewildered and a bit upset. But I succeeded in canceling my contract in the most amicable way possible, and when Mendelsohn telephoned ten minutes later, I said, "In a month!"

I looked around and finally found a room with old Mr. and Mrs. Boldin; he was a retired cigar-store man, and typical Berliner of the era, as was his still black-haired, slightly cantankerous wife. They lived in the housing colony at Eichkamp, at the edge of the Grünewald; their home was a thirty-minute walk to the Reichskanzler Allee, where Mendelsohn occupied the top floor of a three-story apartment house.

How far had I advanced in a year, from the Gleditschstrasse, Prawitzen's lunch table in the odorous little tenement, and the little tearoom on Victoria Luiseplatz, where I had become so well acquainted with the bashful waitress. At that time she had been the only soul I knew in the big, strange city—so much so that when I got a free ticket for the Metropol Theater, where, evenings, I played a grenadier as an extra, I had no one to invite but her. Tickled pink and neatly decked out, she went with me. "You give the ticket to your *braut*" I had been told, and every young girl you could lay a hand on was your *braut* in that old Berlin. We saw from a plush upholstered seat in the orchestra the *Hollandweibchen*, an operetta by Emmerich Kalman. Before the third act, when I was due to appear on stage, I told my fair companion that I had to make an urgent business call, and rushed backstage top floor to dress quickly. She never knew that I was the white-wigged guardsman with the tall headgear of Frederick the Great's era who came on stage and took position at the side of the grand stairway.

Now, working for Mendelsohn, I had arrived after a fashion, and I ate off the Reichskanzlerplatz with Baumeister Bruggemann and other young white-collar gentlemen at the *Mittagstisch*, the family lunch table of youngish but heartsick Mrs. von U., the somewhat neglected wife of a Prussian officer and Junker. An Englishwoman, she had become quite fed up with Prussianism and Herr von U., but she had several children to feed, and did it by means of our financial contribution. Her youngest, a two- or three-year-old boy, was called Joachim, a typical aristocratic Prussian Christian name.

In the office I immediately started out with the addition and corner skyscraper of the *Berliner Tageblatt*, a job for which boyish and jocose, self-convinced, artistic, businesslike, one-eyed, and myopic Erich Mendelsohn had been commissioned by Lachman Mosse, the William Randolph Hearst—or Hearst son-in-law, at least—of Germany. Mendelsohn at once introduced me to Lachman Mosse, who, on his marriage to the old founder Rudolph Mosse's adopted heiress-daughter, had assumed his foster father-in-law's famous surname. Lachman seemed to personify the German funny-paper term *serenissimus*, a cartoon of a high aristocrat or well-dressed prince; but only twenty years later, after his flight to northern California, I found out that he really had brains and was a fine man.

In Berlin, when I designed his luxury office and huge, usually unoccupied desk, Erich Mendelsohn told me laughingly that it was a dummy, for Lachmann Mosse could neither read nor write, nor did he need to. I also became the daily contact man with his business manager, Mr. Hartog. Soon I was the third partner, or joint venturer, on this project, together with the well-known sculptor, P. P. Henning. Although older, he was also a boyish and possibly, as Erich Mendelsohn thought, somewhat irresponsible but splendidly gifted fellow; his wife was a very nice, enthusiastic, and motherly woman. I was happy as associate architect on such a prominent building, and enjoyed the confidence of a chief of genius, and of the owners, men of cultured business acumen.

Erich Mendelsohn was already known at the time for the Einstein Tower, which Henry Kosina had detailed by horizontal sections spaced every fifteen centimeters or less to document its warped, plastically swaying surface. Perhaps he was even more famous for a big poster displayed in all subway stations and promoting the Hausleben Insurance Company. It showed a Mendelsohnian version of the looming and layered skyscraper, and announced a brand-new policy for insuring buildings against old age—like men! It seemed to me a wonderful idea, unless one could, at the start, design them as immune to obsolescence!

Mendelsohn's wife, Luise, was beautiful, tall, statuesque, a somewhat Desiderio da Settignano type, and a cello student of Hugo Becker's, like my bride-to-be. She and her husband were Bach lovers, and he listened to Bach records while sketching with a 4B Hardtmuth pencil, soft and snappy as can be.

The Mosse House met with many vicissitudes, as it violated all municipal regulations by its exploitative, monumental, and yet untraditional towering over well-regulated downtown Berlin. I negotiated with the welfare ministry of Prussia, and I gathered my impressions of civil servants in that neck of the woods as compared to those of Austria. Since then, how many have I seen around the globe! They are fully human too!

Bureaucracy was overcome, however, by expert testimony. At a breakfast given to enlist the support of a jury of architects for the newspaper czar's building project—which was also ours—I saw the high-ranking boss of my first Berlin period. Also there again, with a beer glass in his hand, was the bull-necked, boisterous supporter of the modern, the magnificent Hans Poelzig. His popular title to fame was the circus theater for Max Reinhardt.

The most disastrous experience a building man can have, however, came close to me with the Mosse project. Sand, piled up on a roof slab—concrete which had not completely set in the cold winter temperature—made the slab fail; everything collapsed, falling through a dozen floors, right down into the basement, burying fourteen persons in the debris. The chief editor of the newspaper, Theodor Wolf, fortunately had left his suite just the moment before.

A phone rang at our office in the western part of the city and a breathless voice reported what had happened. Erich Mendelsohn looked at me, and with presence of mind said, "Mr. Neutra, *you* go down!"

Feeling weak in the stomach, I hopped down the stairs to the subway, and while the neat, clean train of the Berlin Metro was gently rumbling along under that great capital, I wondered what I would see at the scene of the catastrophe, and what to say.

Approaching our building site downtown, I saw huge crowds of people, and ever more, straining against a police cordon, afoot and on horseback. I stepped up to an officer and told him I was one of the architects. "You are the *architect?*" he said slowly, and looked at me with a mixed expression on his face. Then he waved his hand, perhaps wondering why I hadn't taken the first available vehicle out of town, or whether he should lay his hand on my shoulder and place me under arrest.

Everybody in the crowd began whispering, and their eyes followed me as, all alone, I walked out of the crowd over the empty paving toward a group of bereft families, some of whose members might be lying buried in the huge heap of rubble. I stood and looked through the opening between the four girders, story above story, and into the sunlit clouds moving through the sky far above. There also stood the contractor's husky but now broken superintendent, the chief of the contracting firm, and Mosse's business manager, Mr. Hartog, directing rescue crews. Nobody knew what story to present to the police.

I was not implicated and the engineers were not at fault, but surely somebody had permitted the piling up of the sand to the height of a man on the top slab, which had not yet set, and which—cracking and crashing—took down all the other floors, with the men and women from the newspaper office sandwiched between them.

Three days later the victims' funeral was a major affair, with Lachman Mosse walking at the head of the procession, his face pale, representative of the grief of all of us. He saw to it that the largest European paper appeared with a heavy black frame around its front page, proclaiming a day of mourning.

While Erich Mendelsohn was away in the Middle East, he anticipated, in his sketches, a good deal of Oscar Niemeyer's expressionism. Meanwhile, in Berlin, I was commissioned to do . a department-store building in Gleiwitz, and quite on my own initiative I designed four novel houses for the suburb of Zehkndorf. Adjacent to each living room, to give it flexible use, was a revolving stage which could, upon pushing a button, be turned to one of three fully furnished sectional bays. The first was a music room; the second, a dining area with the table all set; and the third, a comfortable cozy corner with a good home library. The flood of public attention and news stories about these unusual dwellings, topped by cartoons and hilarious newspaper verses, was terrific. With Berliner humor, the cartoonist for the *Vossische Zeitung* showed the proud owner displaying the architect's sorcery to a guest. Absorbed in bragging conversation, his face turned to the visitor instead of to the revolving stage, he pushes the wrong button and in rolls the bath, with his protesting wife in the nude, trying, too late, to jump out of the tub. Never again has such publicity honored my ingenuity in alliance with a speculative builder. Acceptance and happy service are deeply different from public attention.

Dione had come to Berlin, yet unmarried, ostensibly to study (as mentioned) with Hugo Becker, to whom Luise Mendelsohn, also perfecting her cello playing, introduced her. She stayed with Mrs. von U., who was enchanted by her help with little Joachim. Dione used to take him up and put him on the potty; it was a family training for my bride-to-be. The Mendelsohns liked her, and architect Ernst Freud and his wife, Lux, a classical linguist, became her close friends. We made secret excursions to the Baltic Sea, Stralsund, Eldena, and to Werder, in the pine forest, to drink apple wine.

Then, in 1922, we married in Hagen, Westphalia, and spent our first day of married life in a nunnery in Frankfurt, where Dione's grandaunt was abbess. Our united life began in the Berlin suburb of Eichkamp, under the humming pine trees of sandy Brandenburg. There we had the strangest ménage in my bachelor's half-room. I had concealed the walls with continuous drapes, and we had a tiny sleeping and eating area, with bunks built under the roof rafters, flanking a drawer-stove burning charcoal powder, Northwest German style. In the dark of night my bride would tiptoe down the three winding flights of stairs with the abundant ashes, to bury them in the Eichkamp woods, but the landlord's small black dog would burst out into a high-frequency yapping and betray the secrecy. It was a wonderful study object for a rising domestic designer of happy households. For a lunchtime rendezvous we also had another room rented a mile and a half away at the strategic Reichskanzlerplatz and close to Erich Mendelsohn's office. I had become his associate and collaborated for long after-hours.

We had not plunged into this marriage unprepared. Thirty-five years later Dione recalled her very informal engagement and the start of common housekeeping:

"Our correspondence lasted for four years, and I am ever grateful for this long and slow initiation and gradual understanding of my future husband's mind. Being an Austrian, a foreigner in Germany (as he has been so often in other places later), he was not entitled to ask for a house or an apartment. However, he was able to persuade his landlady to let him enlarge the attic in a housing project, simulate a sink where I could wash the dishes, carry down the bucket of water standing beneath the sink and empty it in the toilet bowl a steep flight of stairs lower down; from there I also could fetch water from a faucet. Of course I had no refrigerator, only a bathtub in the basement, where I floated eggs and butter during the hot summer months. The grocery store was half an hour's walking distance, and I found it quite natural to fetch my groceries in a knapsack. It never entered my mind to ask my husband to do this for me. He had more important things to do, and as I was young and strong and had time on my hands, why should I divert him from spending as much time as he could on his ideas of architecture? I know that these thoughts were not conscious, but came quite naturally because I loved him and wanted to help him."

What a wife, cello student, and singer! Amazement over a lifetime.

White Hope—U.S.A.?

Working together, Mendelsohn and I won a competition for the Mediterranean business center in Haifa. It was a grand, novel project of city planning and urban design for me, too, and my share of the reward, in Egyptian pounds, was large enough to enable me to make the jump to the United States which I had thought about for so long. We packed my self-designed units of sliding door cabinets of my small apartment, now shared with my bride, and left them with a young colleague. They had been the first few pieces of furniture I had conceived.

Loos, Sullivan, Wright

My coming to America was largely due to three people and to the deeply vivid tales which had become meat and drink to me. It was like coming home, really. My first American father was a European, a man who had exerted deep influence on me. He was that most unorthodox architect, Adolf Loos. Today he is recognized as one of the very significant persons in the incipient development of modern architecture. It started as an architecture feeling its way back to a clearer conscious coincidence, agreement, and correspondence with its own time, but, *as I hoped,* to *the all-time human.* With this we are safe, and it carries risks so much smaller than those of fashion. For two-thirds of his life, Loos, who did not share the curlicues of his day, appeared to most of his contemporaries as a lightweight, a funny failure—even a fourflusher.

Although from Moravia, like my mother, he was built and molded very much in the Viennese tradition, being perhaps the most Viennese person I can imagine, except for Agathon, my brother-in-law, but in a more reticent way. He reacted very strongly to the formalism sophisticatedly derived from an old culture. He loved it, and was an open rebel against derivative, stuck-up arty attitudes. After he had completed his year of "voluntary" military service, he spent two years in America. He must then have been between twenty-one and twenty-three years old.

He landed in New York and went through a rather horrible time in the slums of lower Manhattan. He had no money, and he never succeeded even in getting a job as a draftsman. Instead, he did all kinds of chores, from night-shift dishwasher to auxiliary day dishwasher. When he, with his serene trace of a grin and the low voice of a deaf man, which he was all his life, told of his endless job hunts and of finally making a living, he took advantage of the fact that in German the expression is not "dishwasher" but "vessel-washer"—*Nachtgeschirrwascher*—which sounded to German listeners like a washer of *pots de chambre*, a rather disheartening job for a pioneer architect.

Loos finally went to Chicago. He was there during the World's Columbian Exposition in 1893, the year after I was born and four hundred years after Columbus sighted America and the Caribbean Islands which later were to give me also, like Christopher himself, such a thrill and such tough, constructive experience. Chicago was also tough—but midcontinental, not an island to make a landfall, not a natural world port like New York.

Loos had about the most negative experience a gifted, aspiring immigrant can have, worse than that of any Slovak miner who ends up working in a Pennsylvania coal seam. He was a trained person and one of genius. I don't know how good his schooling was, but he was a most intelligent, human young man. In the United States he did nothing but menial work. He never could make both ends meet. But he loved the country. It was an unhappy, unforgettable love. Yet he had the most interesting stories to tell, and in spite of all external failures, he came back to the old country and Vienna, not broke, but with an enriched heart and with the most glowing enthusiasm for the country of his choice. I have never met any person, either in this or any other land, who was as enthusiastic about the "States" as Adolf Loos. If only the United States of the second half of the twentieth century could regain such status in world opinion, and become the image it was to him!

What Loos saw may have been partly illusion, but there was a great core of realism in it, too. To him America was the land of unshackled minds—of people with debunked minds, let us say—of people brought close to life's realities, which are more than all cultural mannerisms and hangovers taken too seriously; realities in a new time, naïvely, subconsciously kept in matter-of-fact working order. People here, as he saw them, had reverted to a sound attitude which had been lost in the old country. At the same time they had golden hearts compared to the pettier or more sophisticated quarrelers back home. He described Americans as the most kindhearted people in the world, and I still concur. One might say that both kind-heartedness and grim-heartedness have economic reasons. Despite the slums, conditions were not like those in various parts of Europe or Asia, where people were, and still are fighting for even a piece of bread, and become naturally embittered in the process.

I loved to listen to Loos's stories, and I still love to think of them. Their validity remained, no matter what I later experienced myself. I had most informally met a great soul, and he had glimpsed deeper into this nation's heart than the superficial enthusiasts. As I recall, one story would go somewhat like this:

"I found myself very badly off, and a general depression had hit the country. I was helping in a little barbershop on Fourteenth Street—which shop, by the way, had a very interesting entrance curtain of glass beads, such as I later used at my Goldman and Salatsch tailoring store on Michaelerplatz. One of the barbers brought me to a cousin of his, a Jewish tailor who lived in the basement of a brownstone house two blocks east of the Bowery. The tailor worked, needled, cut, and also fitted in his basement; but he had a little rear room where he hung the suits. He rented it to me, since there was a short couch to sleep on. Thus I lived with the Jewish tailor and his family, who were very nice people. I stayed for many months, but I could not find a steady job. I tried everything, while the tailor and his wife kindheartedly waited for me to pay the rent. He even loaned me some cash, and I advertised in the paper that I was an expert in heraldry and could design a coat of arms for any new-rich family in New York. Well, I got an order here and there, but I could not make a living, and occasionally had to go back to my odd jobs of the 'night pot-washing' variety.

"One afternoon, while I was running my feet off in my job hunt along Fourteenth Street, something happened on my own street. A fine carriage with two wonderful horses, a coachman and a footman in aristocratic livery, came slowly from the direction of the Bowery. All the kids stopped playing ball, and the street peddlers ceased shouting and looked. The coach stopped and the coachman bent to a passer-by: 'Do you know where Mr. Loos lives?' But he could not readily get any answer.

"Soon there was a big crowd around him, and all the street urchins put their hands on the gold-lacquered wheels and peeked through the windows at the lush upholstery. From his silk hat, the coachman removed a slip of paper and read: 'Mr. Adolf Loos, architect.'

"At once a shout went up from a number of people in the crowd: 'Adolf, he is looking for Adolf!' The urchins began running toward the tailor shop, yelling that a carriage was looking for Adolf. The crowd increased stupendously, shouting in Italian, Yiddish, and Slovak. At the basement door the tailor stood, puzzled, in the midst of all the little boys and girls of the block, who kept calling their mothers to look out the windows and see the show.

"When the coachman learned that Loos was not home, he bent from his high perch and handed a sealed letter to the tailor. Then, while the crowd stood silently in awe and the cooking in all the brownstones was ignored by the women who leaned out the kitchen windows along the entire block, the coachman made the wonderful horses turn the wonderful carriage and fall into a trot over the gay nineties cobblestones. After it had disappeared around the corner, a big guessing game started, carried on in the many languages of Manhattan."

I was sitting in a Vienna coffeehouse, looking at Loos, but I saw Manhattan and the melting pot of the courageous ones who had gone over the sea to the great country of adventure. Loos continued: "That day business and the kids' play was badly interrupted and neglected in this block. Most people stayed at the tailor's, waiting for my return. Meanwhile they discussed the silk hat, the horse whip, the horses, and the carriage's upholstery, and kept up their game of trying to guess what it was all about."

Finally, in the late afternoon, Loos arrived home, tired and pretty discouraged. In the midst of a suspenseful silence he opened the mysterious letter. It was an invitation from a distant rich relative, who had learned of his coming to America and requested in a most friendly fashion that Adolf join a weekend party on his Long Island estate. That was all.

Hundreds of eyes stared at Adolf, and immediately several people put their arms affectionately around his neck; one old Italian even kissed him. A general cheer burst forth, and Loos was lifted onto the shoulders of strong men. But suddenly through the deafening noise Adolf was heard shouting: "I can't go! I can't go like this!" After a momentary desperate pause, everybody agreed that he did indeed look much too shabby to go to Long Island. But one offer snowballed, and everybody wanted to help somehow.

That was Wednesday. By Friday noon everything was ready: collections had been taken up, contributions had been made, everybody in the neighborhood had been busy in clothing rental stores and pawnshops. A smart Prince Albert had been rented which, although a little baggy, was declared almost to fit Adolf's slender shoulders; the striped trousers were supplied by one of the neighbors, and a shirt front, detachable cuffs and collar, tie, silk hat, rather high-heeled dressy patent-leather shoes—everything down to a gold-chained watch for the vest pocket and a camellia for the buttonhole—had miraculously been procured. Love and sympathy had been victorious. And there was also a little gambling instinct, for the race might be won and it might pay.

Loos was shaved by the barber on credit, his little blond mustache was twirled up and scented. The whole affair, after all, was a vague credit deal: "Don't forget us when you are in Long Island." That was the only condition of the bargain.

Adolf looked wonderful when he put his cane under his arm, holding kid gloves in one hand as the other jingled the silver dollars in his trouser pocket.

I sat in the café, looking at Loos: he was wrinkled, sickly, and some twenty years older. Where were all his friends now—those who had helped him to that Long Island fairyland?

Monday at noon the carriage returned, with young Loos a little crumpled and dissipated from his cocktails, but evidently well fed and minus the silver dollars in his trouser pocket, which he had disbursed in tips to the butlers, maids, and coachmen. In the evening, after he had given a glowing account of his weekend adventures, a great transaction took place. The story was told and retold, and new details filled in, while each investor claimed his props—the shoes, the chain, the watch, the silk hat—to take them back to the renter or to pawn them again. People were enthusiastic, but they wondered, what now, what next?

Loos explained that of course one cannot get a job immediately when one is invited to a millionaire's. It is just a matter of hobnobbing for a while with those bankers and captains of industry. But it had been a success, a great success, and they liked him. As a matter of fact, they would like to see him again the week after next. One must play the game. Everybody understood: one must play the game.

At twenty, I was docile and hopeful as I listened to the story of a new world. I took a sip of my prairie oyster, recommended by Loos as typically American, and understood: One must play the game, especially in America. And quite especially when on Long Island, one must be capable of doing as the Long Islanders do.

Two Fridays later everything was repeated. The gold watch, the silk hat, the silver dollars, and the Prince Albert—leaving space for the display of a clean starched shirtfront—all were readied by the friends and speculators east of the Bowery. Again Adolf Loos returned with a picturesque account.

And people continued to hope, from weekend to weekend —until slowly hope and carriage, upholstery and Sunday-child Adolf began to lose their glitter and glamor. Seven-day wonders are everywhere in big New York. The Long Island mirage faded away, and it brought no returns. Adolf never quite lost the warm hearts of his lower Manhattan friends, but to those on Long Island he became commonplace, and also his tips were too small compared with those of other weekend guests. He and his latecomer-arrival American friends strained to compete and keep up with the venerable older Joneses. Perhaps if he could have stood it... But he could not. He decided to pay back some of the well-meaning creditors who had stood by him so faithfully. Fortunately, in the 1890's electric dishwashers had not yet been invented, and some hotels had night-shift openings.

Adolf was called by these new American neighbors by his first name. He had been, was, and remained amiable and humanly attractive to those who ran into him anywhere, but like any marked individual, he was and remained also and always a stranger on a lonely path of his own. Hearty participation of others would flare up for moments, for hours, for hopeful weekends—and then die down, leaving him in his solitude. It was to stay so to the very end.

It may and can hardly be different with an innovator or inventor, any man who sometimes fascinates and then leaves in annoyed impatience those near him, be it now Mozart writing his last piece of music or Graham Bell inventing the first telephone.

Loos continued to admire and love Americans, kitchen chefs, hotel managers, barbers, efficient bank tellers, El conductors, pushcart peddlers, and shoeshine boys. He became to me the Walt Whitman of lower Manhattan. His Americans were extremely fine human material, particularly through forgetting about so-called sophisticated education and culture and those things that were exaggeratedly valued in European countries—especially that cultural capital of Central Europe, which was then Vienna.

This man came from the city with the best orchestra in the world, where there were more significant composers and actors, more applied art appreciation and really cultivated salons and cafés per square mile than anywhere else. Yet in the United States he lived with lowly proletarians and ate and drank among unassimilated fellow immigrants—hardly with the Anglo-Saxon upper crust which might have prided itself on a tradition of its own. Most of his stories were unforgettable, but what is popularly called a "100 per cent" American would rarely appear in them. He was always living and talking with some first- or second-generation Russian, Jew, Slovak, or Italian people he found around Orchard Street in Manhattan. Nevertheless, these enthusiastic, hopeful individuals were all most real Americans to him, and often pathetically, touchingly so. This was the recurrent note: They reflected the spirit of this nation in a significant ever again *initial* stage.

All were in the half-voluntary process of being debunked, and they were all being made good converts to realism—less frozen than before—and to freedom from historical bias, which had somewhat poisoned their bloodstream in the ancient sociopolitical geography of their native countries. At least, according to Loos, they became really kind-hearted people, whereas at home they had coldly been cutting each other's familiar throats for a long time. Of course, a certain amount of throat-cutting still existed, but it was mixed with elements of a good-natured boyish sport. Among beginners in this great melting pot there was even an atmosphere of mellowing hearts—something that Loos sensed as the new American brand of humanism. I may have put some of my own words into Loos's mouth, but his, and later my own, view of this country was never orthodox, although I have come to know a much vaster cross section of Americans, from blue-blood to lowly laborer, including the Asiatic newcomer on the West Coast or on the islands of the Fiftieth State, and in the American Trust Territory of the South Seas.

Loos's story was in a way an optimistic immigrant's version of *Leaves of Grass*. Both these poets, and the vast world of which they sang, fascinated me. Both talked of men and women, and only sketchily about the landscape or the height of the buildings; Loos didn't even mention the Anglo-Saxon "stock company" which acted so prominently in this play and originally populated the country. Nevertheless, he touched upon the effect which this classical country of immigration had on all its immigrants, all it absorbed into its civilization; its potential for rehashing mankind and how its new citizens were being changed. That was his story of mass-molding America, and, if only true, it could now become more important as the nation has, for better or worse, turned into a long-distance catalyst all around the globe; in places behind the tough political drapery a technological civilization of similar quantity transaction also rolls over the individual. Can it anywhere survive for the mysterious chance of evolution? It might turn out close to the crucial question of human growth.

On his return to Europe, Loos tragically thought he could change Vienna with his new knowledge; he seemed then to fail dismally, except with me. I still agree with him, while I anxiously hope the United States will deserve its substantial if not universal following by emerging from the mercurial numerical spirit of power companies, most experienced airlines, Pentagon-nursed industrial and development corporations, into a spirit of shaping more cohesive communities, more human cities. We are no longer young enough to fumble naïvely in picturesque incoherence while personally enmeshed in installment plans so that we can each enjoy his cocky yearly model of this and that as our common denominator.

Loos had walked through the Columbian Exposition, which tried a classical chapeau on the American head. When he lived in Chicago, it just had been, perhaps more justifiably than half a century later, a wild and burly place of great fascination for somebody who wanted to get rid of all the extenuated culture and all the things which existed in the fast-aging Europe of that time. But strangely, with his own modifications, he took the "classical column" attitude back home to a Vienna of the capricious, modish *Art Nouveau* and *Jugendstiel*. It seems that Loos, like most, was impressed by the massive Roman revival of this world's fair—perhaps more than by Louis Sullivan's risky extra tour of the florid new transportation building celebrating the machine and housing ponderous contemporary steam locomotives, now long defunct. I believe I have myself really never got involved in this superficial combat between the "classical" and the novel or even the modish of the moment—even now, when perhaps both are again having a simultaneous and probably again passing revival. There is, however, a human organic *Basso sostenuto* which does not pass, which forever undercolors what we can, must, and will do to remain vital. It is deep below the surface and the light upper crust of sophistication fit to amuse our moment.

When I came to the Eastern import harbors of the "States," nothing grimy, nothing dirty, ever discouraged me. I was so fortified that I saw only youthfulness, a bit unwashed behind the ears. Also listening to and using foreign words abroad, we might often get entangled in happy misunderstanding. Erudite linguistics are a smallish part of anybody's communications. I am afraid I speak all languages badly. English I never had in school; I painfully picked it up in Brooklyn and later tried perfecting myself on Hollywood Boulevard before teaching it to my wife. When on television in Rome thirty years later or for half an hour over the Uruguayan network, I surely succeeded talking native with a foreign accent. Probably it's more interesting to the listeners anyhow. Funny imperfection always is, and often engages sympathy. Facial expression and waving the hands helped in New York.

I certainly didn't come here to find or even see riches because Loos had told me about rags and tailors who worked for Hart, Schaffner & Marx and consumers who learned to go upstairs to Foreman & Clark to save 30 per cent. He hardly told me—except as a fabulous backdrop of the immigration scene—about polished marble, and little about high-grade cocktail lounges and soft society. Rather, I remember him mentioning those prairie oysters of drastic gin. His introduction had been good, and to a kindhearted underground of America, to the people of its sweatshops looking into a rosier future, in a time fifteen years before Sidney Hillman was heard of.

When I actually saw America—Manhattan, Brooklyn, Baltimore, Philadelphia, Chicago—it was just like going to London, seeing some glum poverty-stricken area that recalled Dickens's *Christmas Carol*, and being very enthusiastic because one had read Dickens as a boy. Here were all the grimy buildings and backyards Loos had described in his humanly optimistic stories. If one visited the London of Queen Victoria expecting it to be something like the richest center of money exchange, the world capital and hub of the far-flung British Empire, and suddenly saw critically the masses of people down at the heels, not even able to talk English, one might well have wondered what kind of a top-dog city or resplendent metropolis it was. But once one loved Dickens and the poverty and slum scenery of his tales became endearing, because out of them inevitably some goodness grows, one would have found London wonderful and discovered the resounding humanity in which to believe.

With that kind of an attitude I could not possibly be disappointed. I found New York wonderful. I looked at all its grimy places and considered it all an acknowledgment of what I had learned, a certification of Loos's X-ray vision, which penetrated surfaces and made the future manifest. I even smiled at the Singer Tower and the Woolworth Building, although I had in my baggage and my mind designs somewhat like Lever Brothers and my own Rush City Reformed. Perhaps Loos misguided me as to America as a whole. But his was a beautiful misguidance, a loving prejudice.

There was another man who influenced me deeply. He was vastly different from Loos, an American of the second generation. Frank Lloyd Wright is himself a wonderful subject for a story never told, not even by himself. I am happy to have known this great man long before he gained his country's recognition, and he surely was not easy to know. He may perhaps not even have had an exhaustive self-knowledge, but by others he surely has been misevaluated long and in many ways, humanly, as a reforming artist, and as one competitively rebellious over a long, vital lifetime of never-ending newsworthiness. The older this miraculous man grew, the more witty and clever in interviews and TV he seemed to become. I could stay with him when he was almost alone; he talked to me often. He wrote an autobiography linking great human aspirations which I can appreciate with deep sympathy. I can hear his voice when I read his words.

When I first stood before Frank Lloyd Wright, it was just like suddenly seeing the unicorn or some other fairytale figure one has been searching for behind the rainbow. All I knew about him was from a large graphic volume, really a kind of portfolio twenty by thirty inches in size, which came out in Germany in 1911. It was the most monumental pioneering publication on an architect which had ever come out, and its publication was possible only because he paid for it himself. At forty he strangely was both unrecognized for the significance of his work and affluent through it! I had no idea why he himself should have to pay for this publication and why the story came out far away in Berlin, for at that time I hadn't had the chance to gauge the circumstances surrounding his life which are so deeply interesting to contemplate. The beautifully printed pages of this magnificent volume seemed to reveal to me the fantastic living culture of some unknown people. It was just like seeing pictures of houses for people in another world—an entirely different scene which was impossible in Vienna, because of, for one thing, the density of the living pattern and the historical penuriousness, prejudice, or plain poverty of the Europeans.

Here was an entirely different setting. The foreword appeared in a startling German. Wright himself wrote in a very poetic, often flowery, way, and he could not check the strange, confused attempt at decorative translation; so the text, too, was like a garbled message from Mars, almost incomprehensible. Somehow the meaning became heart-rendingly clear to me from the illustrations. I could only marvel at the drawings and the floor plans; they looked entirely different from anything I had ever seen. These houses really had no walls; rooms opened up in any direction. They almost seemed to have been built in a tropical country where there was no wintry cold at all, which, naturally, wasn't the case.

In the preface Mr. Wright told about how he had invented the "prairie style" and that this magnificent newness was placed in the Midwestern plains of the United States. At the time, of course, I had never been in the Middle West, and I pictured that area somewhat the way it was later described by Donald Culross Peattie, with the strange vegetation, the peeping birds, and the roaming little beasts of a prairie grove and the surrounding land. What I imagined was perhaps like the pampas of Argentina, but still inhabited by red Indians, with tepees as a backdrop, and, in the distance, a thundering herd of bison. In this untouched flat, level, and far-stretching paradise Wright was creating low buildings with tremendous shading roofs and long window ribbons, like those of the venturesome transcontinental trains which looked out on a free, breezy landscape. I had no idea that all this work was in suburban Oak Park, Chicago. It was the more fascinating without such knowledge. I made up my mind that I would have to see it with my own eyes; no one in Europe was doing anything like it. Whoever he was, Frank Lloyd Wright, the man far away, had done something momentous and rich in meaning.

This miracle man instilled in me the conviction that, no matter what, I would have to go to the places where he walked and worked.

When I came to New York and saw what Loos had described to me, it was a sort of homecoming to a familiar situation because I, too, was a poor, lonely immigrant. Dione, expecting our first child, had stayed behind. I lived in Manhattan, in a room for which I paid a couple of dollars a week; it was furnished with a bed and nothing else but a drainpipe running from the upper story to the one below me, and I could hear the people in the washroom above. There was no closet or wardrobe, just a few hooks to hang my clothes on. I lived in Manhattan and worked in Brooklyn—I commuted from the inside out, just to be different from the start. Each day I took the subway, changed twice, finally took the streetcar far into outer Brooklyn to sustain my life. I was living on Irving Place, right close to Gramercy Park, in the middle of the wonder isle, encrusted with grime and mystery. But, again, this was all only a confirmation of my expectations from "the tales of Loos," while Frank Lloyd Wright's picture book and the story it had told me were going to turn out to be quite in contrast to ready reality.

Wright's Prairie Chicago

I had been very impatient to reach Chicago, because there I would see those prairies stretching on to the horizon, with groves in the foreground and communities of lovely prairie houses. So I finally made my way to the midcontinent city, which was then little more than two generations old. I arrived one drizzly November morning at the Illinois Central depot. And here I must interpose to explain another circumstance which caused me to come.

When I was in about the third class of high school, I had read a Viennese newspaper story from Chicago, saying that this grand and mushrooming metropolis had just decided to electrify all the railways within a forty-mile radius and thus purify the air and make life very sweet and clean. *Electricity* at that time was a very new word to me, and it was fascinating to think of all those trains running electrically. I was only a boy when I read this story, but enthusiasm remained.

Twenty years later, I finally was in the place of my dreams, on a rain-gray day late in 1924. It promptly showed itself as different from Wright's story; it was even somewhat different from that of Loos, and surely from what I had read in the old Viennese newspaper. It is strange what fuses and conflicts in our anticipating brains.

Loos never really sang the epos of American machine civilization or electrification, nor had he the chance to live in one of the little communities of America, pioneering or plain rustic. He never really saw the country, but kept recording a controversial and touchingly converting influence of the

American entry port on the incoming polyglot flood of immigrants. He did not explain exactly what the city's implications or impacts were, nor what it was that made for this influence. The human material was changed by something vital here, in the American urban scene and even that part of the city which might be considered slums, not at all outstanding or attractive; he was concerned with what made a *passing show into progress*.

Of course, he didn't see anything in America as glorious as the boulevards of Paris or the Ringstrasse and the great monuments of Vienna. Evidently this was the thing he was running away from. It was too self-complacent and imposed imperial grandeur not natural to human little people. When they came here and went through the grinding mill of immigration, they hardly changed through high civil-service-inspired architecture with a capital *A*. For them it all played and started on a very different, lower level beneath and fronting the Third and Second Avenue elevateds. Later some of them might reach the Renaissance Palace on Forty-second and Fifth Avenue surrounded by commercial skyscrapers.

I have been sketching the influence on me of what Loos thought and saw. I have been talking of Frank Lloyd Wright, whose work appeared to me first in photographs, but primarily in his own drawings and in a text which was garbled and mutilated in translation. From this wonder book, which I read in the library because it was too expensive to buy, I glimpsed a much more rural America than Loos had described, one very much more romantic than it ever was in the last hundred years. If one listens to Henry David Thoreau, who did not live in a big city, one finds that Salem was not an idyllic place even in 1840 and that Concord was more a beautiful name than a fact. Ninety per cent of the New England grocerymen were groaning under impending bankruptcy. The farmers, too, were weighted down under mortgages, and everything was going to pieces according to this wise man who withdrew from the hectic, overcomplicated life of antebellum Yankee-land.

There was no real rural America around most of Frank Lloyd Wright's buildings. The initial majority of them were built just within the suburban sprawl of a fast-growing metropolis, some of whose citizens were making and could spend a tremendous amount of money compared with the pennies which changed hands on Orchard Street, Manhattan. Wright was creating what he liked to think was a revival of the spirit of the prairie in houses of swanky suburban streets. The text as well as the drawings of his beautiful portfolio, with all the charming hollyhocks standing around the open rooms, with shading roofs overhanging the Midwestern summer prairie, had been very much in my mind as I rushed away from New York after having seen the tightly knit Loos portion of America.

I had looked forward to the broad acres of the Frank Lloyd Wright portion of America, but I never exactly arrived there. Maybe I was blindfolded, sitting on a wooden horse, believing myself traveling through and into magic regions, like Don Quixote. I was blindfolded only figuratively, and actually I had been sitting at a coach window, seeing the scenery of the richest country in the world, from Grand Central Station to the Illinois Central terminal.

Finally I was there. It looked old-fashioned and had something like a medieval tower. Carrying my suitcase, I had to walk right around the big puffing and darkly smoking locomotive to gain the open air, which was no less smoky but gray and drizzly as well. The prairies were not immediately visible. My shirt collar turned black in half an hour. At first I thought I must have arrived at the wrong station or something; nothing here seemed to be electrified. But I tried myself to stay galvanized and ready for anything. Again grasping my suitcase firmly, I started from a grimy, seamy old railway depot in what I thought was the general direction of South Halstead

Street. On the muddy way I stalked over one level crossing to another, where ever more dark locomotives were standing, smoking peacefully into the same gray November drizzle.

I was approaching the Stockyards, where I had been invited to live by the only Chicagoan I had ever actually met, James Jackson Forrestall. A lawyer and a Quaker, his own office was in the grand old Monadnock building. He and his wife had become acquainted with me at the Friends' Mission in Vienna, where I had worked to pick up my few words of the most basic English before crossing the ocean. Mr. and Mrs. Forrestall were helping in the Quaker food-distribution program. On his departure for America Mr. Forrestall had said, 'When you come to Chicago, let me know beforehand and I'll put you up at a wonderful place—Jane Addams's settlement." At that time all I knew about a settlement was what I had vaguely heard of Toynbee Hall in London.

While walking west over the tracks and under the rain, I thought of the first Americans I had met at the Mission. Soon after arriving in the New World, I visited some of them in Germantown, and contrasted them with my lower Manhattanites of Fourteenth and Union Square.

The person who had first given me the affidavit necessary for an entry visa was Professor John Fisher from Goshen College, Indiana, who was working at the Vienna postwar Mission and studying Kant on the side. I provided him with a running unauthentic translation, section by section, to prepare him for the lessons he took with a University of Vienna bigwig in philosophy; at that poverty-stricken time such private instruction would cost only a dollar or two.

Professor Fisher in his kindness had afforded me little help with my visa, as the consulate at once spotted him as a Quaker from Goshen College, and the Immigration and Naturalization Service in Washington discovered that campus was a breeding ground for pacifism: three of its professors had been jailed as conscientious objectors during the First World War. Anybody who had anything to do with Quakers was *persona non grata* in the United States then, but I had no idea of it. As a boy, William Penn with his broad-rimmed hat had always seemed to me quite a genuine American figure when I saw his portrait on boxes of Quaker Oats.

Now, in Chicago at last, I followed Forrestall's written directions and climbed, puzzled, over one railway track after another. As I approached South Halstead Street, I saw in the distance the settlement, a not at all uninteresting darkish complex of buildings, standing right in the midst of slums that were quite different from Harlem or the Bowery.

Walking down the street, I noticed some strange and very picturesquely dressed girls standing in doorways or looking out the ground-floor windows of very dilapidated buildings. I couldn't make up my mind about them, but had a faint idea that they might be in an ancient, alluring trade. Later I found out that they were Greek gypsies and that they were wearing typical folk costumes from the old country. They were fortunetellers, so I felt partially right—theirs was a fairly ancient trade—but fortunes seemed controversial in these surroundings, and hard to tell.

I arrived at the settlement house, and was immediately introduced to its famous founder, Miss Jane Addams, who was extremely kind. An elderly friend of the Forrestalls, she had been one of the first to recognize Frank Wright. She gave me a room and talked to me as much as I could understand with my poor grasp of English. Fifteen minutes after I had been installed, I was asked to come down to the telephone in the lobby. "Call from Mr. Forrestall."

"Well, you have arrived," he said. Although he was a Quaker, he was of this age. *Thou* had been dropped for you.

So I answered, "Yes, sir."

He welcomed me and asked briefly how I was. I told him Miss Addams had lodged me with another young man. "You will like it here," he told me. "It is a very interesting enterprise to change immigrants over into Americans, and altogether I tell you Chicago is a most likable, glorious place; it has the best climate in the world—although today it is somewhat drizzly, I might say; but it is a wonderful city if you come to know it. I might tell you that we are now working on a scheme to electrify all the railways up to forty miles out of town, and then there won't be any more of this smoke, which you may have noticed."

"Yes," I remarked, "I noticed it, and I already read in a paper about this electrification—some time ago!"

In this fashion my career in Chicago started. As soon as I had made arrangements to teach certain drafting classes to the Greeks and gypsies of the neighborhood, I got some free time, procured a city map, and began looking for the houses I had seen in Wright's drawings. I told Miss Addams about them; she had known Frank Lloyd Wright as a young man, but meanwhile he had become a black sheep. He had left his family, they told me, and had "run away with the wife of a neighbor on the same street in Oak Park." It was an almost hateful account. When he was young, yes, some of them had known him, but now he seemed to them just a scandalous fellow. Common gossip had given him all the malicious broadsides it could. Later on, when I told Mr. Forrestall that I was going to visit Mr. Wright and hoped one day to get my young bride here from overseas to take her along, he was thoroughly appalled. What an idea—to bring a young woman into "such a den of iniquity"!

My own faith never faltered a bit. I looked around the western part of Chicago, and south, near the university, but nobody could tell me anything about this famous architect I was talking about. People were flabbergasted that I should have picked up the ideals of a great Chicagoan in a European library, and looked at each other in amazement. A few knew that he was involved in some sort of awful thing, and one person remembered that there had been a multiple murder on his farm in Wisconsin. But Wright certainly was not a famous man. He was a terrible man. Had not the Chicago papers brought out lurid stories about him? He had had to leave town—and here I was, coming from Vienna to look for a person like this and his work! That was a very strange thing.

I finally succeeded in finding some of the places which he had built. I would look up all the notes I had made when studying his portfolio mornings in the Art Library at Berlin while supporting myself by playing as a theater extra in the evenings. That was now so far away, and here I was in the country of my dreams.

But where were the prairies, the woods, the lawns? Where, anyway, was Woodlawn Avenue? Once I got there, I would actually find the famous Robie House. My heart always skipped when I imagined the moment: I would ring the doorbell and ask in very broken English, "Is Mr. Robie in?" And so I finally did.

"Mr. Robie? Never heard of him." There was a Mrs. Wilson living there. She had bought the house some years back, and was probably the fifth owner. She wasn't at all enthusiastic about it—but to me it was a lovely, wonderful place.

I asked Mrs. Wilson why she had bought the house. "Oh," she answered, cold fish, "I got it very cheap. The man who owned it had to get out." No, she didn't particularly like it, and she had all kinds of petty criticisms. Nothing was working, of course; at that time the house was already some fifteen years old, and badly neglected.

I had almost the same experience in practically every one of the places which I finally spotted; whether it was in River Forest or Oak Park, everywhere the story was similar. The people whom I had wanted to face, the human beings whom I had seen in my mind's eye and had assumed to be molded by architecture, or especially perhaps those fascinating human beings who had ordered this thrilling architecture of the future and now were living in it happily ever after, were not to be found. For the most part the inhabitants and their furnishings seemed sorry misfits, but their houses were every bit as beautiful as I had expected, and it was an overwhelming experience to lay eyes on them at last after longing to do so for a dozen years. Nevertheless, I was submerged in sad wonderment. I had arrived in fairyland, but the fairies had gone. And the occupants of the enchanted forest looked entirely inconsistent and contradictory to what their setting called for. I was terribly downcast, broken, and puzzled.

My background was somewhat complicated by a mixed-up paternity. Considering not only Loos, an enthusiastic American from Vienna, but Wright, as my father, I was really a second-generation American, and sometimes, like one, a little unadjusted to my co-Americans! I had in this country a third father, who lived in my imagination, a big man, Louis H. Sullivan. Wright's master, he had built the auditorium, the Carson, Pirie Scott store, and many other grand things. Like Wright, and me, he was also a second-generation Usonian. But they were not as lucky with their fathers as I. It is interesting to speculate about the soul impact of fathers. My adopted fathers were great architects. Sullivan's real father was an Irish dancing master; Wright's, a missionary minister who loved music; Loos's father ran a polished-marble business; and my dad in the flesh had started casting cowbells to sound harmoniously. Perhaps paternity is always dubious; everybody is a child of many forefathers.

I went to see all Sullivan's buildings, and found them extraordinary. Here in the middle of North America, I thought, was work which could be compared with what Otto Wagner had been doing in the Vienna of Central Europe. And that was the very highest accolade I was capable of giving to anything built. Sullivan was living in this town, I now found out, and I wanted by all means to see him. I had, in fact, a manuscript of his, "The Kindergarten Chats," which friends of my own friend R. M. Schindler had held and sent to Berlin, hoping that we might find someone to publish it or finance the printing.

Well, I was entirely unsuccessful with this project in Europe, although I tried hard and with all my enthusiasm.

I also talked to a few people in Chicago about it, and they all laughed at me. Sullivan? they asked, —isn't he that old drunkard? He's a pauper now, and is being supported by his friends; each one pitches in five dollars a month. I guess he's living in a run-down tenement or "hotel" on Warner Avenue, around Thirty-fifth Street or so.

Well, I happened to meet some of those people who were contributing five dollars, and they gave me Sullivan's address. Every week either Ralph Fletcher Seymour, Arthur Fred Woltersdorf, Albert McArthur, or John Van Bergen took him to dinner at the Cliff Dwellers Club so that he had something to eat.

I went to visit this "old" man, who, at age sixty-three, was then much younger than I am now. It was a bitter heartrending thing to see him living in a dissolute, dreary situation. I told him that I had come straight from Vienna to meet him and Mr. Wright.

"I haven't seen Frank for seventeen years," he remarked. "He has forsaken me."

"What about yourself," I asked, "are you feeling all right?"

"Well," he answered, "I'm feeling pretty rotten. I am dying. I'm in very bad shape, and I have been forgotten." That much I gathered from his answer.

I put my English words together as best I could. "Mr. Sullivan, I tell you, you are not quite alone. I have come a long distance to see you. Your fame and the influence of your work has been world wide." I now know of how little avail my words could have been.

He said, "I once thought myself that it would be of some consequence, but it has all died down; there is nothing left of it—nothing left to speak of."

He was very broken, while I tried my best to cheer him up. But he kept dwelling on his despondency and lack of following. The loneliness of genius is something horrible to behold.

When Louis Sullivan died, I was grief-striken, and took time off from the office to attend his funeral at Graceland Cemetery. None of my fellow workers, not even the chief draftsman, understood why I would go to such a man's funeral, as "he was nobody really now." Nevertheless, there were a few people at the cemetery, and some of them made orations.

The longest was made by I. K. Pond, who was several years older than Sullivan; he had designed the University Club, one of the reactionary pseudo-medieval buildings in Chicago. I suppose there had been a life-long feud between the Pond brothers and Sullivan, each side representing radically different schools of thought. As I listened sullenly, I. K. seemed to be gloating that all the dead man's ideas had failed and none had ever really taken root. It was very painful for me, although I didn't follow completely the very scholarly diction of Mr. Pond, who was a high-bred person indeed, at that time probably the most cultured architect in Chicago.

But there was another man present, and that was Frank Lloyd Wright, who had come all the way from California, where he was working, to attend the funeral. He had not seen Sullivan in many years, and looked very ill at ease in front of a lot of hometown adversaries; he compensated for it by his dandyish appearance. He was very well dressed, carried a cane, and wore oxfords with fairly high heels. He was acting pronouncedly unconcerned about all the master's friends and foes, and seemed preoccupied with his own antagonism to them or theirs to him. He did not appear to feel as bereaved as I did. I was downcast because of Sullivan's death, but I was also discouraged by my meeting with him in the last years of his life, and by seeing what had become of a great pioneer in my chosen profession. It surely was not very encouraging to a young man. And here was still another man whom I had admired so long, and he did seem to be disliked; he didn't appear affluent either, but he was trying to keep a stiff upper lip, look dressy and undaunted.

After the ceremony I approached Frank Lloyd Wright,

and with a halting voice, told him what he had meant to me. He was extremely appreciative. He took me out for dinner, and later to the Congress Hotel, where he was spending the night. There he asked me, "Why don't you come with me for a visit to Taliesin? I don't have any work, you know. A modern architect can't have any work to speak of in this country—especially not in Chicago." And he started to describe the gloominess of the situation.

Frank Lloyd Wright has glibly been depicted as anything but humble. Yet it was more characteristic of him that the man he called his *master* for a lifetime *was by no means of the former generation*, but one who looked almost of the same age as he. I cherish the photos of that time. Young Frank had been so deeply impressed by Mr. Sullivan in thought, speech, and enthusiastically sketching florid original ornaments. Perhaps a competitive ambition for the older man's gifts of this kind was never again to leave his soul alone. Maybe he would have been in a purer state of his own if he had never seen what was not quite in his nature. When he tried to break away from it fully, at twenty-five, he was better off, although he also broke Sullivan's heart, who told me how he loved him.

Frank Lloyd Wright would have become a great architect even if he never had laid eyes on Sullivan's achievement. But it kept him, deep in his heart, competitive to it, more than a generation after the older friend was in his grave.

The master had left him a bequest of disgust, together with lasting inspiration and cause for never-ending emulation of impressive gifts. It was a mixed package—an occasionally opened Pandora's box, to inherit as a young man and carry along for fifty years to come. I have later often pondered it, wondered about it.

The intriguingly new often tends to attract imitation. At a zoo one can be deeply fascinated by a giraffe never seen before; nevertheless one doesn't, or shouldn't even try to, become a giraffe.

As a whole Frank Lloyd Wright was known to stay the man destiny had made him.

Wright's own unhappily resentful pupil, Albert McArthur, even much more troubled by the shadow of a great man, had painted for me the same glum cyclorama of architectural chances or their lack a week before, coming from breakfast at twelve noon to his office, where I was patiently waiting for him. I had then ended the long, disheartening conversation with the meek question: "Do you want me to commit suicide?"

After Wright's own outburst of pessimism and a dark look into the near future, he had now suggested and, before parting, repeated generously: "If you want to come and visit me in Wisconsin, I'll be glad to have you." I was deeply grateful.

He was lonely, and indeed pleased when I said I'd love to. But I didn't understand why he responded little when I talked about Sullivan and my feelings for him. Now I believe I know; filial feelings often have their emotional controversiality grown into them. In Peking, and for a billion Asiatics whom Sigmund Freud did not know, probably it is not so.

However, Sullivan and Frank were only some seven years apart in age, and had more than a tiff; they had tragedy at parting time. Then again, perhaps it had some quite typical tristesse in it, what the sensitive young draftsman, George Elmslie, watched in Sullivan's office from his frog's-eye view and told his sisters. By accident it was narrated to me much later. But no third person can fully follow such grief.

Once, while I was sitting at lunch opposite Mr. Wright in Spring Green, the mail was put on the table. I opened a letter, and inside was a topaz stickpin, sent to me with an appreciative and hopeful letter. It told me that I was worthy to have the pin which Sullivan had worn in better days and which his friends had now redeemed from the pawn shop. They thought I deserved it for my enthusiasm and friendliness to the old master. Glowing, I, who was nobody, rushed around the table and showed the pin to Mr. Wright. "Do you recognize it?" He shook his head, and I gave him the letter. It was a mistake.

He read and silently gave me back these tokens. He seemed sad.

The necktie pin I have never worn. It is in a bank safe.

In our very first conversation I had already told Mr. Wright what troubled me. I had wanted to see the *people* who were living in those extraordinary houses of his. "As a matter of fact, the houses themselves," I said, "are so familiar to me that I know them by heart." I would not have had to come to Chicago to see them, because I had studied the plans so very thoroughly, but I had wanted to see the people, *the humans, who were living* in them. However, there was something strange about them. "Do you know a Mrs. Wilson who is living in the Robie House?"

"I have no idea who is living in those houses now. But that's how things go here; nothing stays, everything changes." Again he seemed to echo the pessimism of old Mr. Sullivan, now lodged in Graceland.

"Was there a lot of prairie around here when you built those houses?" I asked. "For instance, the Robie place."

"No," he answered, "there was no prairie, it's just close to the University of Chicago; but it was the spirit of the prairie that was recaptured with it and in it."

"Yes, it was," I said. "I haven't been on the prairie yet, but I think it gives me the idea."

Many years later it occurred to me that I myself have so very often gone beyond program requirement, fact, and physical site, and spun a thread, woven a fabric of my own, when I began to design. An architect can also be a storyteller; first of all he tells stories to himself, sees worlds of his own. A little Don Quixote in oneself keeps one going.

And then others will have to get the tale told, full of form and sense. This it will have to be, so that souls take it in and hold it.

I went to Spring Green to visit Mr. Wright, and it was truly wonderful. I felt as if I were in a Japanese temple district, whatever I thought that might look like. Taliesin was completely removed from anything I had known before, and here there did live a man who fitted it. The America which he represented, perhaps all by himself, was extremely attractive to me, although it did not seem to exist except in his mind and now in mine, and perhaps in those of some people I had not yet met. I could only find the human beings to populate this kind of America in Mr. Wright's own realm; there, for instance, Carl Sandburg was a well-beloved guest who would sing songs, with the guitar, and recite poetry.

The ordinary Americans of means and purchasing power whom I was to meet as time went by were not necessarily of Anglo-Saxon stock, but they seemed assimilated to it and often enough to somewhat pedestrian mental inclinations and rational practical ties. The immigrants whom I had seen were half slave to this assimilative process and half free. They were eager to get upstairs, but for the time being they seemed to exist on an entirely different level. They were living in the basement, and there were no basements in Wright's houses!

These straightforward one-story buildings were built right on the ground, under clouds sailing through the blue sky, and they had no cellars and no garrets. It was a strange experience, trying to fuse all my mixed up impressions of the American scene. Has anybody ever fathomed it and been just and fair to it? It's such a big, wide land if one really starts walking through it, with open eyes, instead of shutting them and just speculating about it.

Wright was famous to me, and if I seemed in this country almost alone with my devotion, I surely and most firmly anticipated his future world-wide fame. Infamous to his hometown papers, ridiculous to his professional confreres—whom he, in return, despised for their attacks and irony—he remained master of his destiny. I could understand his feelings, but gently tried to talk him out of them when they bothered him. One morning he received a letter, and after reading it, tossed it to me with a bitter laugh. I expected it to be an insult, but it appeared to be a kindly invitation to participate in an exhibition of the Chicago Art Institute. I pleaded with him to forget earlier slighting behavior and enjoy the slow improvement of climate. It seems more easily advised than done. Everything has its prehistory, and some of it is hard-to-penetrate polluted air one would have to cut with a knife.

He supposed himself to be a regionalist, and was ostensibly reviving the prairie atmosphere. In his mind he was dealing with Americans as one who knew how to house their souls and bodies. But in fact his work seemed, at least on the surface, dubiously fitted to them and their thinking, while, to me, it still appeared of great cosmopolitan significance, although at the moment perhaps not suitable to any particular country I knew. Imitations were appearing in Holland and, very little and lamely enough, in Germany; but Wright's ideas simply did not appeal to the average American. Recognition, practice, or usage seemed largely denied to it in the very region of its origin. I wondered if this always happened to "conceived regionalism," to ingeniously given form, whenever something was willfully created rather than developed from simple inner habit and common outer tradition.

At any rate, this was my second experience with an American scene imagined by a genius, filtered through a great mind. To see an oversized, much more than just gifted man realize how unrecognized some of the sources and aspirations of his work are becomes revealing and perhaps typical for other such extraordinary cases that one knows only from history books.

When given the privilege of listening to ideas of imposing men of entirely different fields than my own—Albert Einstein, Sigmund Freud, Thomas Mann, Paul Klee, or Leon Trotsky—I felt myself imbued with a similar empathy to their icy solitude, although in an often-rarefied atmosphere I surely could by no means follow their cerebrations—always fused with emotion—about their aims as they saw them. Yet empathy is only partially dependent on intellectual capacity of sharing.

How America Builds

Still reviewing why I came to America, it was a bundle of motivations, nothing accidental, and not only the attraction of great men.

There was something else, more impersonal but influential, that slowly started to grow in my mind and color the picture of this great country of newcomers and the "unheard of." It emerged from a simple thought which I had already had in Europe. Maybe it was as partly initiated or generated by Loos but, to my recollection, only faintly so, if at all.

Loos was at heart interested in handicraft, and one of his ideals in this field was the well-finished Viennese cabinetwork which, even before his period, had been obliterated by gaudy Victorianism and then threatened by *Art Nouveau* fashions. Smiling, he would say that the most beautiful piece of cabinetwork was the American oak toilet seat. It was wonderful! Today plastic is used, but in those days there were well-curved and shaped oak seats. Loos became dithyrambic about this graceful but matter-of-fact article, how it was fitted on the china fixture, how neatly it was joined, and how well it would withstand all abuse. He always gave this as an example of American cabinetwork, and his eyes shone with the enthusiasm of a craftsman or a man whose life's work is to hand-shape boomerangs or tobacco pipes or well-finished, unique Cremona violins.

Perhaps this strangely sparked my admiration for the United States' precise though repetitive *industrialized* technology. It became clear to me that for economic and political reasons it comprised almost a whole continent without tariff boundaries and with a terrifically expanded continent-wide market for toilet seats, doorknobs, appliances, tools, and devices—not to mention the export possibilities.

At least the organic common denominator of the species had here a better chance to be served because there was scope and means to support just this! Parochial conditionings would not interfere with the ultimate world-wide problem of *this species, and within it perhaps somehow the biological individual as its vital part, served tomorrow by broader and yet more pointed research.* Was this a queer hope?

To a European it seemed that such a tremendous market would provide the opportunity and give rise to cautious research which would usher in a beneficial, growing, wholesome industry, especially in the field of building supplies, and would create a technology well endowed for and by truly current information. Thus mankind would be furnished with some new equivalent to the output of petty tradespeople, who as craftsmen anyhow had lost their traditional touch with human beings. This country would foster modern architecture as no other could: not only did it have ingenuity and the machines to service a new auxiliary production of broadly adaptable fabricates, but, above all, it had *biological success at its disposal because consumption could be, had to be, widely and sharply observed;* it had the distribution system, it had the mail-order houses and their pattern of distant control. From diet to man-made microclimate in our abode, *biology could win.* Everything basic seemed available to the underlying framework, and the four-day work week around the corner. Democratic individualism would perhaps be allowed to flourish—not mere nose counting and reviewing a thick order book with carbon copies and cash registers. Piecemeal petty research in individual attics and basements could no longer be of this age. The big scale would now and here be endowed.

I have meanwhile grown weary and less credulous that American individualism can now triumphantly unfold with more success than a century earlier, when escape from humdrum standard toil by flight to Walden Pond was attempted. But I won't give up.

It had been my idea that baking bread for a continent without those duty boundary lines Europe suffered from, with cellophane packed shipment and distribution over thousands of miles, should, by the breadth of the market place, justify and make possible scientific advisory staffs of biochemists and dieticians, such as a baker in an Italian or Swiss village could not employ. Helped only by tradition, that little man would dismally flounder in comparison with the up-to-date big company, which would do what is wholesome for the world on current terms. But the United States has some of the world's worst bread, and I was wrong again. Still, one day I may yet be right, and transition may rise to new levels.

One day rich, far-shipping Pittsburgh and other glorious production centers may be model communities, too. Technology may not only be big, fast, and cleverly cellophane-wrapped, but lasting, beyond staccato obsolescence. While there is so much human constancy—for better or worse—obsolescence should not break us or be the idol that promises ever-new big marketing.

Fast-changing supply should not nibble on the virtue of our—thank God—amazing organic steadiness and our pocketbook. Can we capitalize on our inborn stability instead of wantonly impairing it?

I had a friend in the perfume business who laid in a big stock of My Sin; next year he almost went broke. He may recover. But for the moment, at least, it was all superseded temporarily—I imagine, by new sins.

This sort of thing doesn't happen in the country. The plague of obsolescence follows us around particularly in an urban civilization, and we are in need of a Secretary of Urban Affairs to keep everything, especially community improvements, from going to pot so fast, while community plans are so slow. In the midst of the clichés of a quick-turnover age there are still plenty of long-range investments and decisions to be made.

I remember that when I was young, Adolf Loos in Vienna, my deeply admired mentor and older friend, told me, misty-eyed, of his happiness because he had just received a letter from an old client of the past, from whom he had not heard in many years. Loos opened the envelope and, puzzled, found a moderate but still sizable check made out to him, and signed by the client in his almost forgotten handwriting.

Loos read the short letter which said:

"Others of my friends who have built their houses with fine architects, I should say twenty-five years ago, have written them off, amortized them, and many of them are now building a house in a new style. My own house is still good. My wife and I, and in fact all who love us, think it shows no date or loss in refreshing our souls and aiding our life, just as it did in the beginning.

"I believe I am saving a new architect's fee, and I think it is only fair to pay you for it after twenty-five years once over again. I apologize because it is not much in current money, and thahk you for having tried so hard to understand what is in us and what may best last around us."

Adolf Loos treasured the letter and the check—he never cashed it. I have never forgotten the expression on his face, and I am happy that I have met a man like this and have kept his lesson on lasting values in my mind. Perhaps perfumes may change fast, but architectural virtue must last.

At any rate, once I had become familiar with the wider American scene, I found that, in contrast to Europe, there was no great difference between rural and city consumption of refrigerators or Ford cars or anything else that came off the assembly line. The urban dwellers and the peasants were not greatly dissimilar, as they were across the ocean. It occurred to me that this socioeconomic setup, this breadth of market, would tend to feed into a contemporary architecture, whether it was now really prairie style or any other. Maybe such architecture shouldn't be of any set style at all, but just fit the consumership and this kind of social setup, which man had created for himself (in this country) under a constellation that existed here but never before anywhere else. Large control groups are an instrument of our science, and in the United States they would enable the clinician to study subtler responses as well as fundamental satisfactions. The term style became suspicious to me, but my optimism as to the chances for design of our age bounded and leaped, in spite of, or because of, what the greatest men of the region had told me about the designers' misery. All evolution hinged on the individual, his biological mutations; millions of subtle parameters were involved in total differences. How coarse, compared with all this, was the romanticism of old or, for that matter, new styles; how little did the mere stylistic penetrate into the core and heart of our organic responsiveness. I had been interested in man, but now I wanted to give full attention to his means under current conditions.

My research led me through dozens of employments. I worked in places where I was the only draftsman, offices where six or eight people were cramped into a small room on lower Fifth Avenue, producing millions of dollars' worth of cheap apartment buildings. All of us would labor like steam engines, drawing fast a lot of lines and Gothic buttresses and standardized gargoyles. Then I worked in offices that might be termed middle-sized; finally I came to Holabird and Roche in Chicago.

I really didn't know how distinguished this office was, but when I told Mr. Forrestall and Mr. Sullivan of my new job, they showed various degrees of awe, congratulating me as if I had just won the sweepstakes. I had no idea of my luck and important score as a newcomer. The firm had produced many of the most noted buildings in the Midwest, and was later responsible for projects such as the Statler hotels in Washington, Los Angeles, and other cities all over the nation. It was, and is, particularly renowned for its hotels. When I joined the staff, I started working on the "new" Palmer House; it is now very old hat, but then the much older Palmer House, built after the 1871 fire, was still standing. The H. & R. buildings had been among the first large edifices to be built in Chicago during the nineties, in those days when the skyscraper was born. In my time the firm's own office was on Wabash Avenue and overlooked our Palmer House site, which covered half a block. I was in on this grand project from the very beginning, when the first shoring took place and work started on the big caissons which had to be sunk into the alluvium that makes up downtown Chicago's subsoil. As I recall, the hotel had twenty-four hundred guest rooms and twenty-four hundred bathrooms. It had four different eating places on four different levels—structurally and financially—as to typical check, menu, and architectural trimmings.

The project was the most complicated I had ever seen, and it was so interesting that I at once began taking notes and writing it up for myself. In the midst of this job the firm got another comparable one, the Stevens Hotel, and also the Morrison Annex—both with thousands of rooms and baths.

My writing also was broadening, and I started to write a book in German, *Wie Baut Amerika* (How America Builds), on the interesting current means, the modern means, to serve man by a setting now feasible. I was at that time living in Highland Park and traveling fifty minutes on the train going to and from work, and I wrote this book on my lap. Nearly everything I have written seems to have this characteristic hand-to-mouth immediacy of intake and production, of seed and yield. It surely has its cons as its pros.

In *Wie Baut Amerika* I discussed not only the construction of a hotel and what the hotel means in America, but, in general, the composite multipurpose downtown structure. For instance, one could live and die in the Temple Building, which had a church on top—without ever going out. One could have every service, from a haircut and manicure to medical assistance, and one could have Mass said, I believe, buy theater tickets, bet on a horse, eat dinner, open a savings account, arrange for insurance, stock transactions, divorce, and even get (before remarrying) one's nose fixed by a plastic surgeon while waiting for one's pants to be pressed.

My book told what a hotel meant for political conventions, and I wrote about the community role of the building of composite dedication, as it never had existed in Europe, and then went into the detail of human and social relationship problems. Finally I dived into an account of the way in which this kind of building project of box-in-the-box accommodated by one structural frame was produced and brought to realization by a complicated contracting and subcontracting process unknown to a Roman Emperor. I described minutely all the steps that had to be taken and everything that had to be prepared by the co-ordinating architect and his engineering aides; the electrical planning, the plumbing, the heating, cooling, ventilating, the signaling and intercommunicating, and all the various other technical aspects and specialistics.

My story was illustrated by pictures I had taken myself with a cheap little camera. However, I merely hinted that there was also an architectural-design department to co-ordinate *Gestalt*—which must be consumed, too—and tried to suppress how this Palmer House was supposed to look according to "the artist's conception." Unfortunately, my publisher insisted on having at least one photograph of this so-thoroughly-described creation to show how everything finally shaped up for the visual sense. It had to be admitted that the approach to the solution of appearance was as thoughtlessly "historical" as the rest was freshly up to date—if anything can ever be up to date that misses the individual by a worrisome margin.

The picture of the Palmer House, *all finished*, must have jolted the reader who had meanwhile been admiring all the well-organized know-how; for me it almost broke the spell of convincing power. Otherwise the book is still, after over a quarter of a century, very presentable, including its many illustrations, and simply and without bias proves my point that design cannot survive on technological management alone, however imposing.

Intuitive clinical and systematic exploration of human and social interplay was really root and subject of this book. It contained prophesies on the prospects and success of modern architecture in America, which possessed favorable conditions not easily imitable in any other country on the planet. At no time and in no other region had so many individually designed domestic projects in clinical contact with clients of flesh and blood provided such insight as in America, or perhaps in California. Before this, "styles" had been decided upon by the architects of a King Louis of France, for example; his designer served in the retinue for a lifetime. The king was always the one, and almost the only, client in France, although perhaps diverse experience was gained from his changing girl friends, for whom a variety of hunting chateaux were built. Louis XIV was practically the only one to sit in a Louis XIV chair—the rest of the Frenchmen stood around him as indebted courtiers or crouched on the floor, sometimes in squalor, as bankrupt commoners.

While this picture may be a little exaggerated, there was then, at any rate, only a meager control group for an architect to draw upon compared with the United States middle class and its amazingly widespread purchasing power for houses built of commercially produced component parts. Bricks, plumbing fixtures, wall and floor coverings, or hardware and lighting fixtures no longer came from royal manufacturing establishments. Their production, variety, distribution, and absorption by a vast public was colossal.

Although there was a lot of talent in Europe and many stirring new ideas even in the 1920's, much, if not everything, was of a "specially made up" quasi-arty nature. Every doorknob had to be designed by an architect, and there was only a limited upper-crust demand for them, even in a big city like Vienna. Designers lost themselves in a greal deal of hand-shaped detail, made possible by the artisan's low wages and his availability. This sort of thing no longer really existed in America, and there was no such prospect. But a tremendous quarry of standardized elemental supply was as close as the telephone. I wrote something—not in meter and verse, but like poetry in prose—about *Sweet's Catalogue*, and this, in fact, became the heart of my book. I didn't have enough American sense to get paid by the Dodge Corporation, which publishes this annual illustrated building-material directory, but as a result of my book, it was promptly copied, down to its green cover, by a Berlin publisher.

Wie Baut Amerika was immediately accepted by the foremost house in Europe, and at once became what was called a best seller. It was received with interest, I later discovered, in Tokyo, Rome, Paris, and all around the globe, because it reflected actual day-to-day experience and dealt with the miraculous American production, in which the world had become interested, and that organizational know-how in relation to architecture. Soon after publication, promoters considered it worth while to utilize my title for a huge exhibition which was then opening in Berlin. The book sold like hot cakes, and I was aghast when it was completely out of stock: I had kept only a few author's copies, which I had stored in the basement, and by mistake the paper-drive man cleared them all out one nice day. For a long time I had no copy at all, although it was in the public libraries. A few years ago, when invited to lecture in Buenos Aires, I found it in every architect's office; someone had two copies and kindly gave me one. It had been published in 1926.

Immediately after this first literary effort, paralleling my work and learning about building in America and what made it tick, another German publisher commissioned me to write a second book. This little tome was briefly called *Amerika*, with the subtitle: *Neues Bauen in der Welt* (New Building in the World). For it I dug out what I could of pioneers' work. I photographed the work of Sullivan's office boy, Irving Gill, whose friend and admirer I became. I collected the work of my old friend R. M. Schindler, who had contributed and learned much—perhaps too much for his own original good—in Mr.

Wright's office. For his part he broke away, as gifted Burleigh Griffin had done before him, following the painful pattern of individual frustration which I knew in this form only from listening to the troubled souls themselves as they described it.

I began to give my story of John W. Root and his beautifully integrated Monadnock Block; of Louis Sullivan, who mastered rich ornaments of his own gifts and spun them over parts of a nobly conceived soaring skeleton, and also over the concepts of Wright, his great first assistant. After so many years this text is hardly dated, and it still makes worthwhile reading. In the mutual relationship of these men was buried much of the tragedy of the individual, in stimulation and in frustrating competition as well. One may turn into the other without our realizing it.

In *Amerika* I spoke of American industrialized architecture, and, following the enthusiasm of Tacitus for his exemplary *Germania*, so slanted my descriptions that all the world thought there was much here to be taken to heart and that, in 1926, there was an American vogue for modern architecture. This was, of course, a downright untruth, I must now admit: I was terribly lonely, and was just whistling in the dark. One need only look at the magazine illustrations of that bygone age!

In those days whatever could be considered contemporary design spread very slowly, and sometimes almost like a nefarious underground conspiracy. More footloose than the East, the West Coast was reached earlier. Slowly but increasingly the leadership of the big successful architects was challenged, at least in design, by the small-scale pioneer like me, who began to win awards in national competitions. Better Homes in America gave cash prizes; and amazingly announced poor little me, an unknown quantity working in my bedroom, as the top and triple winner in a twenty-minute radio program over a national hook-up. General Electric sent a vice-president to present the godsend of a substantial check to me, conspicuously, at a big A.I.A. architects' dinner. This occasion was intended by G. E. to catch the attention and interest of editors, readers, and advertisers of magazines for the struggler that I was, and many colleagues sincerely congratulated me. The struggle was indeed gruesome at times, and I was grateful when more and more human beings began, even very haltingly, to recognize my efforts. I badly needed some bright spot in my life.

Today the pioneering of one-man offices may be over; it was an interlude of the last three decades. The big American outfit, operating over wide stretches of the planet, modernized itself and once more resumed its power; today its scope is large in everything. It scrapes the sky, serves big business, big politics, and a far-flung armament, from research centers to Navy housing, shore installations, officers' clubs, and launching pads.

My book was the first, I believe, to evaluate the classical large American office, the *big* architectural office which, when I came here, was greater than anything that existed or even could be imagined in the old country. I wanted to, and later did, thoroughly test the mammoth cluster of drafting rooms, but first I worked and made some headway at this firm of H. & R. I didn't tell anybody that I myself could draw or perhaps design, following different principles which nobody else cared for. I wanted to master all these indigenous technical aspects because I thought that *someday human concerns, so far crudely lacking, could only be introduced by someone who could match the current physical dexterity as well.*

In the field of biologically guided design there was hardly anything to be learned at H. & R., but I had decided to learn what that firm's experience could teach. I made such tremendous progress in these technical phases that my superiors tended to leave me doing whatever I had acquired. For example, I would detail large toilet groups for months at a time because, due to the cumbersome bisexuality of our species, which management could not abolish, there were so many toilet groups in the Palmer House that drawing them could keep a man busy for a year and a half! After a while I started to detail vertical paths in this building to overcome gravity (elevator shafts); there were plenty of them, too. After some months, I finally succeeded, due to my little linguistic talents and my much greater diligence, in graduating from draftsman number 208 to liaison officer. I worked as mediator between the various departments on their different floors and Mr. Pellini, the director of design. He had been imported from the Beaux-Arts in Paris, and spoke only French. It was really my good luck that I could talk to him in his language, and understand his queer trains of design thought, incredibly superimposed over the "live and quick"—it gave me quite a value in the office. Here, too, architecture was a problem of feeling oneself into others much more than one of purely technical significance. Bosses and galley-slave colleagues, codraftsmen and clients, are all human beings. Mating, matching, individuals is, and will be, our main issue.

As I watched the departmental interplay, I always glanced across the elevated toward the rising steel skeleton and structure into which we fed our joint efforts. In the end I got acquainted with the production methods of the contractor and subcontractors when I saw these plans and details executed, step by step. Always I tried to meet man face to face. Amazingly much even in this supertechnical world indeed seemed to be a human affair.

During the nineties a wave of structural originality had swept Chicago; big office buildings sprang up together with bigger and better stockyards. Some forty-two railway companies which had converged on Chicago turned it into a doormat to all parts of the continent, wiped their own sooty shoe-soles on its citizenry, but made it a junction for trade, salesmen, politicians, country yokels, and combination-ticket holders. One couldn't get through Chicago without spending at least three hours there, changing depots, and passing downtown department stores and girlie shows. In one account of this strangely motivated metropolis I compared Chicago with sixteenth-century Nuremberg. Neither are natural ports like New York or Antwerp; both are situated in the middle of a continent and solely dependent on man-made intersections of commercial routes—rather than on potentates, like Paris or Persepolis, or on the ponderous seat of political administrations.

The big architectural offices especially had at one time a character of native originality similar to their city's. If one looks at the Reliance Building or at the Monadnock Block, it is obvious that such buildings could not have been designed by anyone who was merely a graduate of any school at that time anywhere. In the case of mightily gifted John Root he may have been the chief designer himself. In the case of Holabird or Roche, it was clear that neither filled that post, but the firm was surprisingly capable of breeding its own designers, its own engineers, its methodic and technological ideas of procedure. And original procedure begets the original product. Such an office was really a training camp for structural talent and a generator of technical determinants of design. Of course, these projects concerned mostly office buildings. They had as base a very skeletonized program of usage and often a minimum human significance. Nevertheless, these structures had themselves wondrously novel, unheard-of skeletons; they were also wonderful in the method and procedure behind their creation, and in form they were very matter of fact, much as Loos had told me. Over the entrance or marquee there was occasionally something "ornamental," some sort of curlicue, which became more enriched or sobered toward the end of the nineties, especially after the decorative and fortissimo and "classical" Columbian Exposition had done its harmful work in clogging the brain with more phony retrospection. Before that, the emphasis had been largely on engineering, based on no other appeal but the economic one, and the results were very much to the point. It was a pragmatic experimentation instructive to the world and consistent with current philosophical trends in America, sounding on from Mills, Latrobe, and Greenough to William James. It seemed that soon what worked and stood up might emerge as good and beautiful. But as so often before in cultural history, we know also today that brain breezes change and may swell to amazing brain storms, sometimes in not quite expected directions.

When I arrived in Chicago, much of that old to-the-point curiosity of technical realism belonged to the past. The big offices had not only survived, they had thrived and become something else. But they had imported their designers from Paris, and they continued to peddle importations. Transporting decorative talent as well as ideas, they subordinated native gifts and made them subservient. To me it was like diving into a degenerate and decadent period of a once-great civilization. But, after all, periodic organic decadence seems to be part and parcel of unending evolution. I became quite aware of this phase of decadence and, incidentally, I think that might be why I was able to break through. I was to make certain headway in a country whose strong main course I somehow recognized, even though I was a poor immigrant without any contacts whatsoever, who had not married the right girl—I mean the niece of the mayor or an important banker—and had no political or social pull. That I should make a career and finally become somewhat reputed can only be explained by that temporary degeneration of the big offices, which provided the opportunity quite good-naturedly to contest them while sincerely praising them in my book. Otherwise, and in general, the small architect did not and could not count at all. Only the big office was a successful machine, with its French designer putting superficial touches like the gay Petit Trianon on the Palmer House roof to camouflage the elevator penthouse and the water tank. This kind of firm was thoroughly accepted and cherished by the captains of industry and the magnates of finance, but it was getting tiresome even to the architectural editors, although they then didn't know much better. And as Frank Lloyd Wright was, in general, to be boycotted, there was little of refreshment left for them to report on. A glance at the best magazines in the years 1923 to 1928 will show how dully architecture was presented. The subsequent development of these media of communication, of often unsuspected significance to our human world, is stupendous.

Under the prevailing circumstances, as I see it now, I had in all my loneliness a singular opportunity, although I hardly knew it. I was taking the thing up from an entirely new and human angle, while on the other side of the fence was machine production, very large and on an imposing scale, but not automatically suited to human constitution and digestion. "Automatically" it was getting tiresome and unbearable, and this perhaps offered me my great chance. I started to become known with hardly any material success to boast of—nothing that figured in dollars and cents—handling jobs nobody else would have taken. I could use the most insignificant objects to quietly make penetrating demonstrations. If I had had big commissions, I would probably have had to conform, and so I did not crave them. Having (as others saw it) pikers or paupers as clients, and working for the normal percentage fee, which on these tiny jobs amounted to next to nothing, I benefited greatly as to freedom. My clients listened to my personal, warm-hearted explanations, which also warmed their hearts, and they would let me offer them more than the ordinary clichés. Gradually stories of my diminutive work began to seep into magazines—not merely those specializing in architecture, but also the popular home publications, even the throw-aways which were distributed to women shoppers from chain-store counters. To be sure, at first the articles combined a pinch of mild editorial ridicule with novelty of reporting, and the editors would always prefer a very bare picture, even if it showed a home, so that the caption could conveniently mention its resemblance to a shoe factory or something of the sort. To gain human appeal was an almost superhuman struggle, and my dear wife and family mother and musician, Dione, most cheerfully helped me carry the stupendous burden. I have no idea how we managed. Nevertheless, the time was opportune—no young architect of the same character or inclinations would have such a chance today, when a flood of nonconventionally patterned design daily breezes across all editorial desks, and illustrations sensationally vie with each other. I never learned or had to learn to look for novelty.

I must emphasize again how much changes during one brief lifetime, especially if one labors oneself to bring about the alteration. When I arrived in New York, the Singer Tower was considered one of the great buildings in the world. As the Woolworth Building was going up, it was the finest example of Gothic, even surpassing the Cathedral of Canterbury in that its gargoyles and other buttressed ornaments were made out of sheet metal; thus the ingenious new technology reduced the dead weight in the tallest building. Backward medieval craftsmen had never been able to think that up or to calculate or fabricate it en masse. I made a few timid remarks to the effect that the building looked like chewing-gum architecture, but the joke was on me—everybody laughed to think that I, a poor immigrant, should have such "original" views about the most wonderful, broadly admired edifice on earth. It was just like a yokel's coming to Athens and making disparaging remarks about the Parthenon. But the Woolworth Building may have different merit; it is no more Gothic than the tower extolling Singer sewing machines is Renaissance; even today no one believes it. Although the wind again has switched and is blowing once more toward a bit of historical association and ornamental flavor, no new animation has come yet to those self-conscious markers of the past.

Quite apart from the architect's talents, there was something like a curse resting on the wealthiest cities of the world—like imperial Madrid of the sixteenth century, or the Empire City of the twentieth. In a supposedly materialistic world, their affluence should logically make them empire leaders, not only in tallness but in deep draft; but this is only in theory. These capitals, like Delhi of the Moguls and Rome, appear centers of gravity for secondhand foreign imports, with little home-growth of individual genius, and, in fact, little to favor it. The Escurial, near the former world capital, Madrid, was rushed to completion, its size and the speed of its construction resembling the dream of a real-estate editor—like, for instance, our own Merchandise Mart. In such cases it must always be the world's biggest footage with the fastest completion date. Plenty of politicians, foreigners, Neapolitans, Dutch, French, and Moors, were on the payroll of Spanish gold. Some made a career, some probably were broken-hearted within.

New York, at least, is the most humanly warm city, with men pathetically ready to weep on your shoulder in a bar or an Automat restaurant—even while driving a cab. It is perhaps the most articulated city of its mammoth size. You can always see nice horizontal water at one end of the street or the other in Manhattan, and in spring or fall there is almost an Italian sky over it all. In my memory, it is even now still a little the City of Loos, where he saw all the poor unabsorbed stragglers getting vivaciously happy after they had, with great awe and admiration, and almost in a ritual, passed the Statue of Liberty on their overloaded ships, in steerage, and then the Ellis Island Immigration Office, with its stern St. Peter turning the key to paradise. This paradisiacal haven of a distant promising skyline is really quite a bit of New York for me and my deeply harbored associations.

The city is lovely in its childlikeness. With shining eyes it is always aspiring to do the biggest and the best, and the dream often turns out to be the Radio City Music Hall after a while, or some other seven-day wonder—or is it eleven days? Now when one goes to see it, one can't understand what people saw in the Pulitzer Tower. They once admired those great monuments of New York, and today they have other great impersonal realty structures, many soon to fade into dusty oblivion, with taxis, to get there, jammed between unloading trucks. Most of these edifices seem second or third hand. In spite of the money available, New York clients have only recently and in a small percentage of cases succeeded in employing a great architect for any job. That agile minds acted so is a puzzle which I can't glibly explain. For a long time during my early life a really new store front in any New York borough, or a modern store interior, was a rarity in proportion to the massive output of construction in general. Altogether, there were not half a dozen truly contemporary stores or shops, not to speak of schools or homes, in New York several decades ago at the time when I, with love, had lonesomely labored on the Universal Pictures Building, with its various stores and restaurant, at the corner of Hollywood and Vine—in 1930, I believe. As I planned the Corona Avenue School in Bell in the early thirties, slowly inching, as a foreigner, into the confidence of a tightly knit political school board, how any precedent would have helped!

Even after the First World War the whole metropolitan area of New York boasted only a few modern residences. I myself finished one on an Atlantic island and others in Connecticut. I could not explain now how I could be trusted and how I lived up to the trust. On these occasions the owners and I combed city and countryside, and kept combing it all over New York, to find a contractor who would catch on and would bid and build. New Canaan, Connecticut, became quite a bit later the first development spot of modern architecture, the first place where repetitively people were building non-replica houses somewhere near New York. And yet minds in the world's greatest town seem more curious, more enterprising than elsewhere. The answer is not easy. New York always appeared full of constructive lessons to the world, and surely it is full of human interest. The coming years, I am confident, will give it even greater prominence.

"California Calls You"

By 1925 it had become clear to me that the United States was a wide, diversified land and that New York and Chicago were only important parts of it.

Once when I was walking down the Bahnhofstrasse in Zurich, I saw in a travel-office window a folder with a palm tree printed on it, and the words, "CALIFORNIA CALLS YOU." I knew only a little English then, and I wasn't quite sure what this meant, but I put two and two together and concluded that I was supposed to come to California. After I had been in New York, Chicago, and Taliesin—more or less a guest of Mr. Wright's, as he had no work or projects—I began restlessly to think about California. I knew it was the only place where he had had anything under construction during my American sojourn.

I made up my mind in the winter of 1925. I traveled with a family now. My wife and first child had followed me from Europe and had the greatest trouble immigrating; passed and granted a visa as a musician, Dione had to leave behind our three-month-old boy. My lovely mother-in-law had brought the grandchild and joined us, wide-eyed, at Taliesin, where for four weeks she, too, was a guest of Mr. Wright. He surely was generous to us. Reunited with our lovely bright-looking child, we now migrated west. On the way we briefly marveled at the Grand Canyon, while our baby boy, left alone in the hotel room, picked and tore to pieces the section of our travel guide book which dealt with America west of the Rockies. Thus we arrived at the Coast unadvised and unprepared.

In California, especially southern California, I found what I had hoped for, a people who were more "mentally footloose" than those elsewhere, and who did not mind deviating opinions as long as they were not political. One could dress up in a different way and act completely as if one were at a Halloween party where one can do most anything which comes to mind and is good fun. All this seemed to me a good climate for trying something independent of hidebound habituation, European or even American, and also for getting acquainted with human minds and human patterns of behavior, so to speak, in a sort of tropical exfoliation. Many of the people who had come to California had not done so under economic stress, unlike those who had passed a hundred years earlier from the Catskills into Ohio or from Ohio into Illinois. In these days, before the sandstorms in western Oklahoma, starvation did not pressure people into going west. Bringing their savings with them, they showed up in the "southland" just for rejuvenation. The most outstanding communities, like the Indiana colony which is now called Pasadena, or Redlands, or any of the older settlements in the orange country, were founded by well-to-do people. They had been successful lawyers, doctors, professional men, or something else, and had migrated and started a college or a church—with subdivisions for real-estate sale around it, to be sure. It was a different sort of pioneering, and it was a fruit-garden country with an "industry in the fields," machine-studded fields rather than shops and manufacturing plants. This was when the sky was blue and smogless. Los Angeles was still a fairly small town when I arrived, but even in the nineties, when the place had a population of only fifty or sixty thousand, it possessed architects like the Britisher John C. Austin and John Parkinson—who, I believe, had carpentry training. They were still calmly practicing approximately the same architecture for the gas company and local bankers and merchants, yet, lo and behold! it was possible for me to get at least some small jobs on the basis of another kind of dedication.

This, then, is how I went west and got a new start once more.

Pretty soon it dawned on me that California had another significance in world history. Architecture and culture altogether—out of which architecture is created, more than by a few "form-givers," and for which it is the man-made physical ambient—had originated in subtropical countries: The South.

It was in Greece, Hellas, Mesopotamia, and Egypt that all the great textbook styles of architecture had their beginnings. Later, when the two Roman empires had degenerated, bar-

barians rumbled in from the north and, attracted as they were by "life in the mild," started to confuse and befuddle an international style, a cosmopolitan style of *savoir vivre* and *savoir faire* which reached from Sussex to Syria. Palmyra was architecturally similar to a Roman Empire place in England: it had almost the same basilicas and colonnaded avenues leading out of town. That empire had been a very international setup; essentially its style was subtropical, and may not have fitted the Nordic countries well. But ideas and forms, not material determinants, remained long-governing. In the Middle Ages the powerful Nordic impact finally affected, among other things, architecture. To use the brotherhoods as examples, the Benedictines produced Monte Cassino and all the beautiful Mediterranean warm-climate-blue-sky architecture of the early, loosely organized church. Later on the same order, the same Christendom, gathering momentum north of the mountains, adopted a Cistercian austerity, even a Nordic grimness, which was all ascetic; the monasteries were steep-roofed so that the snow would slide down onto an earth full of the traumatic experience of bitter winters.

Nevertheless, the ideas of unneurotic tempered antiquity were taken up again and again, and classical architecture was milked by Nordic minds throughout the ages. The sensually subtle which was Hellenic religiosity, much older than ethics or mere geometricity, had already long been superseded by deadpan patterning and Vitruvian canons. Snow lies piled up at Ionic column bases and chilly rains have washed Corinthian caps of Berlin museums; City of London banks; Wall Street, Manhattan; La Salle Street, Chicago. Nineteenth-century colonialism "exported Hellas" on a larger scale, but essentially more Nordic architecture, with its southern pedigree just dryly memorized, long dominated the world. When the colonization of the fifteenth and sixteenth centuries began, the explorers and the conquistadors took it along in great packages—soon mixed up, mingled, and married with a little Renaissance—which they then unwrapped in many southern places. But first fairly Nordic ideas in building and clothing of Madrid and of the desertlike winter-cold high plateau of northern Spain were introduced into tropical countries such as Hispaniola, Puerto Rico, and the *intra muros* of Manila. To lose one's dark-draped *grandeza* and wear short white trunks is a new idea for civilized people in the tropics. I suppose Columbus never gave up the black court dress which he brought along from Madrid. He brought it ashore, salvaged it from the foundering caravel *Santa Maria*, and sweated in it through all the troubles he had in Santo Domingo. In San Juan, until recently, dignified dark suits marked one as a Continental and a member of the upper crust. Similarly, the architecture was often conservatively Nordic. There was no idea of sitting under a mango tree or of living outdoors, teaching, learning, or being in the open air like the Greeks. Window holes in heavy masonry, small openings to let the breeze pass through, were a meager concession to the southern climate. Of course, the Spanish influence sometimes relates to Andalusia, and at least some Spaniards had the Mediterranean air in their blood. But the British and the Dutch were attracted yet hesitant strangers to the south. Think of Batavia in Indonesia, built by the Dutch under coco-palms; it is a copy of Nordic Amsterdam.

Among the form-givers there are those who perhaps have received, like Ronchamp, plasticity and accidental curvaceous charm from the Hellenic islands—but when I say "Greek" or "south," I like to remember the open-air festive rituals of Poseidonia and Akragas—teaching and learning and thinking while promenading under the olive trees of the Academia, in the open colonnades of the colorful stoa, as Plato and Aristotle continued in the tradition of the buttonhole-questioner Socrates. However, there were buttonholes only figuratively speaking. Lightly dressed, he would stand around with a group of disciples on the sunny agora, the southern market place; he never had to sit in front of a fireplace, worried by Nordic chills. The original man, the Southerner, had in many places been overtaken by the last big glacial period, but everywhere he continued to seek his way out of the shivers and into the sun again. He did it with an almost neurotic restlessness, as a Norwegian doctor in Oslo pointed out to me, talking about the travel craze of those ancient Norsemen, the Vandals and the Visigoths. A few fatal times their destination then was south, and if they reached Africa, they would stay—until possibly they went to pieces there.

German souls kept seeking the land where the lemons bloom, crudely to paraphrase Goethe. Even when they remained in Prussia, they built what they understood to be Greek, without really being able to live as the Greeks did. Karl Friedrich Schinkel, the great Grecist of Berlin architecture, became a highly-thought-of master to Ludwig Mies van der Rohe, who had come from Aachen with splendid brick masonry training. Mies was born, so to speak, in the shadow of Charlemagne's cathedral in Aix-la-Chapelle, which has perhaps a few Byzantine motifs from the Mediterranean, but is nevertheless quite a bit of a Nordic cave, or "enclosure" par excellence. Mies has added ever more openness and glass to his concepts, even when he finally, much later, built against the raging snowstorms blowing over Lake Michigan. Walter Gropius, most gifted son of an architect, was born in Berlin; he designed a prototype factory with a lot of glass—on the order of industrial or the Ruhr mining center establishments, which Mies has also seen and appreciated.

As I later learned, having myself left Europe early, these masters in Europe had called theirs an "international style," because it was begot by industry and a new machine-generated civilization, nostalgic perhaps—not really tied to any clime.

But I had heard and followed the call of far-away California, the mild climatic region, to live among the other transplanted ones, enjoying and even sharing a little their footlooseness and a potential to bring the South to life again—not abstractly, not theoretically, but quite warmly in a new concrete and actual way. Frank Lloyd Wright and Walter Gropius, I understand, have not spoken too favorably about California. But it was to turn out the most contemporary southland in search of a way of life for this day. Mies and Le Corbusier have never visited there, as far as I knew. If they had, they would hardly have felt friendly to its cultural naïveté, bordering everywhere on mix-up. Me, Loos had educated, I guess, to sympathy with lowly mix-up.

I did not only long distantly for a new south, but earnestly wanted to exhaust just what I like to call this footloose informal quality, this chance to realize a cosmopolitan return into the "tempered scene," but now on affirmative new terms —living, in a home and in the city, going to kindergarten, to school, in a *new* southern way. In some human future, being unafraid of getting caught by a blizzard on the way home from work will be an actuality everywhere, not merely a dream. In the Northwest Territory of Canada, it may take glazed covered walks and streets (unless the deafening noise of swift air traffic will have driven us all underground in the next fifty years).

But for my moment of history Los Angeles was a very peculiar spot and vantage point. It was clear that this romantically Spanish colonial country of California might, possibly at a premium, become a prototype industrial and research area, emulated by many others who could only artificially develop the *climate control of tomorrow*.

It was specific to my attitude, my career, and the peculiarity of its tendencies that I wanted, with my family and with my first clients, at least, to live through this situation—in all its reality. But then, further, from this outlying post I wanted to see and reach the rest of the varied earth. Δος μοι που ςιω και ταν γαν κινασω. Did not Archimedes in Doric say: "Give me an outside place to stand on, and I shall find a good leverage to move the earth, however heavy it is."

This planet is culturally so hard to move because in matters of sophistication it is perhaps justly run by greatly educated Brahmins and learned Pharisees in a few monopoly centers of civilization. A Pharisee was once a proud top-ranking doctor of knowledge. And seen from Jerusalem: 'What good can come from Nazareth?" (informally, very rurally styled as it was). Well, plenty of good has come from such unlikely outlying places under the sun.

A southland, I thought, was *not* really an unlikely place, but almost certainly it had been the cradle of anthropology in practice and a good spot for the career of our species. I was humble and did not come to "give forms to mankind," but I followed a call to re-adapt, if I could—in spite of the stumbling blocks, biases, and prejudices of "Iowa-by-the-Sea," which then wanted to be all Spanish. I was to fit the now necessary or the long-ago evolved accommodation of man's activities to a situation occurring after the glaciers had happily receded. It was still a situation not well digested by Northerners, but one with a long-range run into times to come and presumably into an eased climate control everywhere to follow suit. Even in a dense Nordic apartment in Leningrad or Toronto natural living stimuli, as here with my clients, would address human senses, and through them anybody's emotional life could be studied and help offered in at least diminutive dosages. In no future can nature be dropped, so that we feel as well in an abstract vast parking place of artificialities as we would among long-established naturalistic appeals.

The open South is the testing ground for the closed-in North. On several occasions, especially and hilariously at a convention in Biloxi, Mississippi, I have expressed my thoughts on "man the Southerner" and his mission and task of converting. Prospectively, we shall have more and more the means to be Southerners anywhere, with our eyes, our skin, our nose....

Summing it up, I felt that southern California was a godsend. It was an instructive new subtropical country, developing surprisingly from quasi-paradisiacal cow counties into an industrialized region—quite different from Manchester and the Ruhr.

It was "calling you" from Zurich and many other points north, and making sometimes silly motion pictures around carefree swimming pools with palmetto backgrounds, which in turn, through movies, would be enticingly shown in places less sunny. But with its mountains and highland forests and snow loads, it was for me a highly diversified training ground. It had educative chances even in and through its failures. California seemed to be the longed-for Southland, even if it was only very potentially a Hellas, and surely not in the sense that Los Angeles had a wonderfully developed Acropolis. That wasn't the case, and in a hundred changing, finally rushing years the whole social-political setup had been confused enough, without a Pericles showing up to hire the right design talent for all the wild growth.

But climatically it favored the launching of new architecture, quite a little closer to biological requirement, a new mode of living. And so I tried my best to launch it. The houses for flesh-and-blood inhabitants, built "with the inside and outside fused," became under this label pretty well known here and there, and Nordic countries followed us in this promising pattern of their own accord and began to build elementary schools where possible in low one-story structures, on ample grounds, even with classrooms opening broadly onto "patios," as I kept urging. It happened from Denmark to Uruguay, as architects showed it to me proudly when I visited. Then, the "Corona School" in Bell, California, fought for and built in the early thirties, had already become something of a prototype. I owed it to the enlightened school principal, Nora Sterry, and the League of Women Voters, who together with me appeared in a dramatic session before the Los Angeles Board of Education, and helped me win the day, and the decade, for a more nature-near, a bio-realistic school design. In cold regions of the world it could not easily have succeeded.

Perhaps for a historical moment we tipped the scale in favor of the South again.

California has at any rate seemed to me a strategic area in which to try to do so. I wished to see redeemed some of the sins committed against living as man had originally; he was really a Southerner before those glaciers and shivers moved in on him and forced him into caves. First, he had lived according to his original physiology, as it had taken shape in the mild half shade of moving green foliage. The problem to me was never quite to forget the essentials and elementals of this, even if its primeval totality could not romantically be transferred into a time of our population explosions. Jean Jacques Rousseau was dead, but biology was a more alive science than ever, and longed for application.

I doubted myself that it all would come about in a systematic way. There was very little systematic about Los Angeles, certainly. The placid South had by ever new stirrings from the outside become embroiled with hectic Nordic tobogganism.

Much later, unfortunately on the day of Pearl Harbor, the Los Angeles County Museum opened its exhibition "The Past of Southern California." I had painstakingly, and with pleasure and conviction, written the script, sketched the layout perspectively and all its features, objects, and dioramas. I showed how, under a blue sky turning grayer with smog, this region had, without consistency, zigzagged and stupendously grown from green cow-grazing counties. Amidst mission acreage, tilled by Indian converts, ample area for neglect and confusion came down to us from fantastic Spanish land grants for a handful of people, unable to sell the meat of their cattle. Later, sheep-wool speculators would be driving flocks of fifty thousand west over the continent, to flourish for a few wet-pasture years and then be bankrupted by drought. Others dug for water and found it stinking. Oil had been struck and made big derrick fields urge out whole towns. Still other people hired brass bands in New York to stage an absentee realty boom over thousands of miles. Transcontinental trunk lines, unprecedented automobile conflux, day and night trucking, and mass immigration went on and on until, within my own life in this tempered country, all the deserts were being occupied and became industrial land, while the citrus groves and the "factories in the fields" subsided, were crowded out by F.H.A.-subsidized subdividers. The whole development became a prototype—also ominous for things to come in many development countries around the globe. California had increased terrifically while I was bending over a drafting board or a steering wheel. When, toward the end of my practice, I raised my now white head, there were five times as many souls around me—but hardly a place left to park them.

This Los Angeles exhibition had for a dozen years been prepared in my mind. It was most of all characteristic for my own curiosity, the special path I had come to see, as to what the future held for environmental, perhaps really "post-urban" design, and to take a hand in it as well as I possibly could.

When I first arrived Southwest and looked for a job, I also thought of teaching. I wanted to teach about my search and convictions, but no college would have me. Then in 1925 the tiny Academy of Modern Art was set up in an old Victorian residence, and I found four or five students. Harwell Hamilton Harris, then a very young sculptor, and Gregory Ain, who had dropped his regular studies in dismay, were among them, and they soon joined my diminutive "office" in loyal effort.

Regular college students began to give me extracurricular, unorthodox but cordial attention, like Raphael Soriano from Rhodes, and as time went on, others from many places and in ever-increasing numbers.

Restless students began to prod teaching staffs, rather than vice versa—in one university after the other. But there was never an appointment for me or to feed my family.

The modernist movement broadened its attitude, strengthened its initial toehold especially in the mild climate of southern California. There a remarkable magazine, *Arts and Architecture*, brought to life by John Entenza, had begun to give it a continuous showing. This magazine has finally gained world readership. I was elated to help it from the start, when it hardly had its equal in planful, practically supported case studies and research on mild climatic living and building.

While these unheard-of ideas and a new native attitude toward architecture slowly gained support, I was with sustained courage continuing my work of a decade on "Rush City Reformed," begun with much devotion in the early twenties. Rush City Reformed was a growing cluster of studies on urban affairs, on downtown and suburban communities, on housing and traffic, on recreation and education in the picture of a township. Later, much has proven to be quite accurate and stimulating prognostics. It prophesied that comprehensive urban renewal would have to take place; and much later I should become member and even chairman of our State Planning Board—a state which has quintupled its population while I practiced planning! It is as if Soviet Russia had grown to a population of a billion during one architect's lifetime, and while he tried to take a hand in molding this growth! Not much of this sort of wholesale review and planned renewal, which I then advocated, was going on in the United States, or in the world, for that matter, in the period between 1923 and 1930. If it was, I surely was not aware of it, and I long felt like a lonely crier in my wilderness, without echo or reply.

Multilevel railway stations with heliports on top; air terminals, directly permeated and served by a steady stream of common carriers on rail and tires which would ultimately feed some thousand air movements, arrivals and take-offs, daily; huge metropolitan weekend beach resort developments, not just idyllic, but suitable to fantastic population growth which I computed; neighborhoods of atrium houses, not carelessly spreading and sprawling, but livable, nature-endowed, with privacy and face-to-face instead of fender-to-fender contact; ring-shaped schools with a space core for after-hours assembly and expansion of a multipurpose room to serve also the parent generation, the school taxpayers—all these and many more ideas, lively as they were, occupied my mind and my pencil. It appeared it would take endless years to see something started under the sun. Despite all the speed around me, it seemed mixed with slowness beyond all possible patience.

Thoughts and graphic presentations of the commercial and shopping links between neighborhoods, with appropriate parking and multistory garages adjacent, and on the other hand with well-preserved pedestrian lanes and promenades and safe, pleasant school walks, fully separated from rolling traffic; bridgings over half-sunken multilanes; ribbon developments of clean, pride-accentuated, commuter-centered industries instead of dreary ones; and a downtown zone completely elevated over an equally complete bottleneck-proof and well-distributed traffic parking level were then of most unusual character. They were ridiculed by those who saw them, as was the time I spent on their development. Some quarter of a century later Lewis Mumford in *The New Yorker* graciously recommended these never-ending comprehensive studies of Rush City Reformed to young planners and architects as an early, almost forgotten prelude to urban renewal, and I felt gratefully vindicated. My friends Harris, Ain, Soriano, and more and more others, as, for example, Victor Gruen, who in years to come would remember these stimulating moments, watched the then quite lonely lecturing effort of mine, listened with constructive minds, and further developed these fragments. Slowly thoughts were improved, jelled, and fused to a panorama of inescapable urban reform, but much still is left to the future.

Officially accredited students were denied me for many years; no university in the mid-twenties would grant me even an assistant instructorship, although I needed it badly. Thus between me and my apprentices, the older man's and the younger man's felicity for this long bygone companionship remains mutual. I have often thought of this wonderful emotional tie and what I learned while I taught. Perhaps that is the most dependable way to do it.

To comfort impatient young men, I can say that individual practice and "clientele experience" got under way very, very slowly, and some of the early, really progressive, then almost unique work such as the previously mentioned Universal Pictures Building right in the middle of Hollywood—with a fully contemporary eating place and all sorts of stores patiently designed piece by piece—has later again been "modernized" in reverse, and strangely altered in the turmoil of our day. It had not yet finally taken hold of minds, even after it stood realized. Now only a few respectable photos of the original structure remain to be compared with illustrations of store design in the middle twenties from coast to coast. Perhaps I was too early to produce a turning point. And a little afterward there were many ready and I was too late. I have often wondered whether priority or lasting quality is the better claim to any historical significance.

I also at last found a client for my prototype of the smallish American home, which was so close to my heart and has always remained there, in the midst of the "big jobs." Ernest and Bert Mosk and their daughter Lona, a good if perhaps a somewhat erratic young writer, owned a steep view lot along Hollyridge Drive, which winds up into the elfin forest so characteristic of the California hills. I designed a group of houses; one was built, and during the thirty years since, has given happy satisfaction to a sequence of owners. But Ernest Mosk, a small merchant and himself a quiet and friendly person who had invested in full the price of $3,000, lived in his home and worked in its garden only a brief six or seven months before he suddenly died of uremia. His disconsolate women, mother and daughter, insisted that he had loved the house so much that I was the man, rather than any minister, to speak at his funeral. I was no orator, but I found some heartfelt, heart-rending words for this, one of my first clients, the first small man to trust me with all his earthly goods and fate, the first little man who had loved me for being an architect. With love I, too, shall think of him always.

Health House, Vintage 1927

Earlier, in 1927, I had begun my work on the "Health House." It was prototypical in another way. I had enthusiastically given it this name because of my deep interest in biological fitness and because Dr. Philip M. Lovell, my client, stimulated me by sharing the same point of view. He himself doubted particularly the pill-producing pharmaceutical industry, with its sweeping propaganda and its slanted research to corner the market of anxiety. I was perhaps not so radical, but I began to think that medicine was best when well versed in prevention, and that city planning and building design might be the most promising package of preventive medicine and a strong influence factor in originating the inner chemistry of wholesomeness. Its full dosage of environment was administered every changing minute of the twenty-four-hour day, three hundred and sixty-five days every year, over at least a thirty-year amortization period! Long forgotten and paid off, the architect, like a ghost, like an evil demon, or perhaps a protective angel, stayed, himself unseen, with his wards or victims; he broke off marriages by cumulative daily devilish irritation or, at last, might make a youngster break away from any family which failed to have a truly suitable two-generation house.

In 1927 architects customarily prescribed Spanish ornament in Hollywood, brownstone in Manhattan, and Cape Cod in Connecticut or New England. Often all styles got mixed up in one block. Frank Lloyd Wright, as I have already said, was amazingly unappreciated and even unjustly resented by some of his clients in California, whose "dynamic stereotypes" he had too brusquely changed, as the "neo-Pavlovians" would say. Mrs. Lovell, however, seemed to share with her sister, Mrs. Freeman, her appreciation for the concrete block house

Mr. Wright had built for the Freemans. One day, to my amazement, Dr. Lovell, of whose new building intention I knew nothing, approached me, with the idea of having me design a house which would not follow Mr. Wright's idiom. Feeling a novice, I at once spoke of my friend Schindler, and to him as well, as he had already worked for the Lovells. Both men steadfastly rejected even the idea of collaboration, because of some earlier unfortunate misunderstandings.

With bated breath I then went up to the so fateful, spectacular, and precarious site, near Griffith Park, and lonely in the midst of all my worries, fell in love with it.

I told myself that mankind, with a new health and population swell in store, would one day run out of level ground. It will have to build on steepness and on prefabricated stilts, with the living area pendant from the roof! Dr. Lovell wanted to be a patron of forward-looking experiment. He would be the man who could see "health and future" in a strange wide-open filigree steel frame, set deftly and precisely by cranes and booms onto this inclined piece of rugged nature; he would love marrying it through view, air, and radiation.

I transposed this program into a unique task through a most laborious series of months, but always worked with elated concentration. At that time I habitually rose at 4:00 a.m.!

As a matter of fact, I had started this routine some five or six months earlier, when I had persuaded Schindler to work with me on the stupendous League of Nations Project for Geneva. Here also, as in my demonstrative California health architecture, the concept was to be southern.

But among other things, I wanted to demonstrate a lake and hydroplane approach, and I developed especially ideas about auditorium acoustical modifiers in the enclosure of the vast hall, which brainstorm won acclaim by the noted European authority, Professor Oswald, and later by the great American acoustician, Vern Knudsen, who has remained my friend until today and through all the theater designs to come.

Our international project was one of three—Le Corbusier's

and Hannes Mayer's were prize winners—to be selected for exhibition all over Europe. Like the ring-plan school of the same early vintage, my ideas on variable "acoustical illumination of auditoria and theaters" found realization, at least by me, only more than a generation later. I had almost forgotten.

That I succeeded in such short order with the steel-skeletoned Health House, which was, as a whole, in its philosophy and in many features, so highly unorthodox, seems almost incredible now. It was, in fact, a strange, unheard-of apparition to be conceived in the general scene of 1927. From a distance it was to be seen on a steep, even precipitous, slope, with the looming Griffith Park hills as a backdrop and a wide outlook south, over trees in the foreground, down to the faraway sea.

I had often thought that suspension construction would save material: a minimum of recessed slender compression columns of metal carried girders projecting out, on which upper floors of much larger perimeter were hung on slender suspension members of minimum cross section. Open web bar-steel joists were used here in a residential building for the first time; they were new and almost unknown. Through their slender trusses I figured I could run plumbing pipes and electric conduits freely in all directions, thus saving money. For enclosure where it was not glass, I shot a thin shell of hard concrete out of the nozzle of a 250-foot hose uncoiling over the precipice; the mixer stood far away on firm ground, up on the hill road. In two days the concrete enveloped the bolted steel frame which had been erected of shop-assembled units lifted from the delivery truck in forty field hours of work. All was detailed and surveyed down the precipice to an eighth of an inch exact, because the standard steel sash, too, fitted precisely into the original skeletal assembly. The building loomed over a swimming pool, also a thin reinforced shot concrete shell suspended within reversed reinforced concrete portals cutting into the slope. It was all a very novel "thoroughbred" of integrated design, a never-contracted-for type of construction. Even the kitchen layout, as well as the built-in furniture design, really anticipated a generation of advances I would have still before me. Willy Boesiger and Esther McCoy have in careful detail biographied my technical labors, and I am grateful to Sigfried Giedion, Ellery Hale, Cranston Jones, and Frederick Wight for later appreciation. But all I did was really only auxiliary, subordinated though helpful, to the principal thought of this demonstration *house of health*. Health—by so far little seen fusion of interior and exterior—would benefit. Through continuity of fenestration, linkage with the landscape, we should draw again on what the vitally dynamic natural scene had been for a hundred thousand years, and make it once more a human habitat. It was indeed a splendid vista and landscape that permeated inward when the continuous but dividable drapes were slid aside.

This was one of the first "houses with textile enclosures behind glass," at a time when the hemisphere as a whole, from Montreal down to Rio, Lima, and Buenos Aires, was still rather virginal in such a matter. It is puzzling to think that a generation later the movement had gained such momentum and breadth in each of those places that a dozen or so distant unknown friends would heartwarmingly receive me at the airport because they knew of my effort so long ago; and also talked of it kindly. Ideas and mind-stretchers traveled strangely even in those days; how, possibly, could I have proceeded from such obscurity and a starvation diet to something like a career, not only densely occupied by effort, but also no longer derided, and even acknowledged? What has this human and interhuman effort been, and how could it, and the far outpost in which it happened, be described at least in fragments? I was *so far* from the intellectual centers where styles are first conceived or emerge in artistic circles; but real life after all is everywhere close by.

Generally, the eating, drinking, breathing, sleeping, thinking, and hoping of these particular clients—father, mother, and three young boys—became the target of my enthusiastic observation. I thought of Dr. Lovell's extrafamilial links—his friends, followers, his human hospitality, the sociability of children and adults, indoors and outdoors. It would all be planted into my program of current southern flavor in an ancient mild climate, and with a client sharing my biological interests.

I would study with Mrs. Westerman, the Lovell's dignified cook-housekeeper, the "naturopath's" raw food and vegetable-fruit diet. These, my nature devotees, ate well, and even tastily. They prepared meals long, and cooked little but thoroughly. It was a complex process to exhaust the fumes from interiors, purify the water—by a most unusual and then experimental fixture—house raw sugar and vegetable salts and everything else within arm's reach. All my later biochemically tinged kitchen studies up to *Life and Human Habitat*, all my thought wrought in bathrooms, sleeping porches, transventilation, subtle illumination for vision, gym courts and pools for exercising muscles and lungs, goes back to this patient example—evolved in the solitude of 1927.

Long before sunrise I started to check every one of the thousand prepunched bolt holes and shop-cut coverplates of my steel window-bearing I-beam columns. Nevertheless, it was all only to the one great end, goal, and purpose: *To service with contemporary means organic life-needs* by the best I could think of!

The construction was no rush job by any means; all drawings had been very exacting. When the house was almost completed, it stood its test of fire most literally. A terrific storm blew an awful brush fire over the adjacent mountainous Griffith Park, and many dozens of homes went up in flames. Our project was piled full of paper while the painters worked in it with inflammable spirits and oils. I hung on the telephone and besieged the fire department, which was being called from all sides simultaneously. I had all workmen use two ridiculously small sprinkling hoses, which, with the lost water pressure of this terrible day, yielded only a little humidity to surrounding shrubs. A hurricane roared, aroused by a sea of tall flames over the park woods, which from minute to minute became more brightly glowing as a dark night of dense smoke shaded the landscape. The furious fire approached inexorably. The case seemed lost when the shrubs and trees near the park boundary caught on fire. I settled back and persuaded myself that watching a steel frame yield might be instructive if observed from close by, but I kept praying. Nevertheless, none of the glass had yet broken to expose the painters' mountains of loose newspaper sheets to the flames, when suddenly the fire department was there and went to bat in the biting darkness of the smoke. Almost in minutes their hoses were laid and the air compression effect simply knocked out the flames. I hardly trusted my eyes. The roaring, wailing ocean of fire and air currents stayed away from us. We were saved. The next morning all was a black-burned and ash-gray desert around the slightly blackened but, in all, still white walls of the gunite.

The house was finished in two weeks, and the nature medico, Dr. Lovell, who had a wide following through his Sunday columns in the Los Angeles *Times*, announced he would show the Health House to whoever wanted to see it. Model or demonstration homes have become common over the years, but at that time such exhibition of a house was unheard of, and thousands came by the hour. Dr. Lovell had men from the Automobile Club of Southern California direct the parking a mile away in the valley. As always, they did a magnificent job, but at three o'clock that afternoon a car broke down, and suddenly some three thousand visitors at this hour alone were trapped beyond return in the house and on its mountainous grounds.

It was a quarter of a century later when I again saw a large crowd on the same spot. The house had been sold after the Lovell children had grown up and left home, and the new owner, unbeknown to me but knowing my name, invited me to a second housewarming! The guests congratulated me and looked at it as a new but interesting house—"perhaps a little radical, but very attractive," I heard someone say. Nobody seemed to suspect that it was a generation old, and the new owner kept mum. The building had not aged—only the landscaping had wonderfully developed; the horrible fire before the first housewarming lit only the scene of my memory. I shuddered to think of it—in a most unfortunate moment, all the work of my devotion, all the momentous steps forward, laborious for me working alone without any helper, would never had been realized, and probably would have been forgotten for good.

Through Asia and Africa

When I had finished the Health House, I caught my breath. It had been an exhausting one-man job. Instead of hope, fatigue was my main share at the moment. I looked at my wife and our two little sons, Frank L., named after the admired prophet not honored in his own country, and Dion, named after his mother, as we had already chosen the feminine version of the name when the newcomer was expected.

Could batteries be recharged, conclusions drawn, a future course mapped? We decided to see Switzerland, Austria, Europe, our old friends and our relatives again. However, as I was first to be welcomed for lectures in Tokyo, where I might compare other people's urban affairs, learn of the problems in development countries, find the common denominator, we parted.

Dione and the two boys were to take a slow Norwegian freighter through the Panama Canal soon after I departed as a low-class passenger on a Japanese steamer, which was to cross the Pacific in nineteen days.

A fellow traveler was an impoverished, adventurous, tall slender young nobleman; later I was to visit his old family castle in the Thuringian Forest. One night he awakened me shortly before midnight to see a ship we were encountering on the high seas. Sleepily I climbed on deck and looked at its sparse lights moving through the immense darkness. It was a Saturday night. Ten minutes later Sunday had started. But a quarter of an hour farther along we passed the international dateline, and then it was Monday. I had lived over three days in half an hour. I no longer felt young. I was still, in spite of having bathed at a Hawaiian beach, tired from the infinite single-handed work of the past years; perhaps I had reached the end of my course?

We sighted Yokohama one bleak morning, and it was the first time that a dozen new friends and anticipating young men in my own profession—as I understood and represented it in a contemporary way—received me very cordially in a foreign land.

Tokyo and Osaka then were something like a quarter their present size, it seems to me; Kyoto was almost untouched in its antiquity. All was so unbelievably different from my own background, and yet so close to my feelings of treating space and nature or giving emphasis often only by surrounding restraint.

I was a bit dumbfounded living through so much friendly hospitality granted me and seeing so many listeners crowded in a huge hall when I spoke of a new architecture which we might share in the future. Seeing, hearing, smelling a scent from the tiny garden court, enjoying one's inner senses of position and muscle strain in following a zigzag path and gently climbing a gooseneck bridge over the lotus pond—all seemed to make an art of subtly knowing man's many and fused responses. Even tasting and drinking tea out of exquisite tiny pottery, whispering a couple of hardly audible syllables of poetry—whereas we Westerners would loudly recite and declame—all expressed my own respect for the "value of the small" but decisive in human life and biology. Here the sensational and the fashionable seemingly did not stand—not yet—on a pedestal.

I felt happy from Kamakura to Nara, and wrote a series of articles which *Die Form* published in Berlin on how the Japanese lightweight house fitted Japanese music and modes of living and privacy, how furnitureless small rooms corresponded to Japanese sociability, manners of eating and diet, as well as those of dancing and watching the dance. The rich and the poor, the urban wealthy and the peasant, all had the same standard of dimensions, from tatami floor mats, sliding door panels, to *tansu*, built-in drawer sets. Detailing and finishing were as simple and normalized as they were superbly neat. I had been striving for all that, and I was no longer alone. A Japanese publisher brought out the first compilation of my designs, a small portfolio daintily tied with a ribbon, with a text by Kameki Tsutsura. Other friendly books and many articles have followed; they recognize our natural kinship, without thinking of my being at all imitative.

Whenever I have been in Hong Kong since—or walked through its crowded and often steep streets with boy and girl students of the university—I have referred to my first lonely acquaintance with the strange island free port to which I sailed from Japan.

Many of my quick color sketches remind me of this first encounter, which has stuck in my mind, like those with Singapore, Colombo, Aden, or Port Said. Everywhere, it appeared to me, human beings, in mixture and in clash, held nevertheless a common denominator beneath their biological individuality—in spite of ethnic variety.

Only a few years ago I was in Macao again, and it really looks different now. It is overrun by Chinese new arrivals, as are Thailand and Singapore. It is the illicit exchange spot across the iron curtain that Hong Kong cannot be so openly.

Seeing Macao first in 1929, it struck me as a real Latin city, with merely a certain suffusion of the Far East as Marco Polo had known it. I was a young man then and the weather was very tropical in July. I walked, as I always did at that time, to know a city—never using a ricksha, never using any vehicle at all.

I saw on top of a hill a church whose silhouette particularly interested me—an old church which I guessed was Portuguese baroque of the 1580's or 1600's, much earlier than, say, Ouro Preto, Brazil, which I was to experience fifteen years later.

I felt my way through large crowds up toward it, and finally to a steeply rising plaza of cobblestones, situated with the main portal as backdrop. A monumental set of free steps was leading up to the front of the church. At that moment I discovered that there was no building at all, that there was *only* a front. Most of the church had been destroyed, I suppose, by earthquake, maybe hundreds of years ago, but the front was still there, with the entrance arch to the middle nave, the side turrets, and frontal statuary. I walked up, sat down (wiping the sweat from my brow), and looked down onto the inclined plaza. As I rested, another man came up and joined me. There was some sort of a ritual character to his behavior when he stood still. Soon another man approached, and he, too, seemed to follow the same strange mode of taking position. I looked around and wondered. There was nothing in the way of a shrine, only an empty opening. It looked like a vacant eye socket, so to speak; there was no eye in it, no windows, no door in the door arch. But some more people came. They all came as for a kind of worship or service, and they all gathered around me, looking at me gravely. I wondered what was happening and whether there would be some chanting of choirs or some litany to elevate the soul. Nothing of the kind happened; they solemnly remained in a very attentive attitude, standing as if they were listening to some strange tune I myself did not hear on this hot July noonday. This went on for approximately thirty-five or forty minutes; no one spoke to another or to me, and I myself, of course, was unable to speak Portuguese or Chinese.

Afterward, the people slowly started into a loose formation, and wiping their foreheads, walked down the plaza over the cobblestones to town. After the last trickle had disappeared, I finally went down, too. When I met the Chinese with whom I had an appointment—and whom I should later join for a most interesting venture, which I will relate farther on—I asked him whether he knew what took place at this church.

"Oh," he said, "that church is known coolest spot at noon in hot season. People go up there because everybody know wind blowing straight east-west through old church, now gone." He swept with his hand along that disappeared nave and through that still remaining entrance door.

So they went to get the best of a small climatic boon. Then there was absolutely nothing ritual about it—or was there? I looked, somewhat puzzled, at my Chinese friend. He talked a pretty poor English, although he had lived in Detroit several years, and my conversations with him were always incomplete.

I was and remained greatly impressed by the ritual regularity of the microclimate in front of the defunct church. Its thermal benefit cooling effect had at least given rise to an orderly tradition by the people. Usually one thinks that *singing* or *seeing*—the auditory or the visual—comprise a ritual. But it seems there may be a "thermal ritual," too, as had evidently existed here for years and years; the evaporation on the skins of these sweating people and their moment of noon contemplation was very much aided by the longed for, cherished breeze. Every God-given day they went slowly and gravely up the steep hill in all the heat to make the most of a little cooling. It was something to give thanks for, and it was done in solemn silence.

Yes, I thought, no matter what, there is a traditional, ritualistic behavior, with a simple, basic underlying biological need. Perhaps that's the way it always is. A repetitive action had sprung up, a natural "shape," or pattern, of acting, with thermal and locomotor elements woven into a reiterative social event. It is highly important for anyone concerned with human beings and with the housing and molding of their lives to recognize such patterns and, if possible, their origins and physiological background. This kind of base, safely lasting, can be distinguished from any mere superimposed artificialities.

Being aware of the inner workings of a patterning process which gives shape to our life will become more easy for the designer of the setting if he accepts and values biological realism as underlying the life of all creatures—including, last but not least, ourselves.

A Chinese standing under the portal of a fallen-down Nordic-Portuguese *barroco* church, a wild derivation from Greco-Roman antiquity, may be in a strange setting. But the evaporation of sweat droplets simply makes him feel as good as anyone else. Sure, there may be something of accrued stylistic byplay in front of and behind the building façade. Essentially there exists a common, an international human denominator for us all; this thought appeared to me comforting in a world of strife over pronounced differences. The designer, sometimes unwittingly, becomes a sort of applied naturalist, calm in the midst of all cultural wrinkles: old or new, in the last analysis they, too, are always in a measure derivatives of nature within and around us.

Biological realism is an issue below, beyond, and versus the inventive game of superimposed artificiality which we are likely to overrate. The basic "baking rules of our natural layer cake": life, the cook, adds one acquired conditioned sentiment on top of the other. I began to cling to this picture.

Ideas like this glowed in my mind during my journey, always following the sun, through land after land. Man everywhere appeared to be dressed up and decorated differently. The icing seemed varied but, after all, the cake came from the same bakery.

All man's progress is due to the exercise of his super brain endowment, which, quite "naturally," seems to lead him through inventiveness into an ever more involved, perilous out-of-bounds region. Animals do not live under such a threat; humans do, and for them the risk rises with every patent application. Since Adam and Eve were expelled from the green campus of paradise for their condemned curiosity, wise men and moral educators have worried about it, and ever since the people of Sodoms and Gomorrahs have had to be smoked out for their perversions, the sin of antinatural behavior.

Human inventions seem to corner and crowd us into artificialities, into new conventions, rituals, ceremonials, games with very complicated rules. Whether we like these games or not, first it is necessary to understand their rules, and that in itself seems to me as much a satisfaction as the contrary is frustrating. You will say, "To hell with bridge or canasta" if you don't know what these people are doing as they shuffle their cards so intensively. I've watched Europeans looking with blank faces at a baseball game, Americans with raised eyebrows in a Mexican bull ring; I've talked to Mies van der Rohe's disciples who may not understand and thus do not love the game Le Corbusier is playing or vice versa. A game can be superb: it cannot be properly judged or simply condemned if we don't care to know its rules and objectives. Satisfaction here depends on this knowledge, as in all that is added to the course of nature.

It is funny and fascinating to hear somebody explain a game the wrong way. If you see someone eating, you don't wonder or wait for interpretation. Nature is self-evident, and needs explanations and thundering prophets only if things have become perverted.

While sitting half the night on the deck of that Japanese steamer in the Indian Ocean, I had begun musing about design essentials which would *not* be rules of games that come and go.

Natural satisfaction, the satisfaction of a biologically suitable situation, does not depend on any of the "frontal-lobe exercise," as I call it, of logical intellectual convincing. Organic endowment that has been and is being adapted to the natural scene for millions of years is much more than following a game—in fact, it has grown out of and sprouted from this natural adaptation. And so the whole organic being is harmoniously involved—unlike, for example, belonging to an esoteric group in a small café on Montmartre, trying sincerely to be "all eye" for an impressionist canvas. It would be tricky perversion, an artful game, not to use the whole of our brain, of our organic system. A few may learn to rely on one sense almost exclusively. Hopping on one leg may be fun to another few, and for a while—but babies keep on being born with two legs to walk. No speculation or best cause will change it.

A view of organic wholeness and lastingness versus the passing show, puts again a bit of eternity into design, which has so often become related only to the current and next issue of the fashion journal! No, we are not quite "so different."

Of course we want to be good naturalists of post-Darwinian evolutionary creed and never stop watching the individual specimen, so meaningful and full of potential to the species. And again, with respect, we look back to slow-moving, almost perennial steadiness. To look back and see the large, the vast, control group of human beings of the past is also a necessary postulate. Even before the Altamira Caves were painted, people had the same eyes as we do now, the same ears, the same inner-ear acceleration sense, the same nerves recording the muscle movements of dancing thighs and feet and of rolling eyeballs and turning and tilting heads. They had the same chilled backs in winter, the same sweating brows in many a summer, and the same anticipating, worrying, hoping minds which function brightly and darkly, all with a lot of glands in action. *"Tout comrne chez nous"*—we are still the same kind.

True enough, when we look through the latitudes and longitudes of time and space, there are, as already mentioned, ample and varying "baked-on" conditionings over the natural bottom layer. Each of us constitutes a thick layer cake of such secondary conditionings. They are firmly baked on in one lifespan, from the prenatal months of gestation in the womb, over the shock of birth, the years of toddling, growing, maturing, and aging. It goes on until finally all baking is over before the last telephone call to the funeral parlor, when our life heat sinks to the temperature of the grave.

Then mneme, over-all organic memory, ceases. Memory is self-identity all over; it does not sit in a particular spot in the body.

In that deck chair under the tropical stars, I pondered how humanity can be served by the designer.

Man needs to be comprehended in his congenital constitution and his further accruing nature. We must see first things first, and never ignore that common denominator of the elementary. *So far we have not properly served it in housing man* in all his fine responsiveness and small or sweeping activities. Lots of attentive work lies ahead.

Time is passing, a flood of scientific information is now at our disposal. But man has not yet been served, except piecemeal, often accidentally, hit or miss. In all his inventions, *he has only in snatches been grasped by himself,* whatever Protagoras said about him—that he was the measure.

He has indulged, and recently more than ever, in the artificiality of a million seldom co-ordinated appliances, installations, technical instrumentations, not always following his measure. He has been busy making and breaking the rules of his own games, busy creating fashions and conventions and getting tired of them, sometimes fast, sometimes too slowly. But universal principles beyond game rules, organic tolerance to guide him in this behavior of inventiveness and "progress," have not emerged. Specialistics won't do.

I had worried about this early. In the midst of life I began to seek and scan the sky for a lodestar while immersed in this obviously perilous passage through tossing activities, where our progress into fantastic energy transactions, velocities, masses, and distances needs more urgently than ever dependable and co-ordinating guidance. It cannot be just a game, maybe with rules agreed on, for one, or a hundred, or a thousand afternoons. Afternoons come and go fast. Organics are here to stay. For all practical purposes they are a given quantity.

Our busy, ever smaller planet can now be observed seven or ten times a day by one watcher, rushing around in an artificial observation moon. It is not practical economy that has propelled this sort of advance. Money is probably all right, but we can waste a lot of time making it, even in the missile industry of our progress. Organic resources can be seen ominously wasting away like green space and breathing time. Driving through the greatest know-how country, every eyeful through the windshield shows both stupendous investment and frightening waste of natural opportunities. What one sees—outside of the national parks—usually looks bad. Every site once had a chance, before being bullied by bulldozers, studded by telephone poles, with current transformed in bulky cans, with the sky over our heads crisscrossed by wires of the local utility company, and the atmosphere generally mistreated by the company of man.

Every site was a "resource," every site was once a shape akin to man's powers of perception. He was adapted to nature in her many stimulating impacts on him over half a million years, and this only begins to cover his background and his organic pedigree, which should be respected. I wondered while I went down into that second-class cabin in 1929, and even after I closed my eyes in my berth to sleep, I kept on wondering.

All the novelty—quick turnover, humming wheels, myths—of our industrial civilization cannot break down or dissolve into insignificance the natural rule of adaptation—or the troubles of failure to adapt, once the biologically possible rate of this vital process is overstepped. The long-range affair of survival can only be ignored by a designer who is, up to insanity, innocent of such biological realism. "Man alive" is his eternal project and program, and must be it. Man, woman, and child, and the things about them, around them, have existed a long time, but have not been grasped in their best meshed linkage; rather, they have been disturbed in it. Length of coexistence does not yet mean comprehension. Electronics have always existed, but only now do we know anything about them with an arrow to ourselves, and control them. Man, too, has been with us for long ages, but slowly, much too slowly, do we, on more reliable, newer, also objective, terms, get acquainted with the particulars of his endowment and begin to suspect that he responds as an entity, not in a few childishly mechanized "departments." We have a long, long way to go toward achieving any harmonious control of it all. We had better get started.

...and I fell asleep for that night....

Before the Portuguese church in Macao I had seen some Chinese move into a thermal-locomotor pattern, all on a deep-down organic base, somewhat as a swarm of tiny phototaxic night flies would perform a visiodynamic dance around an electric bulb. Nature, from such organisms up to man, manifests herself in shape and is full of shapes. Men simply must continue—not break—this natural principle of shapefulness, at which the "utilitarian-wise" always sneer.

On my trip I heard many languages spoken, and often wondered what language may do to our behavior. I thought, as so often before and since, of the word *figure*. In the English language it means both "shape" and "number." It has been effective to human minds for a hundred thousand years *in the first of its two meanings!* By comparison, *its second meaning is almost ridiculously recent.* Even now there are some primitives who can't count above three. But naturally we are more under this recent impact, as human beings, in spite of their famous conservatism, strangely are also always ready to discount, mistreat, or forget earlier good practice for the newer stuff. So often our progress is paid for with loss. For counting a million leaves on the tree in the foreground or deciding myopically on a lot of decimals, we may lost sight of the shape of the woods and the landscape—and how much we need them.

Shape—perhaps we live by it; perhaps the dangers, the awful chaos that is death and amorphous nothingness, are not just a myth! Space is not Euclidian or Newtonian for any creature; such concepts are recent wrinkles. For thousands of years and generations it has been perceived every moment of each life. Shape—broadly and in sheer endless experience—precedes paper geometry. The physiological geometry began with the innate relative rectangularity of our *up* and *down*, our *front* and *back*, and our *right* hand and *left*. We orientate by physiological co-ordinates and exist by sensory shapes which surround and stimulate us—stimulate our positioned bodies and our life processes.

What might be a good definition of *shape?* What is physiological space and physiological time? It is by no means a clockwork mechanism, with measuring sticks and slide rules to worry about. At the outset it has natural inbred rules, not artificial ones. This "naturalness" of the issue makes it stably dependable instead of temporary or merely ephemeral and fashionable stuff. The best architecture is less fickle and more irritation proof, fatigue proof. Design of the human setting, the planning of human communities, is not a seven days' wonder, barked out in sensational headlines. It has a long-range amortization, and it does pay back.

To sound, satisfying shape, there is obviously an inner dynamic corollary right within our skin. In its reception and impact, shape is the cause of well-rounded organic, especially nervous energy transactions, in and throughout us. They are very much in contrast to the damaging reactions we show to chaos and confusion. In such situations energy phenomena also take place, but they are characterized by mutual interference, and finally perhaps eddy away into ambiguous, unresolved, confounded patterns. Endocrine discharges thus activated are correspondingly in conflict and undecisive. When evaluated by a psychologist, what happens here will be given a negative accent and be called anxiety, discomfort, bewilderment, irritation. Shapeless offerings and surroundings leave a human being confused and unable to command an articulated memory retention, on which *the continuity of our conscious existence*, our lasting self-identity, depends so much.

An architect feeds us digestible memory patterns, "mnemic material," or we are troubled by him and frustrated, we lose our security.

Ambiguity or vagueness on any level of nervous transaction is valued negatively by us. Feeling that way is not just a matter of taste. It might be lack of acuity in seeing or hearing. It might be a level, but in one spot slightly slanting, floor in an old house, or the deck of a boat that minutely starts rolling and pitching. Such things are bewildering to our sense of position and acceleration as well as to our muscle senses, while we notice that we must try to keep balance. We know we have not had a drink too many and, alarmed, we think it must be something suddenly wrong in ourselves.

A faint odor, hard to define, a shape with fuzzy, changing, or hard to determine outline, are tiny phenomena that are difficult for a human being to live with. When we drive a car through the night and suddenly things become ambiguous in front of our headlights, we step on the brake in just such alarm. Are perhaps our eyes failing?

Perceptions which do or do not yield clear shapes and patterns most evidently play in or are projected into outer space and time. Those nervous corollaries of theirs unroll with lightning speed within us. Our living body is their playground.

The primary space-time is *sensed*, observed. Without an actual observer, it would become a game of misleading abstraction. It was Albert Einstein, whom I had the privilege of knowing in conversation and correspondence, who introduced the "observer" into the Newtonian-Euclidian scene. Of course the architect's client, *our* observer, is of flesh and blood, which has existed for so many millions of years on our planet.

"Flesh and blood" stands for life processes playing in a vital physiological space-time. In this space and time the existence of flesh and blood means sense, nerve, brain endowments and reactive characteristics.

Muscular and glandular activations accompany every such space-time experience, whether we roll or lift our eyes, turn our heads, or walk on our legs through the center nave of a famous mosque or of Chartres, or any other great architectural composition. When we tilt back our head to the vaulting which looms so high, the inner-ear sense records this tilt. Our organic relativity simply governs all we experience. Indeed, every speeded up or retarded movement of ours adds and fuses important experiences to the merely visual ones which are hardly ever "still." A frog's eye, and ours too, first and characteristically grasps motions at the rim of the vision field.

We hear the reverberations of our steps on the stone pavement, and this auditive phenomenon illuminates the space acoustically, as the candlelight illuminates it optically. The thermal senses which motivated that ritual in hot Macao are also here at play. Even the slight air movement caused within this low-tempered cool interior space and, consequent to it, the slightest evaporation of the constantly exuded moisture film on the skin of us watery beings, as well as the heat losses of radiation into the moist stone walls, all is perpetually of record in us.

The osmatic, the smelly, exhalations of these old tall stone walls and of the microbiotic life sustained in its pores give specific atmosphere to this ancient space as compared to a "church interior, Scene 6," on a Hollywood movie lot, built quickly out of new hardboard and plaster. Architecture indeed is and starts as an omnisensory affair, and grows into the infinity of a human soul, a realm beyond present terminological description.

But first of all it is indubitably a striking phenomenon of inseparable, tightly linked senses, taking in together every moment. The tall steeple of the church seen on a postcard or travel folder in our lap is very different when viewed bending over backward, thus beholding the real looming thing and much more wholly than by vision only.

The design activates our muscles and glands. It invites us through the entrance door, beckons us to walk along a precisioned space conceived by a good architect for impacts in series. And now, the parallax effect of nearby columns and arches moving fast, while distant ones move more slowly, makes us partake fantastically in the grand architectural offering of, say, that triple-nave church interior, as deep within ourselves we feel the action of our thighs, feet, toes, our breathing lungs. With a deep sigh we stop in the transept, and will remember, beyond any words, the moment of turning around.

Our space is always the interplay between our organic endowment and the stimulating circumstances surrounding us. Even if we have *ceased to be conscious* observers, we still richly respond. Clear consciousness is only a tiny part of our organic life.

If we are shot into space with fantastic acceleration, it is evident that the stimulus constellation we must face is very different from that of daily life on earth. Tests and trials have been set up to prepare us for such new stresses and strains, for the dissolution of usual stereognosis, that normal automatic link between our senses—in fact, for many other normal, necessary linkages in our organic being. Thus "human engineering," or connection between us and inventive manipulation of engineered, inorganic devices outside obviously becomes necessary. In Soviet lands and ours this new necessity of space research may someday bring attention of this kind also back home into our living quarters and urban scene. The thought has made me gleeful: Things I hoped for are coming true!

For decades I have predicted that the same care was required also for less spectacular situations than those in outer space. The housewife in the kitchen in all the cumulative irritations and fatigues of a working day is perhaps entitled to as much scientific curiosity as the astronaut pilot of a contemplated space ship. After all, passengers to the moon are not yet as numerous as occupants of tract houses. Small, subtle deviations from the biologically practical are more insidious, and not less interesting, because they are subtle. Being unobserved does not make a thing less dangerous. It is not the car we have seen, it is the car we have not noticed, that kills us.

The minute, the tiny, the individual, deserves watching. Home design may only *seem* a smallish task! The large, the big project, so decisive for architecture, has something impressive but fallacious in it. It is certainly not the primary learning and training ground.

Removed from real human beings, the practice of dentistry would never have had a high development. Learning through mediaries that an unspecified person has a toothache will not do. One must open the individual mouth and see the individual tooth and cavity at close range individually to fill it well. While doing so, one can ask: "Does it hurt?" An individual will answer.

Seeing a prospective client and his wife brings the architect close to the true clinical experience of men and women as they are really built. It gives him an insight into such various muscular and nervous fatigues as these people remember from their past dwelling place, and into their endocrinal discharges, which color their daily lives emotionally and their outlook into the future.

In designing a classroom, a theater, a living room, I have often thought: Humans do not dwell in nondirectional space, as abstracted by the surveyor or geometer. On the contrary, there is much directiveness, directionalism, *born* into everyone, with vision built into the frontal eye sockets, with vision fields tapering out to lesser acuity sideways, while the space behind remains forever disquieting, ill controlled, suspect because unseen. None of these are "rules of a game." It is all practically perennial.

One of the principles of engineering honestly is not to torture materials, maltreat and force them into forms and functions foreign to them. The supreme commandment, however, should be not to torture human beings, the most precious material daily trusted into our hands, and to respect their subtle strains and stresses. Only if *they* are kept functioning right is the design functional—it is human.

For the last thirty years I have not had a slow contemplative boat ride over a long distance, with some ports of call shocking me into new turns of thought. Sitting on deck with sun and moon rising and setting, many thoughts came and still reverberate.

From the almost eternal biological common denominator I love to think of, I every so often returned to diverse and exotic regionalism, to ethnic behavior characteristics which would reach back a comparatively short millennium or two, and to passing circumstances which are different every few years. Even in this passing show I noticed with amazement that the stranger does not necessarily long remain a stranger. He can sometimes be more empathic and intuitive than the local inhabitant who has gotten used to it all.

Back to Europe via the Orient

In Macao I stayed in a Chinese hotel which was at that time a booming place. These hotels have disappeared now because there are no wealthy Chinese merchants visiting Macao from their country. With the iron curtain down, they remain on the mainland, if they exist at all; it almost seems that all those who have reached Macao are fugitives. Many have no money, so they try to make some.

Thirty years ago many Chinese, big farmers and merchants, used to come from across the border into the Portuguese colony to have a good time with the sing-song girls. They came to drink, and especially to smoke opium. They stayed in hotels which were seven stories high, with the two top stories devoted to all the entertainment you can imagine, from Chinese opera to all kinds of honky-tonk variety shows, dancing, and so forth. The Chinese hotel guests would have their rooms on the various floors below. Every room had a ceiling fourteen feet high, but only a few had an outside window. The partitions between rooms were only half as high as the ceilings, and air percolated through the whole solid block of the building.

Walking along the endless corridors, one could see the Chinese playing mahjong. They would play all night, with an entertainer sitting there looking like a flower. She would just sit and look pretty—that was her job. The players would smoke opium, and some would already be lying on the floor on a cushion, half asleep and evidently having pleasant dreams. The others would continue the game, and they were not so silent. Mahjong is very terrible from an acoustical, or auditory, point of view if all the doors are open and the partitions are half-high: One hears the mixing of the mahjong tiles all night until one almost goes crazy.

Every so often people would leave the entertainment section of the hotel upstairs and go downstairs, but I must say that their behavior was always very much more orderly and much less annoying than that of Americans similarly breaking up a late party. As a matter of fact, they were very quiet; they would not be drunk and they would not engage in any brawls. Everything was very orderly, but the mahjong mixing was tedious.

I was staying in this hotel with my Chinese friend. I had met him on the boat, but had lost sight of him when I arrived in Japan. By chance, as I was walking along the quay in Hong Kong and passing the Great Asia Hotel (a Chinese hotel now no longer in existence), he came up and told me how happy he was to see me again. I asked him where he was going next, and he answered that he was going home. When I inquired, "Where is your home?" he replied, "My home is in Kwangtung, and I haven't been there for seven years. First I'm going to Macao."

Perhaps I should go to Macao, too, I had remarked, whereupon he suggested that I join him for the entire journey. And here we were.

My friend's preparations for his trip home soon began to interest me. I saw him bargaining with various taxicab drivers and finally asked him whether I could perhaps accompany him a little farther. I had no idea that I would ever have the courage to go into the interior of Kwangtung or any other part of China by myself, not knowing a word of Chinese. And it is not a tourist traffic area at all.

He said he was delighted and that I should certainly come. He invited me to his home town, which was some—oh, he estimated, two days' automobile trip away. But, of course, the automobiles would have to go very slowly.

I was in no hurry, and was delighted at the chance to see something of the interior. We met at the taxicab stand, where coolies had brought my friend's baggage so that the two drivers would not have to find the way through a very difficult maze of small streets. There was indeed a lot of baggage. He brought all the treasures of America home to China, and God only knows what was in all the boxes and bags he had accumulated—highly interesting things which he was lugging home either as gifts or for himself. Finally all was stored away in the taxi-cabs or on their roofs, and packed to the brim, we set off.

The taxis were somewhat old-fashioned, similar to those in Paris at that time—in fact, at moments they looked rather like something out of the sixteenth century. We drove about three or four miles and then the road ended. Once out of Macao, we just traveled over the ground of China, uphill and sometimes sideways through some little areas between rice paddies. The drivers evidently knew how to manage under such conditions. I was sitting in one of the cabs together with my friend, and it was very bumpy indeed. So we drove on for a long time at a very, very moderate speed.

We arrived someplace where several women suddenly came out of a little adobe hut and began to talk. They looked to me like civil servants of some kind; in fact, they were revenue collectors, concerned with inspecting the baggage before we crossed a county boundary line. There was a great deal of palaver. The sun was shining on my head, and I crawled back into the taxicab, which was also very hot. The conversation continued for a long time, with bowing back and forth and discussion of what to do; but no one opened the bags to see what was inside. Finally, the deal had been made, some coin was passed around, and we went on. Every few hours we would reach another boundary line, usually not far from the county seat; and the whole process would be repeated. The world was much divided.

All the villages looked like medieval towns, with cobblestone paved roads or streets leading through very narrow gates, city gates, within a fortified wall. The outside and the inside of the wall were usually studded with shrines or actually made out of ancestral worship shrines. Through their shrines these saints, ancestors, or holy men acted to protect the citizenry and the community against the marauders and the brigands of the open fields, who evidently were expected any moment, and did actually come every so often. Sometimes the war lord also came to take monetary contributions for his campaign; these communities would close all the gates and try to bargain for a discount rate on duties.

The landscape was a rolling plain, and often we saw water buffaloes working in rice fields which were in different stages of growth. I have since observed Chinese communities, for instance on the mainland of Hong Kong, where the plots are much more regular than they are in Kwantung—practically square, like a Roman castra, or encampment. But the Cantonese towns have more the character of medieval accidentalism, and the shrines around the fortress walls are very picturesque. In this accidentalism there was, however, a great regularity and orderliness of orientation. The buildings all had the same kind of glazed tile roofs, the same pitch, of course, which was suitable for that kind of a tile, and all the gables were directed uniformly. The windows of any significance were equally orientated because everybody seemed to know from which direction the wind blew and where the sun rose every morning to benefit or to bother. So, in spite of a first impression of haphazardness or accidentalism of architecture, there was a great biological orderliness expressed in appearance and the relaxing harmony which goes with it.

Finally, after a long trek, we reached my friend's village. It didn't look very much different from the others I had seen, but of course it was the one we were to enter. We had always by-passed the other villages, following roads that went around them, and this was really highly admirable. The Chinese were greatly advanced, long before such a scheme had even been propagated in America as a good idea. There was no passing right through the towns and making the inter-city traffic and life of the citizenry miserable by unnecessary or avoidable TO HU-WA-BOHU, as the Old Testament with horror calls chaos.

At my friend's village we parked the cars under two huge trees. There was substantial shade, which I enjoyed greatly because immediately another palaver began, just like the ones at the county boundary lines. This time it was not about any contribution to be made; it was just that everybody came to see the returned son of the town. It indeed seemed as though the whole town were there, but I later found out that, because of a certain dignified pattern of conduct, my friend's own relatives kept away and waited to serve him his first tea in the house of his birth. I didn't notice it at the time. But I saw a lot of other people, old playmates and schoolfellows, everybody coming to greet him. Naturally there was a great deal of conversation in rural Cantonese. I suppose he told them all about Detroit and the business college in which he had been learning accounting beyond the skill of an abacus, and so forth and so on. I more or less had to surmise it, because I didn't understand one word of the conversation itself.

Finally this also ended, and the men started to unload the taxicabs. Under no circumstances could the cars have entered the village gate, as it was much too narrow. However, there was no lack of people to carry all the bags, all the boxes, birdcages, and everything which this collector brought from great Detroit. We watched the loading and unloading of the carriers and finally entered through the gate. As I mentioned, the streets were just like medieval town streets, the place did not have the character of a village in the European sense. Some streets were populated completely by butchers, some, by candlemakers and various other craftsmen; and, of course, there were "merchandising" streets which had a bazaar character and which one would find on a much larger scale, let us say, in Cairo, Canton itself, or in Istanbul. Most of the streets were narrow and well shaded by abutting buildings, and I thought wistfully of the idiocy of the new "city planning" which had been enacted in Canton. I had visited there a bit earlier and had had to find my way through a city of several millions in the throes of remaking and renewal, with broad avenues broken through; the sunshine glaring on an unbearably reflective paving; and a terrific traffic of busses running in all directions, their destinations inscribed in unreadable Chinese, of course; a crowd and jam of rickshas and bicycle rickshas, and so forth—all the things one may find in Bangkok or Singapore or any southern Asiatic city. Many places are becoming unlivable because of "modernization" of roads.

But the little old town in Kwangtung was well shaded. Mats even hung across the roofs of adjacent and opposite buildings, so that there was shade in the middle of the narrow street. We walked over various irregular piazzas and market places, everything cobblestoned, some on the slant, some on level grade; the whole town had a somewhat undulating hillside character.

Finally we stepped up a wide and narrowing street against a group of buildings unmistakably of a domestic character; all were orientated in a uniform way, and all gables ran parallel to each other. My friend told me this was his home. "This is your home?" I exclaimed. "This is a whole town in itself."

"These are the houses of my various relatives, my uncles, and my brothers," he replied.

We finally approached the major building, and I saw a girl looking out of a window in the second story. Her face betrayed terrific excitement. She was evidently a sister of my friend. She giggled and disappeared without reappearing. We entered the house, and I had a short glimpse of a tile-paved space which opened onto a patio with Chinese landscaping; the planting differs from Japanese work in its greater symmetry, but demonstrates the same penchant for dwarf trees and fantastic shell accumulations.

While I was looking around, my friend touched me on the arm and pointed at a woman standing beside me, squeezing her fingers and perspiring in excitement, and he said, "This is my mother." I bowed, and he turned around and said, "Now I'm going to show you a very interesting park."

I was dumbfounded that he didn't even give his mother a kiss or put his arm around her. He just said, "This is my mother," though she hadn't seen him for seven years and was almost fainting at the great experience of his homecoming. It was evidently not in the pattern of social behavior for him to show any excitement before a foreigner, so he immediately started to lead me toward what he called "the park." I did not understand what he had meant when he said "the park," but we went through the rear patio and immediately started climbing one of the hills in back of it. And there was a densely planted garden. On the top of the garden was a sort of a summerhouse, or really a small pleasure pavilion, which my friend was particularly fond of, and had even partly built himself, he said, together with some of his relatives. He was deeply depressed to see it in disrepair. Finally we walked on through the garden and entered what looked to me like a copse, through which stretched a continuing path; still we went on. It was a beautiful walk, only a little bit hot that summer day, but I couldn't understand why he was taking me on an excursion through the woods as soon as we arrived. Suddenly these woods opened, and I looked down from the ridge over large, long parterres, very neatly kept, with hedges of cut trees, perennial beds, and large, symmetrically and geometrically grouped rosebushes. The whole scene reminded me a little of Versailles. It was an entirely stylized expansive park, and my friend's use of the word was entirely deserved.

Most astonished, I asked, "Now, what is this?"

"Oh," he said, "this is the park; it was given the city by a relative of mine."

That's all I could find out. Naturally, conversation between us was always in a rather sketchy English. Even in Michigan he had been staying with a Chinese family and had talked with them in their tongue.

I was surprised that anybody in such a humble village would have a park like this, or "give" it to the community, because it was really fantastic. I stopped asking questions as we went through a long parterre and approached a building positioned in the middle of the whole marvel. It was a long, stretched out, well-tiled, roofed building. My friend knocked at various entrance doors until one was finally opened, evidently by the major-domo, or caretaker. He immediately broke into great exclamations at the prodigal son's return from America. Of course, they knew each other very well, and they engaged in an excited conversation which immediately drew the womenfolk from other rooms. We were standing first, but soon were seated and served some tea in a cool, sheltered porch, which was really open on all sides and was just a roofed living room without enclosure on three sides.

While these people were conversing, I walked about the room, and was suddenly struck by a photograph hanging on the wall. It showed several Chinese grouped around three people: a fat American, an even fatter she-American sitting beside him—they looked rather coarse and funnily dressed up seated in this group photograph—and beside them, a wonderful-looking slender, very cosmopolitan-appearing Chinese. When I saw the latter, I immediately felt that I must know him. I tortured my head, but in the first moment had no idea where I had seen him. The whole scene and experience was so strange that it took me quite a while to collect my thoughts.

Suddenly I remembered where I had encountered this man. It had been quite recently, perhaps a week and a half ago, at a Chinese hotel in Canton. The dining room had been somewhat like a second-rate West Coast Chinatown restaurant, with the usual tastelessness and untidiness, but it overlooked the Pearl River. The tablecloth was white, though rather spotty. The food was excellent, but the architecture was makeshift, possibly put together by somebody who had been the third helper of a San Francisco contractor and had returned to execute this ten-story hotel in Canton. Seated at a table, I began looking at the people who came in, wondering whether I had any ability at physiognomic diagnosis. Those sitting around evidently were visitors from the flat country coming in to Canton, but I decided that it was extremely difficult to recognize and actually judge people in a foreign country, from my own impression, especially people of such a racial divergence. I finally concluded that I would never know who was upper or lower crust, except perhaps by the clothes, and that I wasn't even clear about them.

At this point my meditations were interrupted by the appearance of a man entering the dining room with a young, very good-looking girl. He was perhaps fifty-five, and immediately it was clear that he was a most exquisite human being of the highest grade. With a start I realized that I had been wrong in believing that a Westerner wouldn't be able to judge people because they were Chinese. The two sat down at a table and ordered some food, and I noticed, both from the waiter's deference and also from that of the other people in the room, that these were quite aristocratic guests. I watched them and wondered whether the girl were his mistress. He was a pretty old man to have such a young, wonderful-looking woman with him. I couldn't make out who this couple was, and finally gave up. But I watched them eat, and noted the way they used their chopsticks, because they were not eating European style, although there was a white tablecloth on the table. I had spent quite some time meditating about them, especially the gentleman. And now he was the man in the photograph!

I rushed over to my friend and asked, "Will you please come over for a moment and look at this photograph?"

He assented, and when I had showed him the picture, he said, "This is my relative, the man who gave this park to the village."

"You mean to say he gave this park—he owned this vast park and gave it to the village?"

The answer was Yes. Unless I misunderstood his English, that was what he was telling me. He added that the man had also given two or three schools to the village.

"Two or three schools?" I wondered.

"Yes, he was the minister of education under Sun Yat-sen, and one of the leaders of the Nationalist party when it was still in its prime."

"Oh," I remarked, "that's interesting. Tell me, why did he give this park to the village?"

"He was born here, this is his home town."

"Oh," I said, "now I begin to understand." I gathered additional information on this interesting man. He had been trying to tear down the shrines and evidently was a man of very new outlook. He was a person of great progressiveness, one of the great figures of Sun Yat-sen's China. Then I asked, "Who are the other people I see here in this picture?"

"That is the American consul in Macao."

"That's what he looks like," I added wistfully, "and this must be Mrs. American Consul."

Thus I was suddenly more positive that it is possible to judge people from a photograph, no matter what country one lives in. Still, generalizations are unjust, and I have, of course, seen very different American consuls, different in looks, demeanor, and wives. I tried to convey my vacillating thoughts to my friend, but he was not a philosophical kind of man. He had just barely been through a business college in Detroit, and Detroit possibly might not be a place for technical trainees from abroad to acquire a profound philosophy, either.

Years later Detroit's more practical quality seemed confirmed to me in Marseilles, when I met a French Frigidaire salesman who had received a year and a half of training there, selling refrigerators. Then he was let loose in southern France. He had been chosen by my architect friends to translate a speech I was invited to make to the natives at the Marseilles *Unité d'habitation*, built by Le Corbusier, but here it also seemed to become evident that Detroit is not a place where people are groomed for interpreting or translating profound conversations into *langue d'oc*, the Gallic tongue of the South.

The man in Marseilles probably had proved capable of selling a sufficient quantity of freezers, but around us was an audience composed of various kinds of people, even friars and monks from a nearby monastery, young architects and others who did not speak or grasp the Detroiter's idiom. My English was Greek to them, while my thoughts in turn baffled the Frigidaire man. Linguistics alone do not make for confusion. It's more than that, at any rate. My Chinese graduate from that Michigan metropolis was a match for the Frenchman. They both proved masters of neither subtle language nor penetrating thought. No matter where they had acquired their particular worldly skills—others would have remained foreign to them. I have said it before, and it merits repeating: Sometimes the right kind of a stranger can penetrate—feel himself in—more deeply than a local, and without the clumsy misleading of an interpreter.

Europe—U.S.A.—1929

Between three meals a day, musings, and conversations with a mixed group of hopeful or resigned, vivacious or dull, travel companions the journey went on. One of them soon departed from our company.

I saw my first and only burial at sea in the Indian Ocean. It was night; the Japanese captain tried to read the small print of a psalm by flashlight while the British flag was being spread over the burlap sack in which our fellow passenger had been sewn up, with a few short iron bars at the foot end. The propellers of the *Asama Maru* were stopped; from the stern of the ship, where the cages of the tropical-bird trader stood, we heard the swishing of a few wings and, every so often, little birds, escaping singly or in groups, would sail out over the wide sea. With a soft splash the sack was let into the deep down dark. The midnight wind blew my hair into my eyes and, like the handful of other passengers, I covered my head again.

Sitting on deck chairs and promenading between stern and prow, I also thought over the Buddhist architecture I had seen, the Hindu temples, the rubber and tea plantations with laborers who earned ten cents a day. I sat under the stars not only alone but also with a young Dutch engineer who told me all about tin dredging in Malaya. It was a slow, long-winded way west—in the main always west.

Past Aden we squeezed through between Yemen and Africa, and in an open automobile I left the shore of the Red Sea to cross the real naked desert. My eyes were fixed on the clear, clean-cut rocky mountain escarpment of the Nile valley, until they became inflamed from the fine invisible desert sand blowing into them. Toward evening, when I approached Heliopolis and alighted in the lobby of the old sumptuous Shepheard's Hotel, I thought that by this time my wife, whom I had left *behind* in California, was now *ahead* of me. With the two little boys, she must have passed through the Panama Canal, and at this moment her freighter was perhaps following some course into the Caribbean Sea.

Strange, how world-spanning my family affairs had grown! I was about thirty-eight, and my situation was anything but settled, although I had worn myself very thin, checking those steel shop drawings of the Health House, and had lectured in Tokyo and Osaka to thousands of touchingly appreciative colleagues. All those memories mingled with dreams as the night air got stuffy. I had as yet no idea whether I would stay in Europe this time or take up my tenuous path of life in the United States again, which then seemed so far away.

In Cairo there had been a wild uprising. I heard machine guns clatter and saw the mob fleeing through the streets. I remembered the good advice to watch out for shot-down high-power wires, which curl around your feet and have a way of electrocuting you. The best thing to do in case of a revolution is to step into a doorway. Experiences came in curious juxtaposition. The patient stone-polishing workmanship of the pyramids' interiors so far from revolt impressed me as much as the sun-glaring mosques and minarets against the blue of an Egyptian sky. Much later, Egyptian students came to join and work with me.

I saw Naples for the first time, Pompeii, Stromboli erupting, and took a night train from Marseilles to Paris. By that time my little family was probably sailing through the middle of the southern Atlantic.

The Parisian railway station, the new apartment of Doris, Dione's younger sister, in the Faubourg St. Denis, the Metro, the Palais Royal, the boulevards and sidewalk cafés permeated by the gasoline stink of busses—all stayed in my memory while the train took me to Brussels, where the delegates of the young Congres International d'Architecture Moderne (C.I.A.M.) were meeting. From afar I came to represent America—wasn't it wonderful? It was then that I met Henry van de Velde, with whom I should be friends again thirty years later in Switzerland. I treasure the thought of my last lengthy meeting with the wise old man at the Ageri Lake a few months before his long, fruitful life ended.

With Le Corbusier I went to see the Stocklet house, which Joseph Hoffmann and Gustav Klimt had created twenty years earlier. I saw this remarkable building again thirty years later when judging the competition for a cultural center for the Belgian Congo in 1959. It is an endless amazement how memories with a cargo of emotion become our intensely deepened property and ever again our precious means of self-identification.

Back to Paris I went, and from there to London. In a little boardinghouse I waited for the Norwegian steamer to berth at the Victoria and Albert Dock. Here our family reunited. It was a bank holiday, and a one-horse cab took us over cobblestones to an ancient transients' lodging I had found and where I had made everything ready to put the children to bed. Then we walked the streets of London.

Next day we walked to Victoria Station and stowed the youngsters and our luggage into the train. I went to make a short telephone call and my wife waited for me; when we returned to where we expected the train to be—it was gone, and with it our two small children. First we turned pale, but then we comforted ourselves that Dover was not out of the world. In fact, we suddenly felt like newlyweds and free as birds, without family or baggage.

Later we found our boys at the Channel coast, well taken care of, and passed over the water to the Continent, through Paris, and crisscrossed over Europe.

In Zurich, as in many places, I found myself already known and even invited to express my ideas. Upon returning from the lecture hall, I found a wire from Rotterdam, signed by a man unknown to me: C. H. van der Leeuw. He suggested a meeting in Basel the next day, and I accepted, thinking he was possibly a poor free-lance writer or reporter. I came down from the apartment where I had been visiting an old doctor friend of my wife's, and at the curb stood an elegant new Lincoln car, colossal in size, with a charming young-looking man and a lady official of New York's Russell Sage Foundation. They were on their way to an international industrial-relations conference. Mr. Van der Leeuw, a millionaire industrialist and owner of the Van Nelle tobacco and tea interests, was the president of this influential body. It dawned on me that *Wie Baut Amerika*, written a few years earlier, might have aided me in this world. My very kindly received lectures in Basel and Zurich and this visit by a strange magnate could hardly have any other explanation than that some people found my views promising. It was strange to think of it, coming, as I did, so to speak, from outer space, from my far-distant outpost.

Mr. Van der Leeuw invited me and my wife to his house in Rotterdam, and a few weeks later we actually arrived at the *Kraslingische plaslaan*. It was the most modern house I had ever dreamed of: An assembly of technical novelties, from English sheet rubber to cover the floors and winding metal stairways to microphonic conversations at the entrance and from room to room, exhausts for cigarette smoke as soon as it left the mouth; organization down to a complicated dashboard of switches over our guest beds to activate all kinds of illumination, move the window drapes, electronically turn on hot and cold water in the bathroom. It took us only half an hour to understand Mr. Van der Leeuw's explanation of all the colored knobs, and feel at home.

Our host covered Holland with us. He said he liked my work and my ideas—and arranged for me to speak before Dutch audiences in Amsterdam and Rotterdam and meet with all modern leaders in architecture. We slept in Rietveld's pioneering house in Utrecht, saw Zonestraal and Hilversum, and became thoroughly informed about modernity in Europe. For some reason Wright's reputation in the Netherlands had then somewhat declined, and all international style, to which I have earlier referred, had evolved, as it were, under Gropius's and Le Corbusier's influence. As always, I seemed then and long after to be somewhat an outsider, with my very American interest in procedure and southern background and with my physiological concern, as expressed in the Health House. But, after all, I was only giving attention to what Leonardo and many humanist artists of the Renaissance thought worth watching, *to know* man and thus see him in his right proportion in the center of the picture. I think it is no accident that of all places on the nature-near southwestern coast there should exist a special collection of "Vinciana." My friend and physician, Elmer Belt, has given it to the university for his physiological interests.

Yet while watching, to know man and thus serve him, "The Book" of mine, which everyone seemed to have seen, had been read apparently for its technological revelations on American know-how. Alvar Aalto, still a young man at that time, came to shake hands before I spoke publicly in Frankfurt, and smilingly related how he had used *Wie Baut Amerika* to convert Finns of influence and means to overseas progressiveness. Idealized Americans became examples, as idealized Germania had been used by clever Titus Tacitus to reform Rome. I have every so often thought of this ancient interestingly recurrent leverage to change "our" things by a legend imported from abroad.

After a short lecture trip to Cologne, where I pondered the Romanesque-Byzantine universal culture in a world of once much more intimidating travel distances, I decided to go back to the United States. It was not so far after all. But, as on my first journey, I had to leave my wife and sons behind. She stayed near Sigmund Freud and his daughter Anna in Vienna with my oldest boy, who, as now became sadly clear, had in his speech center been injured in birth, to be unhappily impaired for life. Our second son, well, healthy, three-year-old, gifted Dion, was cared for by his grandparents in Zurich, while I myself crossed the Atlantic a second time. Dion later studied architecture on both sides of the ocean and, as so many cosmopolitan young men, joined and significantly aided me in much work of distant days to come. My thanks to fate.

For the moment I lived in New York, rather poverty-stricken, in an old brownstone. But newspapers again ran long illustrated accounts of the trip which had taken me through so many countries, and I had trouble avoiding reporters in my shabby quarters. The reason for all this attention was that the New School of Social Research had just been finished by Joseph Urban, and Dr. Alvin Johnson, the president, invited me to give the first three lectures in the new auditorium—to test its novel acoustics, as it were. In my patient audience was a small, very attentive man who later turned out to be Joseph Hudnut, then Dean of Columbia's School of Architecture. He sat through all three lectures, looked at all slides, and wondered, perhaps. But after the talks, he graciously expressed his appreciation. That he pushed, years later, an invitation to Walter Gropius may well have had its roots in those evenings.

    I had just been a guest for six weeks in the Bauhaus and spoke enthusiastically about its earlier and later period, and its older and newer masters. Altogether the reception was favorable. The newspapers became attentive to modern architecture, and the first exhibition of this sort of building design was being prepared in the Museum of Modern Art, right in the cultural import harbor of New York. The show was then to tour an amazed back country.

    In Europe someone would occasionally tell me: "Just the day before yesterday a big American car came through here; in it were a man with a red beard and a young man with tousled black hair. They said you'd build the new museum in New York." In the next town someone else would have talked with the two in the big car and would have heard the same tale. I greatly wondered about it. However, Philip Johnson and Russell Hitchcock, who had just returned from their trek through Europe, evidently must have misunderstood. Perhaps they had thought I might have the chance to work on the new building for the Museum of Modern Art, but it did not come to that at all. Notwithstanding, I am thankful to them that a neat model of the ring-plan school of my 1923 vintage became part of the museum's first American exhibition, of new architecture, which I endeavored to help in its travels from coast to coast. *It was to take this school thirty more years finally to find its actual place on earth.* There was, I am afraid, little of the go-getter in me, and mine was no cliché of a dizzy success story.

Yet almost simultaneously, the Museum of Science and Industry asked me for a diminutive, actually steel-built replica of the Health House; it was, as it were, an isolated curiosity piece, and they paid $600.00 to Harwell Hamilton Harris, then my faithful disciple (of, I believe, third-generation California stock), who built the laborious steel model. He did it in a garage in Pasadena over a period of months. He surely worked hard. The last time I saw this neat, indestructible piece of work, it was in the museum at Rockefeller Center and pretty well forgotten.

In this science and industry show, as in other situations, I had passed as a sort of engineering wizard—"artistry" was not considered one of my attributes. My health and biological writings did not seem to belong on an architectural library shelf, and perhaps to this day they have hardly found a legitimate place there. Anyway I was happy to hear of Eastern colleagues now; Loenberg Holm, Lescaze, Howe, who paralleled what was prepared in the West sporadically, from San Diego to San Francisco.

There are now excellent historical studies whose accuracy easily surpasses my memory as to how all came to pass. And at present the East and Middle West have their great galaxy of designers and architects who are recognized everywhere. I had looked forward to it.

One day, while I was still in New York, a phone call was relayed to me by my landlord, who lived downstairs, and I rushed from my room with its thin-worn furniture for a memorable conversation. The man on the other end of the line said he was Homer H. Johnson. He asked me whether I could spare the time to have lunch with him at the Banker's Club downtown. I was dumbfounded. He also told me of the friends who would be present at lunch: Arthur Vining Davis, President of the Aluminum Corporation of America, and

Jacob Gould Schurman, United States Ambassador to Germany. Catching my breath, I mumbled that, since my calendar was quite filled up, I would have to think a moment, but, I said, I might find time to do so the next day.

At the appointed hour I walked over the heavy carpeting of Wall Street's social headquarters, and the club manager led me to my baldheaded, extremely amicable host, who, in turn, introduced me to his friends. The luncheon was superb, only psychologically somewhat disturbed by my growing restless curiosity about its purpose. Naturally we talked a great deal about my world-girdling trip, which they had read about in the press, and of my encounters in Europe. Nothing else happened until the friends had taken leave. Now, over a cup of black coffee and a big cigar, Mr. Johnson explained that Alcoa, the Aluminum Corporation of America, then still a young company, might participate in redesigning "Pullmans of the Highway" for the then well-known White Motors Company if the chassis were changed over to this novel metal. The question was whether I could come to Cleveland to look at the situation, with all expenses taken care of and on a per diem of $150. He suggested this very modestly, apparently fearing that I might turn him down; obviously they needed an "outsider" to push progress inside of old "White." Actually it was a fantastic compensation at that time, especially for someone who had lived on meager lecture fees, had no prospects for tomorrow, and was staying in the cheapest sort of rooming house near Third Avenue. To recover from the shock, I cautiously said that I still had one lecture to deliver the following week at the New School Auditorium, and he suggested that meanwhile I pay at least a first visit to the Board of Directors in Cleveland anyway. They wanted to get going.

And so I slept for the first time in a private Pullman compartment, was installed in the swanky, dignified Union Club (again, with very thick carpeting), and made an utterly successful appearance before all the board of White Motors. The aluminum president had won out against their flabbergasted technical director, a man of conservative leanings, by dispatching me into the battle as light cavalry! As often before, I had not even understood the battle layout while riding into it full blast. With a contract like a motion-picture director's I later returned and busied myself, assisted by a staff of engineers, designing novel "Pullmans of the Highway." It proved a splendid training in planning prefabrication, also of units not on wheels. I also studied the redesign of the production plant and a new layout to prepare it for the switch-over from making a composite hardwood frame with steel links, to manufacturing an all-aluminum chassis.

Evenings I displayed a quickly rented tuxedo for all Cleveland society to see, but sometimes when unobserved I fell back into the old habit and sneaked out and into an American diner to have a hamburger. The H. H. Johnsons, their lovely daughter Theodate, a fine musician, and everybody else were extremely nice—Cleveland gave me, so to speak, the key to its city gate, probably because I had such high-standing hosts. I was even confronted with eligible heiresses. Fortunately, I was no bachelor, and remained, myself, free, but gained twenty pounds from good dinners. My wife hardly could trust a photo from which all my leanness had vanished.

One member of that Johnson family was Philip, then the young enthusiastic promoter of new architecture I have mentioned; later he would become a leading architect himself. He must have spoken about me to his father.

After six weeks, mission accomplished, I took a train to Chicago, where a Mrs. Steele was managing the promotion of a contemplated Industrial Art School. Although $150,000 was in the bank—lots of dollars at that time—it seemed that the Art Institute balked at the "practical" teaching program which was being considered. I was to help by lecturing on my experiences in Asia and Europe.

At the Blackstone Hotel people, all in evening dress, banqueted and paid, I believe, five dollars to listen to me in the presence of the city dignitaries, while I talked again about such things as the Bauhaus. "It sparked the audience," Mrs. Steele and the other initiators assured me. I spoke as much as possible about Mies van der Rohe, whose guest, active day and night with his students, I had just been in Dessau, and it was very probably the first time that I made his name resound from banquet-hall walls in the city of his later destiny. It was just the way I had extolled Gropius before influential Hudnut. I am happy to think that I could play this role. Walter Gropius, on his early first trip to this country, had been good enough to come west with his wife for a short visit with me. I always cherish the memory of his surprise phone call in Los Angeles. "Gropius here. I don't know whether you remember my name."

"For heaven's sake! What do you mean, whether I remember! Where are you? I'll come right away to pick you up...."

It is strange how fateful tiny moments may become. This friendly visit in my solitude made a propagandist of me for his coming again and an enthusiast about his taking a hand in the United States.

The affair at the Blackstone was generally considered a grand success and the school in Chicago seemed rather assured. The board of trustees even offered me the directorship. I graciously bowed out, all the time uncertain about what in the world I would do when I reached California once more. But for the time being I wanted to see again my subtropical workshop of a nature-near architecture.

Some years later I was delighted to receive Mies when he arrived in New York on his way to Illinois. I took him right into the theater on Broadway to see my friend Clifford Odets's brand-new tenement drama *Golden Boy*, faithfully whispering translations into his ear until all the people around viciously "shushed" me. I wish he would have at least once come to the mild West Coast, so inspirational to living as I have tried to help my clients live. All put together, the piecemeal realizations, slowly accrued over many years, could have filled an entire garden city. Wholesale housing projects, however carefully I studied them on the basis of these many "life" encounters, could never quite have solved the fine points of individual accommodation and human mooring places that the single projects did.

At least I endeavored to evolve a vocabulary for them, grammar and syntax, but I heartily agreed with Mies on leaving everywhere a little empty elbow room for personal expression.

The Van der Leeuw House

My second start, seven years after the first in 1923, was almost as uncertain. Again my wife had been left behind; again my mind was directed with emphasis, but it was also, in practical getting on, fairly blank. And while I seemed to have a name elsewhere, in California I had little recognition.

I felt happy, when, a month later, C. H. van der Leeuw, the Dutch magnate, suddenly announced by wire from New York that he was flying to Los Angeles to see me. He came for only a day, and the Health House was the main stop on his itinerary. He saw it in the flesh and loved it. Full of praise, he was driven about by me in my third-hand ancient Chevrolet.

When I pulled up at his hotel and we shook hands for goodby, he looked at me and said, "Why don't you build a house for yourself?"

Taken aback, I answered, "Oh—errrrr—I have not the funds to do any such thing."

He pulled out a checkbook and asked, "How much do you need?"

I almost toppled over, fingered the steering wheel with one hand, and grabbed a handkerchief to wipe my forehead. "I could not accept such a gift," I said.

"Well," he retorted, "I'll loan it to you without interest. No? All right, you pay me three per cent and you build your house. How is that?"

Finally I heard my voice accepting, mentioning a ridiculously low figure. He signed the check; I closed the car door and contemplated him entering the hotel lobby. The apparition had dissolved, but I looked at a check which was a little sweaty and crumpled in my trembling hands. With my own eyes I had again seen one of those unicorns. It had had the horn of fortune over its top and now it had left a fortune in my hand. Or was it what is called a Dutch uncle? My metaphors and mythology got mixed up. I fingered the check, put it carefully in my breast pocket, and took it out once more. It was there, all right. Later I parked the car twice on the trip home. Each time the check still proved to be in my breast pocket, and I knew I was completely sober. I concluded it had been a windfall. That is what it was. The thick woods in front of my nose seemed to have cleared.

For a year I wondered what to do. Mr. Van der Leeuw's letters urged me to build. But I wanted to make it a full-fledged venture of research. Unknown as I was, many a nationally known manufacturer was willing to help with my experimental house for health and human comfort. Pigeons seem to fly and join other pigeons. My idea was surely novel in 1931. Nobody dreamed of such a house, as a look at the architectural journals of those years will readily reveal.

One of my main objectives was to *prove that man is stable, that new architecture is no passing fashion*, and that, unaltered, it could still be good a generation later if well suited to human responses. It was possible to make an *enduring* design while watching with love and clinical knowledge our senses, which had been millions of years in the making—our eyes for light, ears for sound, fingertips for touch, our propensities to shiver or to sweat and lots of other organic concerns, often deep below consciousness. Their perpetuity of needs would supersede mere passing fashion.

Nevertheless, or often because of these stabilized most general considerations, I could well use various kinds of standardized prefabricated materials, fittings, and fixtures, and, amazingly, still create an individual whole.

In *Wie Baut Amerika* I had described the methods of the American building industry and their effect on future design; now these findings were judiciously used and practically realized, as, for instance, in metal sash sizes from a catalogue and in fold-together or sliding doors of metal-framed glass, which I hoped could one day *become* standard!

But I wanted above all to demonstrate that future, ever greater populations on our earth, who would have to be housed with land economy, could have plenty of privacy, interior variations, and refreshing richness of daily visual experience almost in a nutshell—at least on a lot unusually small.

The basic structure of the house in the middle of the metropolis, facing Silver Lake, and soon to grow around a patio, was wood in a so-called *balloon frame*, which was to provide greater elasticity in case of earthquakes. "Knock on wood"— earthquakes are never fully predictable, and I have since learned much more about lateral stresses. But thirty years of California shakes have not even cracked the cement plaster. Perhaps they will do it this year!

Libby-Owens furnished me a sandwich of plate glass and aluminum which I had thought up. I used it both as wainscoting and as material to mirror the heat rays, and using the heat of the shower, quickly to temper the bathroom. Other sorts of *novel heat mirrors* were built into all walls for winter economy and summer cooling. The type of insulating material *varied with each side* of the house to fit sun, radiation, exposure, and to make inhabitants happier. *Exterior soffit light expanded rooms* into a softly lit exterior; photoscopic or color appeal tapered off into the dark, where impoverished night vision alone would have shown only black and gray. I became an ophthalmologist by practical avocation, and have kept to such thinking ever more, using it finally to explain, thirty years later, the design of the Los Angeles Hall of Records to the County Board of Supervisors, and, amazingly, winning applause with such an explanation of the occupant's well-being.

Privacy behind the large plate glass front was *optically in-*

sured by the reflection of that outside illumination. I made much studied and judicious use of *indirect lighting sources;* they gave the room a greater visual calm, and also helped to *eclipse the border between inside and outside* when the first was reflected inwardly at night from the large window areas and mysteriously mingled with the light spread from the exterior roof overhang onto the greenery in open air. Providing light for reading the newspaper was not the primary purpose of this illumination. Rather I saw in it *an emotive stimulant,* changing endocrinal discharges and biochemistry.

We humans never have really lived in static nonvariable light, and soon yearn for the dynamic declination of stimuli. Static lighting might become a pest.

Baked enamel metal facing and pressed fiber boards were at the time excitingly new to touch and sight, and the resiliency of cork floors was rare. But I counted correctly that their appeals would endure. Roof gardens overlooking lake and mountains were uncommon in a city of red "Spanish" tile roofs, but view terraces, too, have remained a good thing. The house looked much more spacious than it was, and a lot of subtle planning went into just that. In the next hundred years of birth surplus, I told myself, *the small must be stretched.* Screening with foilage provided that much coveted privacy on a sixty-by-seventy-foot lot—really a diminutive property for any American city, not to speak of the sprawl which had overtaken my "new South."

If everybody householded land in such patio or atrium houses, Los Angeles would have 40 per cent of its size, of its pole lines, and endless expensive roads. It might have half its traffic to wreck nerves and half the exhaust gases to pollute the blue sky and breathing lungs! It was a somber prophecy to come true.

The Van der Leeuw research house, VDL, as I called it in honor of the backer of the experiment, was tightly sandwiched between its small old-fashioned neighbors, which on their part made only a minimum use of their own lot areas. Awkwardly they stayed below the level of the sidewalk and the street which ran along my cherished Silver Lake's shore. I planted way beyond my lawful lines.

Our house was the first to rise to a commanding view of this lovely water. From the electrically vibrated prefabricated concrete joists over the basement, which I promoted with a new manufacturer, over long and frustrated studies on radiant heat, to the flat-top aluminum-coated roof and mountain-view roof terrace, the house finally turned out to be a novel sample of material, energy, and space economy, but with satisfying spaciousness enlarged by mirrors.

Everything had to double for something else to yield increase and elasticity of use, even in the breakfast roomette, the table of which folded down over a washtub. The kitchen had access to drawers which could be heated or cooled and which opened both ways to serve refreshments or complete meals directly into the living quarters. Later on, electric operation of double sliding doors, six stations of an intercommunicating system and hi-fi over headboards of beds were installed; and still later, when my heart condition became ominous, I also added an elevator to my bedroom on the theory that it was better to have an elevator in the closet than a skeleton. The intercoms grew to nine stations at my bedside. Everything else, even most of the furniture, has stayed put for thirty years. The great flexibility of the house has permitted having married collaborators and various apprentices with full privacy in this modifiable structure, and sometimes more than a dozen of staff have helped me and contacted me in my bedroom, where drafting easels folding down over my body and three telephones supplement all the intercoms. Trees have grown to woods and tower over this Van der Leeuw research building— of which neither we nor our friends have ever tired in a generation of family raising, living, and later mostly working.

The house has shown no sign of depreciation or obsolescence through these three decades, while other residential and commercial architecture in those and later years went through many changes of taste, only to accept similar solutions and conclusions in the end. At last hard-boiled practical men seemed convinced; the investment in contemporary design was proven safe. It was even good investment, liquidable investment; sales prices after ten, fifteen, twenty years were a multiple of the original costs. Buildings of such design were found to be a more stable value in this quick-turnover world than the most celebrated automobile models of full-page advertising glory. Banks, building and loan associations, insurance companies—dreadfully reluctant at first—slowly began to help finance this sort of project and even to build their own offices in a contemporary manner.

Mr. Van der Leeuw had truly helped the long-ago prophecy of *Wie Baut Amerika*, that an industrially advanced country would interestingly turn contemporary. He has decisively aided the answer to the question: Can or must "contemporary" be a procession of passing fads? Aren't seasonal fashions, like those in ladies' hats, contrary to the obligations of the long-range investment adviser—the architect who is trusted with all the scraped-together savings or strained credit of his client for his active prophecy and a future happy ever after. Famous architecture of past ages was often concerned with eternity, and had a tinge of it. I wished for it, too.

After all, there is something long lasting and very slow evolving about the human species. Organic systems like ours are in a steady, only slowly shifting balance. We must not be fickle in housing them, nor zigzag sensationally when we play with life.

In a way a house is the successor of the womb. But after leaving the womb, social interaction starts; the "post-womb shelter expert" shelters more than an individual—even if that individual is a bachelor—and he himself never works alone nor with his bare hands.

In the foregoing narrative of the successful endurance of my own "research" house, novel materials, unusual devices, and special installations seem to dominate. But to assign it importance because of these innovations alone would be not only inaccurate and wrong, but definitely misleading. It is not mechanical assembly nor newly advertised fashionable gadgets which have made the house immune to obsolescence, but rather their proper use, incorporated into an over-all *design planned with foresight and insight into human beings*, respecting the *species and the individual* as well. A random assortment of novelties added to the design for the sake of modishness will become obsolete as rapidly as the particular trend in popular taste. But if these new inventions on the technical market are fused into the design, applied with an understanding of man's biological nature of longest standing, and directed toward its needs, the house not only will outlast the fashionable real-estate tendencies but—much more important—it will also sympathetically influence the lives of its occupants and visitors, and lastingly benefit them.

We must ever again consider that however well or badly trained, the architect, either way, has far-reaching powers. He is often hardly suspected to be a destroyer as well as a benefactor. Concerned with housing and thus with shaping the lives of others, the life of the whole nation and culture, the architect surrounds us inescapably, inevitably, with his influence or his negligence: in smoke-filled suburban railroad stations, in waiting rooms to depress a commuter's morning; in office towers with an artificial lump-sum climate, figured out by an arithmetic shortcut; in congested traffic lanes; and when he brings us "home" into row houses, differentiated only by variously colored entry doors. But his influence extends far beyond our immediate daily fives; it literally confronts us from morning to evening, works on us "from cradle to the grave," from the maternity ward and infant nursery to the funeral parlor; no escape....

It does us good to remember often where we came from. Nine months before birth we are housed in an ideal, miraculously, especially adapted formative environment, in a place on which nature has lavished untold skill and wisdom—the expectant mother's body, the maternal womb. Under its primary primeval conditions the human individual is premolded gently and safely so that it is well equipped for its fast growth into childhood and adolescence, for the maturing into adulthood. Finally it will have to wither and fade into senility, and, as an individual, cease. Biological destiny is shaped from genetic essentials; there, in the uterine peace, *it takes form, to play and function* over the few or more decades of life. The old Greeks would have called it "play of the gods," instead of a wondrous "play of nature." Anyway, it is miraculous!

This original environment is intimately fused with the organic make-up of the individual; there exists no contrasting independence between the two. The embryo is floating toward birth in a setting of a well-conditioned equilibrium. It has always made me think that in this pre-stage of life, no sudden resistance tests are being passed, and yet it is obviously a preparation for later passing of such difficult tests. The exercises for this coming hard reality get under way most gently. There are first no temperature shocks; the pressure of the surrounding liquid medium is so evenly distributed that the inner ear—the vestibular sense of acceleration and changing body position—is only gently stimulated. The dealing with gravitational pull will become, for every second of our journey over the earth, an issue, from our bottom to our top; for the soles of our feet, through our entire frame and perennially balancing musculature—no bed, no chair, no flooring, will ever be as gentle to us as this incipient floating. Often a longing for it returns in our dreams.

Hearing begins slowly and is confined to muffled noises from the outer world. Even if mother drives downtown, the screeching of brakes and the rumbling of trucks do not reach ears which will later be abused so much. Taste may be stimulated when the fetus works its jaw muscles and opens the mouth to the fluid of salinity; smell is not yet developed, and the eyes are closed. But they will open most promptly upon birth. Then man's most brainy sense, the complex visual one, immediately becomes avidly active to acquire slowly its complex training, at least in some of its component parts. Kittens can wait to open their eyes, the much more cerebral man child must not wait even a bit until daylight, shadows, and colors begin their deep appeal. Whether the birth itself really is a shock—as Rank thought, a trauma—may be biologically doubtful, but the sudden exposure to a completely different environment is at least a serious matter to a young organism as yet unadjusted to it.

What happens after delivery? Only a few minutes before the baby was still in its protective dark uterine surroundings, and now it lies in the maternity ward; eyes wide open, staring into the glare of a Luminaire, nationally advertised for hospital use. It is protected against microbes by the nurse's face mask, because for two generations we have respected Pasteur by this ritual of shielding. But forty-five infant colleagues yell their heads off and the high-frequency sound in the room is too reverberant for baby ears. Why do they yell so complainingly? No other high animal throws a litter of forty into a nest that smells of medications, or feeds them according to the clock rather than the stomach; and above all no other animal takes its young up and out of wet diapers to expose them to thermal shocks, in sharp contrast to months of embryonal enjoyment of never-disturbed warmth with mother. But from now on all life takes place in a heated, air-supplied man-made room.

In the moment it is born, the human baby is, together with nurse and obstetrician, delivered right into the hands of the hospital architect, who will remain as powerful as he is as yet innocent in his ominously influential practice. We must ever remember it; he is to substitute for nature's infinitely subtle care, with which she makes a bird build and feather its nest to fit every wrinkle of microclimate in the particular choice of site, in the properly shaded and properly sunned forking of two tree branches, where the air will move in anticipated flow over this miracle of a minimum home-establishment, reflexively built. Birds and bees, fish and fowl, survive more safely by nature's automation than big brain-endowed and brain-ridden man—guarded, prodded, harmed, and helped by a member of our fraternity of architects.

We have still to learn to grow equal to our assignment. One day, however, we shall, when we get tired of sensationalism, become fascinated by the fine nuances and steps which lie between nature and her perversion, between blooming and withering of vitality. This fascination for the vital includes all aesthetics. *Form is an age-old, eternal utility.*

At the beginning of his life the human individual is promptly involved with the architect, who arranges the reception room of our outer existence and all further physical setting. It is a long-lasting interplay, one which reaches way beyond and below the "materialistic," mechanistic, and stylistic level to basic affinity in a chemical and emotional relatedness to our surroundings and fellow men. There is nothing more noble or religiously higher than insight into "one-cast" homogeneous human nature, and honoring it. The splitting off of the "beautiful" from the "utilitarian" is not a method of explaining anything convincingly. It has no simile in nature; neither in nature surrounding us nor within ourselves. The way bees are spaced in and around their hive, the vital spacing of birds in their rookery, baboons in their East African thorn trees of the high veld, the giraffe, with his long neck to browse in their tops—all are prehuman precedent for feasible organic and social grouping and interaction of individuals with nature, balanced in and around them. But how much more complex are individual human brains, how much harder to provide with a resilient setting which must continue to resound the background of hundreds of thousands of formative years, from which we can never secede.

Empathic understanding of vital needs becomes the basis for work of the *architect who continues nature's accommodations* for human life. He is empathic not only in his in-feeling with his client, but also, as we shall see, in the association with his own coworkers. People who execute do not want to be mere cool-tempered helpers of an "executor." They never have been such in all the past of great architecture.

Indeed, the so-called architect is really, as he will be in the future, a group of people, often a whole team of specialists, not only of varying abilities, but with all their emotional particularities, emulation, differing rhythms of creativity, and really deep-rooted individuality. Each human being has billions of brain cells firing in different patterns and with velocity differentials in fractions of seconds. The team is the necessary nucleus for successful comprehensive design—it is the core of our whole cultural development and future, and what best keeps it together is enthusiasm that surpasses all the merely rational. One could call it well-induced and harmonized biochemistry. Regimentation and intimidation is the other more gloomy alternative for spontaneously working together.

A young architect who wants to serve only reasonable clients and is mad at the unreasonable wife of the owner makes the spectator doubt who really is the least reasonable, the wife of the owner or the inwardly fuming architect. Human beings are wholenesses: lots of emotionalism with something intellectual somehow inseparably molten in and alloyed.

The narrative of these autobiographical fragments may well finally lead toward one culminating deliberation: Is there a contemporary kind of cognition which, better than ever before, sees and appreciates *the individual and its biological value?* This cognition extends way beyond rational verbiage and deep below all hard economics and fiscal facts superficially serving only numerically specified masses. Is the individual helped or harmed by its houser, who should know that biological profundity beneath all building programs. Plumbing of this depth will lead far into the anthropological, even animalic past. It seems to be certain that the individual, as always, is and remains the potential for future variations such as have been momentous mutations in the endless years of that organic past.

But the individual in man, the bearer of a miraculous superbrain, remains a factor of hopeful and endless stimulation in our ever broader, flatter society. His sparks of communication have a power of mediation and range which will traverse all earthly, or perhaps planetary, spaces and periods of history. A new fertile statement of individual interdependence may now fit into our age of penetratingly detailed science. It goes way beyond the vague and beautiful poetic metaphor of our "enmeshment in the universe." This may be as true as ever, and yet we must learn more and more about more kindly mating of individuals, harmonizing their grouping in a suitable common setting.

A potter can become a philosopher over clay, potting bench, and turntable. Baruch Spinoza meditated while he ground lenses for spectacles and telescopes.

The architect first learns to view the world through a fine narrow-angle lens, which turns here and there to take in a long pageant of trusting clients. From face-to-face experiences a bit of generalized wisdom may ultimately grow. Through this and from here spreads more than mere logic over streets and squares of the city. In it still resounds some of the feelings the architect's own heart may have harbored in hoping for a happier future, as everyone does who plans, builds, or for whom another is called to plan and build.

Programs and Problems

THE PROFESSION of the architect is really wonderfully soul-bound, and is socially as well as technically conditioned. The historian can rightly remind us that architecture's consumership has been undergoing changes. In some of its heydays, palaces were built for dynasts who gloried in the designs of their retinue of slave architects. These men were lifetime employees; it was also impressive to them to have a follow-up job and finally to build a perennial tomb for such a potentate. Sometimes kings let the head of one of their architects be chopped off, for safety's sake, so that no competitive ruler could have him as a designer. Thus multiple experience was restricted.

The rewards of such a one-client architect were a series of kingly nods, always from the same patron over a long run of time, and the budgets were covered from the sweat of the subjects and the toilers of the kingdom, anonymously, or perhaps by contribution after a rapacious war. Budgets were no problem. Quality was pretty strictly individualized, depending on whether the ruler was arbitrary or traditional or conservative.

In contrast, the future will be "the best for the most," half a billion square meters of housing a year, in many levels, on top of each other. Possibly each quadra in Brasilia, or quadruple superblock in Stalingrad or sector of quick-growing Johannesburg, may have a figured-out "individuality" of its own.

Perhaps from the top story or an especially prominent roof

garden one will at any rate see those clouds colored by a sunset.

What if we started spending ever better brainpower on making ever smaller space ever more sensorially bearable, biologically enjoyable! Nature has given us ample precedents of teaming density in most tolerable equilibrium of need and fulfillment. What she has done by endless adaptation we shall have to do by concentrated design and subtly applied science.

Otherwise, what may happen to the individuality of the many millions, *each one* personally living on the half billion square meters per annum? As long as the human brain is still evolving, it never can be at its wit's end. A way can be, must be, will be found.

At any rate, between the past Versailles of one king and the necessary mass accommodation of the future, where a little mishap or error may suffice to ruin that best for the majority, I have had, and we all have had, the perhaps never-to-return happiness of living in a transition period.

In Vienna, the city where I grew up, possibly one-tenth of 1 per cent of the population comprised families who occupied their own "homes." Most of the people, like my parents, were nomadic inhabitants of apartment houses which themselves were not always really "more beautiful or better" than what had been built before them. The "liberal era" after the revolution of the last mid-century had crudely crowded huge masses of employment seekers into industrialized cities. Dwelling needs kept mounting. Now, a housing project in my home town moderately scrapes the sky. I guess crowding will never stop, one way or the other. Getting close together will have to be continually refined. Tokyo, ten millions; Buenos Aires, six millions; and this is not the end. Someday, six hundred years hence, standing room may give out, Harrison Brown once told me.

I had no idea that I would ever have an almost placid chance to build for many individual families, meet them in the flesh or plumb their souls. Here was an elementary chance to gain insight. Their responses to my diagnoses and tentative proposals as well as to my enthusiasm in serving them turned into creative impulses. This multitude of clients housed individually in all their activities; the growth processes of their families; and unique, often even peculiar sites, which became ever-varying places of anchorage in all kinds of large and limited landscapes—all these have given me knowledge of a huge control group mostly only very moderately endowed with money or property. Borrowing and building middle-class—even adventurous lower-middle-class—Americans have at least for a short run in history been personal consumers of architecture. I have come to know my clients with greater intimacy and in greater variation than the architect of the Pharaoh or the Roman Emperor of the past, or the architect to the masses of tomorrow. With the population densities of the future we shall especially have to learn all about most minute human responses and not ride roughshod over what is biologically bearable.

Even in my day I have given rather colossal dedication to the design of mass service buildings, be it for education from nursery to university, large housing projects, theater and community buildings, spiritual and sportive gathering places, medical centers, prophylactic clinics, commercial cores of cities, or wholesale planning tasks. Compared with all these perhaps worthier efforts, that which was possibly the best part of my life—my kind of endeavor for the individual—may well be, and probably is, a passing phase. Let us assume it is so. So was the age of the saurians, and my little record may not last as long as paleontology. Perhaps in the future even more "economic facts" will force what are called our "best solutions," or maybe only second-best ones, bulldozers still will generally play a greater role than today. I have very often thought this over in relation to what I endeavored to leave behind me. The best of it was refreshed humans, heartily satisfied clients who were kind enough to receive me on any weekend with open arms.

I was deeply delighted if they actually sent me flowers, and I cherished and collected near love letters, often after years. It all came upon a highly personal serving of someone by feeling with him. I joyously blush at the thought.

Of those letters only a small sprinkling have come from even the best multiple or mass accommodation I have conceived. Charlie Eames once wrote me touchingly after living full seven years in an apartment I had designed. But in such projects there seems generally to be a somewhat less intimate or instructive relationship from person to person. Yet when I look back over my life, exactly such a growing together with real human beings as my clients for single houses has made me truly happy.

My best hope is to leave behind me studies of how outer nature can be made to relate to the inner nature of man, studies and realizations of those *psychotopes*, spots of soul satisfaction, of human beings recognized and gratified, not for the moment, but for the lifetime of their group—or at least for the amortization period of their loan (to simulate more hardheaded talk!). And still these latter facts of financing, of banking, of paying back loans, of taxation and fiscal rigmarole are amazingly different in various places where I have practiced. They may soon be forgotten—and will remain long forgotten while individual lives go on to be factual, the real thing.

A book published about such individual, personalized effort may soon be like a collection of reproduced fossils out of a strange world of by-passed "economic factors," which have now become puzzling relics. But the individual, as "*a minority report on potential*" and of mutation, may well and probably forever influence the endless biological drama of evolution.

There is lasting insight to be gained by taking the individual seriously. Such an illustrated book could seem something like a little, but not yet fully exploited, mine of crude material. It would be valuable to analyze it for my early, probably immature attempts to minutely evaluate *nature as surrounding*, to correlate with *nature within* human beings, all individually alive and intertwined.

For myself, I can say that in all the later large-scale projects I could use very much of what my individual clients have taught me of man, woman, and child. It was and is an inexhaustible apprenticeship. I can only thank them from my heart.

The particularities of my clients have always been very inspiring to me; the largest portion of my familiarity with human beings comes from this contact in action. It stems from my clients, and the knowledge thus acquired benefits others in spite of the fact that they all are so diversified. A down-to-earth businessman naturally is very different from a great film producer or his female star. The artistic temperament lends winged shoes to one, while the other walks on down-to-earth boots, and some are down at the heels.

Clients are individuals above all, but they could perhaps just for simplification be described as fascinating variegated types. Let us characterize them, tentatively at least, as: the imaginative; the timid; the conformist; the rebel who enjoys rebelling against neighbors and the community or group in which he lives; the hard-headed, slashing economist; the conservative saver-on-general-principle; the finicky anticipator of trouble and in-advance-head-shaking maintenance specialist. Some have a specific anxiety, or a truly well-groomed specific crush on the inventive. Interesting is the spree-man, who gets much kick out of picturing himself as daring and dashing.

What makes it more complicated is that wives of all these people very often have been chosen by them or followed them *for contrast!* They are nevertheless, of course, an intrinsic part, often the outstanding part of the client, who must be recognized and served as a group personality, be it now a matrimony or a board of trustees.

There is also the worrier per se, who by nature always finds scruples to gnaw on him and who simply can't take possession except when he has worried his fill. The house, or anything else he wants to acquire, is not his own unless he has dearly paid for it with this self-torture.

Again there is—as I have designated his propensity—the "T.P." who can't feel himself an owner except by a perpetual *technical participation*. In his perhaps petty but passionate technical interests, he may forget *himself,* of whom he really should know something and much more than he tries to. He mixes into the small and large detail with more curiosity than knowledge, often without any inborn skill, but always with much and true relish, a touching childlike participation just "to keep company with the adults" in an age of technical catalogues and clippings.

Then there is a relative to the spree fan, the strutting gambler who pictures himself the cavalier and likes to believe, in particular that his life is not a studied rational game but a wild, amusing chance in a million. He gets it all by chance. His black horse wins at the race. He loves to tell the story of how he came to get on it by sheer accident. His big Cadillac or slender, precious Lancia is really like new; he gets it after it has only been driven eleven hundred miles—a gorgeous car he just happened to run into by smiling luck. He sees himself as an easy-going lucky guy, model Sunday child, and "here it is."

Here it is, what everybody will envy him for. It is not that he might have selected a really dedicated architect. The salient point is that "he never worried about this house." The guest is aghast, while watching arbitrary material, form, and oddity prevail: it must be a half cone, with a sunken understory fireplace and a floating balcony above center, with two other semicones for master and guest suites, partly with glass roofs, attached at each end, and the wall of petrified-tree-trunk masonry. It surely looks fantastically daring to the head-shaking visitor. The owner enjoys this eyebrow-raising, and with pronounced casual smile, he says, "I told our architect we need a living room and a guest room apart from our master bedroom—he went home to his studio and here is what we got.

It suits us fine. The 'big' magazine sent a photographer, who stayed a week and took a hundred and twelve pictures in color." He chuckles and shrugs his shoulders, watching us from the corner of his eye to see if we are toppled over. Every type is impressive to himself and wants to be to others in a certain way. Perhaps this is even a prehuman trait and part of our organic make-up.

Now, to go on, there is, by contrast, the man who closed wonderfully tricky contracts to get the better of every one of the subcontractors—carpenter, plasterer, roofer, and all—by his self-cherished cunning or admirable acumen. He is nobody's fool, not only when it comes to house building. Even his enviable ventures with women—marvelous creatures—ventures properly controlled, are amazingly inexpensive, not by luck, but by his prudent foresight. He knows the winning setup. Why let anybody mess around with it? He gets by fine, while other dopes pay through the nose....

After all, these are only very crudely sketched roles in the comedy of life, not to be taken quite as seriously as that. Honore de Balzac knew that there was a *Comédie Humaine*. The architect may well have stage fright, but he stands during the performance mostly in the wings and at the switchboard, to implement the play instead of making it a fizzle in plain view.

The wealth of individualities is richer than any cartoonish exaggeration can be. Attitudes, inborn or conditioned, are startlingly diversified however one tries to type them. All these people have trusted us, all are human beings, and through and underneath their peculiar personality, lovable—from the most blue-blooded New England aristocrat of great wealth to the recent immigrant, in hope of going places but as yet with a minimum borrowing capacity. Quite apart from their pocketbook, they represent a wonderful variety of human beings, and deserve all our sympathy for their enchanting, inspiring trust. The deeper our feeling for them goes, the greater the promise of lasting benefit. Their own sympathy is engaged by earnest but joyous service on their inner problems and our amazing comprehension of their own aspirations and peculiarities. These, of course, must be probed for factual reasonableness plus emotional balance, all rolled into one, and then sometimes humbly and gently curbed.

Such a mutual grant of sympathy grows into creative capital, more precious than any other funds. Building, if there ever comes a chance for it to anyone, is a major event in his life. A human being can hardly be satisfied through the realization of an idea cut and tailored for another soul. In subtle traits, people are so different, and they surely enact their differences, or want to, at least, when they build their homes. An architect must grasp that, know souls if he wants to serve them, save them from disappointment, from the despair that closes in on them when settled with the wrong setting.

Each human expresses physiognomically a good deal to the observant clinician. Tiny but significant and lasting features of the face are molded by habitual expressions, and active face and gesticulation convey a wide spectrum of fatigue, apprehension, or enthusiasm. Sitting calmly or fidgeting in a chair, a movement of fingers, hands and arms, a film of moisture adding a little extra glitter to the eye, a hesitant clearing of the throat—all expressive behavior illuminates an attentive conversation if one is ready to see and hear. Without ever being in the nude, souls become silhouetted, manifested. There are activated senses, muscles, and glandular discharges, and much of it is revealed to us without conscious vision. Even the choice and wearing of dress is highly indicative; it scarcely conceals, but discloses.

He who wants to help human beings for decades to come—maybe for the rest of their lives, must not disdain straws in the wind, or even in that light breeze which refreshingly picks up tiny but bright and indicative bits during a discussion of a building project, for instance. Full expression in words is not always the best communication. One may be distressed or even annoyed by the overprofessional listener who is an inquisitive stickler and tries to pin one down.

The architect may well have to become an applied physicist like the engineers who collaborate with him; he may have to be an applied economist, like realtors and bank appraisers; but above all he must be an applied physiologist and expert on giving nerves, glands, and muscles what they continuously need from the outside, because he presents a setting to human individuals or groups of them. This is his primary function.

I have enjoyed running the gamut of American society, from building for poor schoolteachers, artisans, secretaries—they were the first to trust me, and I loved them for it—up to university regents, decision-makers of the Navy, Army, and civil government, or magnates of commerce, men with bigger bank accounts, who, late in life, also met me. The human hopes set on projects of buildings, small or large, all had something in common.

All American projects, even comparatively modest ones, tend to look opulent to those abroad, who see them in illustrations. For many years people in Denmark, Venezuela, not to speak of poor and overpopulated India, could follow our building operations and strange prosperity only with raised eyebrows. Frequently this impression is generalized in rather erroneous ways. But often enough innocently human playfulness, which in a Mexican village is cheaply colorful, turns undeniably extravagant in Manhattan night clubs or behind downtown airline counters, over which tourist tickets are sold to countries of picturesque poverty. Extravagance might be amusing, but it ominously flavors the American scene, often with souls soaring and again pitifully plunging, perpetually unbalanced by the economic barometer!

Budget, Mirror of Destiny

Many years ago a motion-picture producer had been good enough to talk to me repeatedly, most interestingly but vaguely, about the house which he would build. As they say in the movies: "Any resemblance to real persons and circumstances is merely coincidental." One day, he suddenly telephoned in a terrible rush. I sat down with him in his grand office, in the vast and busy studio, and he said he was now in dead earnest. Sick and tired of motion pictures, he wanted to devote all his time to building a small house of his own. He proposed a budget, also then very modest, of exactly $9,200, which I should keep sharply in mind! "I am at the present time making fourteen thousand a week," he said, "but I want to give up this damned rat race to be completely free to work with you and supervise the house myself."

Cautiously I suggested that he had better keep his job with the studio for two more weeks at least, as the budget seemed to be—well, rather small, especially in view of the fact that he immediately started to talk of an elaborate adjacent workshop where he could enjoy modeling and burning large-scale ceramics, which he loved doing but now had no time to do. I hinted also that I knew of a man who possibly would be willing to supervise the little house for less than $14,000 a week. But he did not want to hear of that. He looked forward to that pleasure himself. "Building a house is like dancing on a meadow," he said. "You can't let someone else do it for you."

I felt with him here. We signed with a construction budget of $9,200—and, as a curiosity, I believe I still have this contract someplace among old papers.

We proceeded with the utmost economy, using on the outside only one coat of paint, omitting $75.00 for insulation, etc. Economizing is sometimes a soul satisfaction, and everything was figured down for a man who had given up his job and had no income and, in fact, was tired of the world, like Saint Anthony in Egypt. I admired, esteemed, and loved him in his mood of resignation, and in all that followed, in all its fluctuating intricacies and very human contradictions. We might be resigned and withdrawing, but still not quite! A man says much when he says, "Evening," to quote Hugo von Hofmannsthal.

Four weeks later, the producer with hesitancy and yet enthusiastically stumbled back into life. It had beckoned again! He closed on his personal account a contract to film an adventure story laid in modern Spain, with a wonderful director at his right hand, a find of which he was very proud, and a grand, agile actor cast for the main. At once, now sailing under his own fire as an independent, he saw beauty in the making, imagined bulging box offices around the globe, and, on second thought, we speedily added a zero or two to the budget for the house.

In the next few weeks the shooting of the film went on, and at the same time a precipitous augmentation of the architectural project. The day came when the first "rushes" were shown, with a couple of acid business experts watching at our side in the dark. When the lights went on, their faces were solemn, their conversation was unsympathetic, at moments injurious. They decided the picture would be a flop, and to my consternation, most of the augmentation had to be taken out of our plans. It kept bewildered me busy as a bee—but I was not filling the honeycomb, I was emptying it all that sorrowful night.

However, the next day, after I had made the changes, one of the experts had a lot of bright ideas about the film. He suddenly became almost as enthusiastic as the producer himself. Once it had been decided how the protagonist would open the door to a pergola corridor—looking out on a magnificent seascape and sunset—where the young girl would just happen to be passing by with a hatbox in which she was carrying a million in paper money—whereupon would ensue the dainty, touching love scene which had been passed by the censor beforehand—everything was O.K. and everybody was unanimous; the actor really was the genius for which he had been cast. And the sunset would be photographed with the right kind of filter. We also had the right man to do the shooting, with lots of camera experience. It was a natural! Then and there, on top of the frontal porch roof of our house project, a patch of tropical, watery marshland was simulated, "obviously dating from before the last glacial period" and populated by reptiles and an amphibian fish, which the dealer sold us with a discount as he had just been turned down by the director of the zoo. There was now also to be an artificial rain, to stream freshly through a jungle planted on the roof and collect in a monolithic basin of iridescent marble—at night it was kept full of waving shadows by means of a fascinating system of illumination. Beauty was the best thing to which one could turn one's purchasing power once one had it—a thought held much earlier by Pericles. And he had, of course, been right, as long as his other affairs, like the Peloponnesian War, did not go sour.

The master's bedroom was surrounded by a stainless steel grating which I worked hard to invent, heat-reflecting but so finely woven that it was practically transparent in certain lighting and gave full view on the waters of a moat of magnificent square austerity. By pushing a button, the illumination changed so that the grating, together with the polaroid bedroom windowpanes, turned fully opaque and impenetrable to the eye. Hardly any curtain, not even of the most precious textile, could have done that.

No doubt about it, the property was way out of town, and a man with a big income from a successful film like the one in the works could easily be molested by kidnapers, who might try to cross the moat beneath the pendant optical grating during the night. It was also clear that this medieval scheme of protection was in a way primitive and outdated and would have to be supplemented by electronic devices to do away with any intruders who entered the moat as soon as they got their feet wet. Thus, flipping a switch on the complex control panel over the night stand in the bedroom would suddenly electrically charge the water of those protective basins.

The idea was that while the producer, now back in his métier of long hours, was sleeping late in the morning, his Persian chauffeur would, before breakfast, remove from the moat any bodies accumulated during the night so that they would not pollute the air when the sun rose in the hot climate of the wide mountain plateau, surrounded by a large acreage of terraced land. It had been acquired for solitude, which now had to be counterbalanced for security. One thing calls for the other, and when you say *A*, you have to say *B*.

As an architect always must do when he serves a mobile-minded human being who is the football of fate, everything had to be figured out to the last detail. However, to my embarrassment, I must admit that we ran into a big extra when we suddenly found that an electric incinerator would be necessary to dispose of the bodies fished out of the moat. This detail had completely escaped our attention.

Once when the producer was already leaving in his car, he lowered the window and directed me skillfully to incline and to mirror the ceilings of his sleeping quarters, not so much to see himself, for example when lying in bed, distorted or multiplied, as to have the illusion of being on the bottom of a southern sea, surrounded by tropical fish, which were really in the aquarium-like pool beyond the plate-glass enclosure. We tackled this optical problem with energy, and it and the large suspended cobalt-bearing pool skin cost as much as the original house.

There was one item which first astounded me when I brought the magnificent bathroom plans to the owner, but it is no more proper for an architect in a successful world of free enterprise—or probably anywhere—to be surprised at any time than it was for a chamberlain of the Borgias a few hundred years earlier. I had to feel with the man from dear old Hollywood when he said, "Take out all the locks of the bathroom doors." Worriedly he added, "It is my experience that there is always somebody in the bathroom, threatening to commit suicide and blackmailing you, unless you can get in freely." In a moment I adjusted myself to this natural anxiety of a wealthy producer of a world-conquering film. I also could understand that bullet-proof glass for all the windows was indispensable, and that a man of restored substantial income needs inconspicuous submachine-gun emplacements, so located that he could cover all housefronts from the inside without having bullets ricocheting from any columns or posts in ill-conceived positions. To my good luck, the artilleristics and militaristics of my past helped me in these matters, to defend a just cause.

Thus, following function faithfully by form and layout, I had adapted myself to the current idea of a budget when the motion picture had its first showing in a small town in Iowa. To my terror, dependable reports reached us that there had been quite some yawning in the audience. I saw the producer arriving back home on the premises in his private limousine from the airport. (I should explain that he was almost perpetually on the move from and to a plane and had a subscription on traffic tickets, for the necessary speeding. He had chosen his site so that he could reach in short order the Place de l'Opéra in Paris, figuring twenty-five minutes of fast driving, being genuinely Persian auto-chauffeured, and make the liner at Burbank for old Le Bourget, then still *the* aerodrome, where he was expected by his Parisian chauffeur, to take him in forty minutes to the Café de la Paix. He was really in a handy location for commuting.)

Now, after the sinister failure in peripheral Iowa, my client wouldn't be thinking of Paris, of the brilliant center of the world, which he loved so much to have in reach. He looked tired, haggard, and heartbroken. We telephoned Mississippi Glass long distance to postpone the bullet-proof glass.

Like human life, the budget was seesawing up and down during the whole construction period. Toward the end the producer started on a gay play, with a musical comedian whom I found as funny as did everybody else. He was such a scream that in the last moment we flew in two full plane loads of extruded aluminum sections from Chicago. They improved the appearance of all the shower enclosures and of the library of rare pornography in the translucently enriched, transparently expanding winter garden, which in its spaciousness was fused to the bachelor bedroom.

Balzac, like any great novelist, loved man—bankers, chamberlains, pawnbrokers, princesses, prostitutes—in all their hopes and downcasts, while writing that *Comédie Humaine*. I felt with my clients in no less a manner than Honore, kept faith as he did to his humans as they rose on the crests of the wave, sank into valleys; some of them in poverty resourcefully reaching the good life, some derailed by wealth into a picturesque landscape of gruesome disappointments. Fortuna is the old gamble goddess of colorful mix-up then and now, here and there, with capitalist stars or Communist politicians, with timid souls and daredevils. She is always at it, probably always amused by it. Nothing human ought to be foreign to an architect. Perhaps even more than a writer, he can learn to feel with the dramatic ups and down of souls unfolding in a very concrete quest and hope for happiness; and suffering before his eyes from changing fortunes. He learns to be not a rationalistic logician in the midst of watering mouths, or a sanctimonious preacher, but perhaps a humble warner—and then an encourager of what may really last in our responses. Very much later I have seen my client, now white-haired, revisiting his long-sold estate. He walked from one great spreading tree to the other. All he had fondly planted from five-gallon cans. Their smooth bark of once upon a time had very much changed. But he still loved them, and I too, even more.

Everything can be overdone except Nature; she is the secure pole in the madly spinning dance of human notions.

From the beginning life has been good to me through informal lessons and not-too-tough-to-solve tests in human interplay. This was especially true early in this "much-more-than-a-game" of being an eternally enmeshed individual. The members of my immediate family were not at loggerheads, at least not at the time when I, the youngest, stepped into the group. Earlier, some interfering uncles had bothered my much older siblings, but a quarrel between my parents and my uncles about the independence of my brothers lay back in the past like the legend of the battles around Troy. The family, disemburdened of all intrusion, breathed purified air. My parents, left alone, were far away from any cold war, but set a precious precedent of human fusion. Only now have I learned to fully appreciate this as my good luck.

An architect is always enmeshed with other people. If he feels incompatible with human beings because he is unable, or too proud, to establish an empathic relationship with his clients, he is certainly a failure, and should sadly withdraw. Like a doctor or psychiatrist, the architect, too, must surely never be annoyed by his wards, their complaints and problems. In their place and predicament he would probably not be superior. Rather, beyond *technical* professionalism, he should be prepared to understand and relieve never-ending strains and stresses. If a husband and wife do not fully agree in his presence, and live in friction with each other in the old house, he ought to remarry them in and to a new one. And keeping the divorce rate down is his great task.

But marriage is only one of the endlessly manifold cases of valuable grouping of human individuals which may be helped by environment. It might be quickened in going to pot by depressive and frictional arrangement of the setting. Even a bachelor is not as single as he may at first look. An architect should see human beings as always involved with other human beings, although they are silent in the programing council or children who do not negotiate bank loans. Babies, however, will grow up during the amortization period, leave the house, build their own families, and carry benefits or wounds from their early home. All through life such reverberative waves are distant controls over vast time stretches.

Pain, Despite Success

A fine balance in listening to the vociferous and to the slight heart murmur of the monosyllable will help the architect to diagnose relations between wife and husband or husband and wife. Social custom may make a German or Spanish husband say what an American husband never would say: My wife won't come along to talk, she agrees with me! Don't believe it, even with a Moslem married to four wives! Better crash the gate to the harem and talk with each of the four; undoubtedly it would be extremely gratifying and instructive. Be suspicious of unanimity—on which the long stolid future of a building in daily use will be gnawing, until it flagrantly falls to psychological pieces.

I wish I had always been successful, but one must be satisfied with what I should gratefully consider a good batting average. This may really be an understatement of my luck, I would be happy to think. But perhaps the story of at least one failure in which I was involved will be fair and instructive. It almost broke my heart. Without much special technical explanation, the story of a house project can easily be related, and it will reveal what it may do to humans—which appears to me to be the really deeper issue.

Mr. and Mrs. O.—he, a merchant, she, the mother of his five children—bought a ten-acre orange orchard on a California hill, with the most wonderful view of a vast valley to the southwest. He, evidently and conspicuously, had the conviction that being a fruit farmer was a lovely idea for everybody concerned. All during our early conversations he was utterly optimistic, especially on matters of budgeting, and the house which he wanted to put on this very spacious property was proportionately spacious and of expensive materials.

I spent a great deal of time warning him about the cost, especially pointing out the solitude of the location and the distance of supply sources and subcontractors, from plumber to plasterer. Mr. O., who was by no means a rich man, remained persistently optimistic, while Mrs. O. was indecisive and continuously given to change of heart, it seemed. My worry, however, became almost an obsession that these plans, when completed, could not be built from the money allocated or available. Even during the latest stages of the working drawings, when everything should have been fixed and approved earlier in the preliminaries, very vital changes and additions were made, causing us triple and quadruple work.

What was worse, most of the changes seemed also to add to the cost, and no warning seemed to help. Finally, when the building was staked out on the property on the top of the hill with the tall trees, Mrs. O. suddenly claimed she had not understood the so-often explained layout. It was as if from timidity she instinctively wanted to delay the start. But again her husband demanded that their wishes for a drastic revision should be satisfied, and we continued.

Mrs. O. was by no means domineering, but really a person of feminine charm. But she was, it appeared to me, given to complaints. Her husband, in spite of occasional pugnacious interludes, loved her, and their marriage seemed to be a success. I always cherish seeing people get along and instinctively do my best to help it. My sympathy was engaged in spite of her somewhat plaintive voice and perpetual vague disappointment. Without it, she could have been quite an attractive human being, although perhaps taxed by her duties as mother and housewife of somewhat prematurely ebbing vitality.

When finally a contractor had to be decided upon, Mr. O. said that he knew of such a person who would work for him, not on a lump-sum contract, but by the hour. This sounded perilous. I begged to meet the man, to explain the plans to him, and make sure that everything was understood before such a loose arrangement was concluded. Mr. O. deliberately made it impossible for me to become acquainted with the contractor, supposedly his friend, who was living in another town. No clarification in conversations was possible, despite all my requests. Very thoroughly documented and detailed plans of ours were put into the hands of a man entirely unknown to me, which of course caused me no end of anxiety.

The construction period seemed endlessly long, and although we were not reimbursed for supervision, I traveled very often to the distant premises. Almost secretly, and with practically the air of a conspirator, I managed to get to know the man who was working there. Without permission of the owner, he tipped me off on all the delaying changes which were now being made during the actual construction.

Again, it was Mrs. O. who put on the brakes and posed demands, often based on her quite puzzling ideas of personal aesthetics, and each time I would have to go through a frenzy of effort to digest these changes and try to fit all the adjacent parts to the changed ones. In so many cases before I had seen that my passion to be *inspired, not amazed*, by individuality—if only well understood—would also yield refreshingly diversified individuality for the building—even with an unexotic, safely syntaxed form-vocabulary and without arbitrary self-expressionism on my own. This had practically become my creed, and it has worked for many years.

Although my activity was not at all called for, I tried to get the contractor to help me in saving as much as possible of the originally achieved precious integration of design, in spite of ever-renewed and endless readjustments. I wanted to preserve the first wrought-in value for the owners, who tended innocently toward a patchwork of afterthoughts. Of course, I know that one is always wise by hindsight if one has not clearly foreseen things. Maybe there *are* no thoughts from scratch, but only afterthoughts?

By this time, however, all my assistants had lost interest in the job, which seemed to adapt itself like a chameleon to changing invisible inner psychological scenes, while the outward site over the green groves remained beautifully constant. Single-handed, I endeavored to stick it out. My fears of cost (as caused by the owner's wife, by himself, and now also even by me, as I tried to preserve some of the original consistency on behalf of those who had originally given me their trust), bothered me a great deal. I again started to plead with the owner over the telephone to stop his unreasonable procedure. For good measure, I tried in my heart to remember that we all are complexly built and are not simply "reasonable" creatures.

The owner had periods when he became quite appreciative of my voluntary effort, and at least listened to my explanations of what was being lost and what better was to be salvaged. Without meaning harm, it is always easy to take advantage of a devoted man who is possessed by his vocation and obeys the conscience of a mission rather than a contract.

I hardly saw Mrs. O. or spoke to her at all, and, what has rarely happened to me elsewhere, she seemed to be resentful and unappreciative of all my efforts to bring the project to fruition. She seemed impatient, not to further it, but in fact to hold it up.

After about a year of construction in slow motion, and the greatest zigzagging and indecisiveness I had ever marveled at, a point was approached when the people came close to moving in, although the job appeared never to come to any full conclusion. By that time the husband also had been completely worn out by the changes and delays, but, gritting his teeth, he kept on.

To my great and happy surprise, the work of the contractor, who had been an unknown quantity to me at first, more and more turned out to be simply excellent, and all my fears in this respect were really unwarranted. I had hardly ever seen more splendid carpentry work, rough and finished, and there was expensive stonework done under his supervision for a front wall and fireplace which was beyond criticism. I began to like the man and his craftsmanship.

At this juncture I chanced to meet Mrs. O. on the premises one day and gently discussed painting and colors with her. She could not mistake my sympathy, became quite friendly, and seemed happier than I had ever known her to be. I was elated and happy myself to see the long green fruits of devotion ripening in color. We came to a fine agreement on the last hues to be applied. In an hour of understanding we were very jointly occupied by the same endeavor. I squeezed her hand in gratitude for this relief. Heaving a sigh, I drove down from the lovely hill which so long had been a kind of Calvary for me.

After about six weeks, by which time I hoped everybody would be happily installed, I telephoned Mrs. O., suggesting that I would visit with her in her new home. I was dumbfounded by her reply over the telephone, which was most resentful and unexpected. She who had determined the form of the house in endless protracted conversations with the contractor and her husband, always ignoring me up to that last meeting, now suddenly told me that apart from colors the house was a complete failure, and that she was unhappy ever having gone into it.

On my request to help me by explaining, she described the changes, which she herself had caused in layout, as unsatisfactory and hateful to her now, and also all the modifications she had forced upon me in the later stages, with which I had complied. At first speechless, I tried to mention that I had endeavored to please her when I made all these revisions, demanded by her and so costly to me.

She replied that if I was an architect anywhere as good as my reputation, she would never have had to advise me what to do; on the contrary, I should have had valid, convincing advice for her instead of letting her flounder or take her own medicine. She blamed all her indecisiveness on being left helpless by me. This was far from a true interpretation. I had tried so often, always in vain, to fit my advice to her malady of zigzagging, and I fully despaired of this telephone conversation. To be sure, a doctor should not let his patient medicate for himself. But must he not have his ear to the ground or to the patient's chest to hear the faintest reverberations which may help his own insight how to medicate?

Yes, I almost despaired in my long-acquired faith that the truly potent inspiration should be to me the "inner universe" constellations of those for whom I was to create a future setting of many years to come. In this case, it was clear that I must have wrongly mirrored those deep-down motive powers.

I kept on puzzling about what had happened since I had seen Mrs. O. so content before the color samples in the almost-completed house. She had observed it in all its stages hundreds of times during this year of construction. Now she said she could not live in it. The most important rooms would have to be radically changed into different positions and different relationships to each other. The fully equipped kitchen with its plumbing installations was to be on the opposite side where the master suite had been, and all these nightmarish transformations would actually have to be made now. It looked like a frantic last effort to undo everything, turn the clock back. Tearing out all the structural walls and the plumbing installations, rough and finished, was fantastic. It threatened another construction period of a year. This poor woman appeared almost raving, like a patient in a psychopathic ward, struggling not to be forced into the treatment room. I remembered how gentle she had been the last time I saw her on the hill, absorbed by merely visual harmonies. The thought flashed through my memory that immediate visual impressions, and especially color vision impact, may enrapture sense-sensitive persons so much that all other hidden soul conflicts are momentarily at least overcome. I took heart and asked to meet her and talk things over with her peacefully.

Although she said she never wanted to see me again after my bribing her with color, I decided to go there and at least reach some conclusions on my own failure. After all, this house was indeed very neatly built, and on the most wonderful site anybody could wish for, I persuaded myself.

Meanwhile I spoke over the telephone with the contractor, with whom I had had no contact for many weeks. He told me that he had just returned from a sanatorium, where he had been recovering from a nervous breakdown. He said that he would not, under any circumstances, make those changes, and that they would be absolutely crazy. His despondency and unwillingness perturbed me still more. He had been with the

O.'s for over a year, and Mr. O. was also in great despair. We all were, in fact.

I still suspected a great overrun of cost. When I asked, the contractor gave me a complete breakdown. I was flabbergasted. The cost had stayed below the budget in spite of all the irrational behavior of the owners. The man was a pearl of a contractor—but now he was a nervous wreck.

Once more I went up through the fruit orchard and found Mrs. O. alone in the house. She practically closed her eyes and ears, and again showed the utmost resentment. She repeated reproaches that this house, and I with my compliance, had wrecked her. Suicidal as I felt myself, I listened. She went on ranting about how impossible it was to manage this house and garden, both of unwieldy size. Not having grown up on a farm, she would have to depend on help. One of her children was still an infant in arms. How could she keep this place clean, on a mountain where the wind carried great masses of dust from unfinished excavation and planting work, with one maid after the other leaving her in spite of the best pay because movies and dates were so far away. Here she was in solitude with her small children, trying to manage an unmanageable estate, way out in the sticks. I had overcome and enticed her, a babe in the woods. This house was not designed for a woman like her, who was unable to handle such a novel, difficult situation.

I meekly mentioned that her husband had wanted all this and had often lauded me for my plans. Here she broke into a real rage.

"Yes, that is how you men are! He lauds you for your plans, but he drives off to his business in the morning and leaves me in the lurch, alone every day—every day"—and she turned away not to show her frightened, despondent face.

Now she spoke as a woman against un-understanding men, of which I was one, sharing with her husband the responsibility for her misery. I was deeply moved, away from all anger of my own, to a sympathy with tortured human beings, advised, unadvised, ill advised. Suddenly it overcame me. I saw that she was right, after a fashion, and truly and beyond any doubt unhappy. This was not the played anger of a person who perhaps does not want to give due credit and compensation or even draws self-assertion from blaming others. Here in this beautiful spot I saw one of the most genuinely unhappy persons I had ever laid eyes on. And I had surely contributed to it by worrying about wrong things like expenses, overlooking the true problem, and comforting myself all the while that I was pleasing her by following her directives and what I misunderstood as whims.

At that very instant I began to see the affair in an entirely different light. For a year Mrs. O. had tried to halt her fate. She could not do it. Her husband really had failed her by his superficial aspiration to live as a country squire on a hilltop in an ambitious and sumptuous house, ridiculously large and inaccessible for domestic help or helpful neighbors. He had successfully implemented his unsound scheme through a first-rate craftsman-contractor who finally went into a psychiatric waiting room himself. The contractor had completed a large house at a very reasonable figure and with exquisite skill. All this had been a surprise to me, and made my warnings seem ridiculous and ill taken. The possibility of direct failure on this score, which never occurred, had monopolized my own brain.

On an entirely different score, this man's marriage was ruined, not because he failed in his technical and financial plan, but *because he succeeded in it!*

I, on my part, had failed to see where the real precipices threatened, and had become quite involved in feared flaws of execution, false fears which never materialized. Thus involved, I completely missed the human issue and never sounded the necessary warnings; I should have heeded the woman's subconscious but obviously rising anxiousness, which proved quite justified in the end. Too much concerned with building finances and technicalities, I had overlooked her human maladjustment to the entire program, which, as I saw it now, had caused all her indecisiveness and pale sleeplessness. We were all engaged in a mistaken scheme that unfortunately succeeded. Her earlier happy marriage was really developing toward a spectacular crash. Planting and transplanting is almost a worshipful act in anthropology, which does not deport itself as mechanistic.

I prayed that time could somehow heal the situation of this woman. But how could it, with all hopes invested in a big home beyond salvage, a home containing sufficient of her choices for her to love it, yet threatening her self-confidence enough to make her hate it. All their money and credit was now tied up in this house. The thing went round and round in my head like a creaking mill wheel.

In flashbacks, I now saw that Mrs. O. had most consistently shown trepidation, but I had never even come near to interpreting it properly, nor had I tried to relieve her well-based anxiety by advice to her husband, which in turn might have hit the target. Instead, I had only helped him in his ambitious craze, and looked for ghosts while most obvious, real dangers escaped my attention. I could not wash my hands of it—instead, I buried my face in them.

Mrs. O. mellowed when she saw my own unhappiness, and she cried. I almost did, too. This beautiful masculine dream had surely ended in a woman's nightmare.

That I could prove I had done much more than I had agreed on paper to do, has never given me comfort. It was not difficult to imagine how the children would suffer from such a situation of friction between the parents, of a household which had proved too much for a hysterical housewife, a woman from town transplanted as a gentleman rancher's wife without the suitable stamina or means, who in defense and despair had turned to daily nagging and complaint. The O.'s had returned to nature, but they would not be noble savages or romantic primitives, nor would they find soul-balance. We were no longer living in the time of Jean Jacques Rousseau, Paul and Virginie, or Chateaubriand. A carport for three automobiles was necessary to exist here and not be carried away to a dead end in the sticks.

I faintly remembered the rural housing colony I had designed forty years earlier in Europe, the angry townspeople insufficiently turned villagers, and how architecture indeed can spread despondency and break marriages. On such occasions human beings blame one another, not their settings, which often underlie their tension, irritation, and fatigue. Human interplay is so dependent on environment—designed or misdesigned.

What is the future? I am certain that in our ever greater artificial density of population, we must somehow even more comprehend nature, comply with her, and remain faithful to her. The "huge property" may not bring us there, and is increasingly impossible in practice.

I had not helped. We had together, but disunited, barked up the wrong tree. Without overrunning the estimated cost, a splendidly executed design of an architect, with his dedication deflected by the wrong blinkers, an innocent paper project frozen into static reality, may impair and wreck lives, families, campuses, or communities—anything planned hopefully—if important underlying human issues are misunderstood or are beyond the "feel" of the designer. He can be a pest, a plague to mankind.

It was most comforting to me that I at least could recall many another case of luckier comprehension, when people projected themselves by contemplated building into their own future, optimistically and also worriedly. This is indeed an occasion, a time when one needs a friend and a professional of good will and insight, versed in life beyond mere specialist professionalism. He must be a conscientious human being, like a good doctor, who knows human vitality and debilities. He must know longings and how to happily manage the longed for. I have seen much in forty years of growing, but I have never seen it all!

No individual client, like the Joneses who very personally want a home, no group client, or community, like the city of Athens, building its sacred shrine, the Parthenon, can rationally or clearly in words fully express the needs of what is to be designed. The planner must dive through all speakable concepts into often yet dark bioreal depths.

An architect is not a "caterer to stated requirements"; rather, programs may blossom under his creative attitude.

For good measure he shall first and always act with devotion on a small individual scale, as does a family doctor. If in a case he diagnoses the given program, he should not by shorthand take it down as of nominal value. He will do that as little as an attentive doctor will occupy himself uncritically with the subjective report of a patient who also worries about his future life instead of accepting it on face value. One expects that he will look kindly at and through the one who trusts him and who happily does not stand quite alone on the wide field of general human clinical experience. There the architect learns and gains special insight, to devote it later to further and broader human tasks, to "the greater union," progresses to vast comprehensive vistas. Perhaps he is enabled ultimately to serve a whole nation, or mankind itself—beyond all the often imaginary and yet so perilous cleavages—into happy harmonization.

What we have in common with each other we can better feel emotionally, "on the go." *What makes us different* entertains our critical faculty. I say "entertains" because human brains characteristically distill enjoyment from criticism.

We all tend toward exaggerated pride and pleasure in emphasizing our peculiarities, dwelling on ethnic distinctions, our subtly diversified creeds and geographical distances to the next island or the other side of the railway track. This is a constitutional trait, feeding into self-assertion, and deepened by continuous social conditionings and clichés. It severely hampers the chance of world peace and dwarfs the grand issue to see the ecological continuity and unity of the entire woods.

If anything interrupts human homogeneity it is far less nationality—Japanese, Eskimos, and Zulus, north or south of Dixie—but biological individuality, even within our single family, with stomachs of very different volume, shape, and position, and windpipes of remarkably different diameter, and so many oddities of variation. Union used to work only through long tradition or enslaving force. But happy fitting individuals together, by greater penetration into their significance and essence, may be indeed the main future task after a "renaissance" of individual pursuit has proved no longer in the cards, as little as small sovereignties in warlike clash.

Instead of giving the greater union peaceful consideration, we keep on worrying and warring about states' rights and liberation of nations which are even willfully constructed. Human rights have much more of an individual biological base. This humanism of what we add to the earthly scene moves always again, and more so, into strategic position. On the globe, on Main Street, and at home our building expression shall shift from frozen tokens of conflict to monuments of promising cohesion.

From a Past Battlefield to a Future Cosmopolitan Scene

Queer paths lead through barren wastelands to unexpected greening, branching projects, and to programs which develop broadly and astoundingly beyond their original scope. A program is the first small, dry-looking seed or perhaps somewhat colorless cocoon, out of which, quite suddenly, a miraculous butterfly unfolds—the spirit of a building. I have found that so throughout my life, from my beginner's years until this day.

One summer, when I had already succeeded to a point, I was invited to give the keynote speech for an industrial workshop at the University of Arizona in Tucson. It seemed indeed a pleasant privilege to be as helpful as possible in a development area of our own. Mayors and governors were present, gathered to further the state's industrial development. My remarks about not forgetting people and nature as being also close to the core of the issue were received most favorably, and one of the journalists in the audience, John Riddick of the Tucson *Daily Citizen*, then courteously invited Mrs. Neutra and me to take a trip through the desert to the Mexican border.

It was a Sunday, and it happened that I could not return an early telephone call from Washington before we set out.

While driving past the Saguaro cacti, Mr. Riddick, an intelligent young man, told me much of himself and his background; he was a graduate of the University of Virginia and had done postgraduate work at Columbia's School of Journalism. I interrupted an interesting conversation and mentioned my need to return the East Coast phone call if there was any chance of doing so in the midst of this wide arid desert. Mr. Riddick remembered a Texas cowboy who years ago had settled some miles off our road, and had established a ranch, hanging on to civilization by one lonely telephone wire. Kingsley was his name, and also that by which the Bell Telephone System had baptized his isolated exchange. We swerved off the road and soon found the rancher, wearing a vast broad-rimmed Texas hat. Stolidly chewing tobacco, Mr. Kingsley guided me to the telephone. While he had a gin outside with Mr. Riddick, and Mrs. Neutra had a more ladylike ice-cold soft drink, I talked with Washington, three thousand miles away, and learned in short order, amazed and catching my breath, that I was being considered to design the Lincoln Memorial Museum, as I understood, on Cemetery Ridge in Gettysburg, the battlefield where the great statesman had delivered that grand, short, wistful, and prophetic address. In a flash, before my mind appeared all the humanity of that often saddened man who soon after was to die by the hand of an assassin, and at once I thought that this should not be a battle monument, but a shrine of the American nation.

I came out walking on air, put my arm around Riddick, and

bubbled, a little out of breath, "What do you say to that? I just heard from Washington that we might build the Lincoln Memorial on the Pennsylvania battlefield where Lincoln's memory still resounds, and here I am from Los Angeles—actually, I should say, from Vienna—in the middle of the Arizona Saguaro cacti. Imagine, a Lincoln Memorial at Gettysburg!"

I expected Mr. Riddick, and possibly Mr. Kingsley, to kiss me on both cheeks, not to speak of my wife, but I got quickly chilled. The man from the *Daily Citizen* looked me over from head to foot and then spoke gravely. "Do you mean to say that we are going to spend the taxpayers' money to commemorate the defeat of the Confederacy?"

For a moment I thought he was joking, but he was in deadly earnest, and I remembered in a flash that he was a Virginian. I had heard that Southerners were still fighting the War Between the States, but this was a clean-shaven young man from Columbia University, not a white-mustached colonel.

"Defeat of the Confederacy!" They had not told me any such thing. They told me over the telephone that I was to do something on the order of a memorial to Abraham Lincoln, at a hallowed grove of old trees, a museum and a reception center for many visitors to one of our national parks. Before my eyes was tall Honest Abe, of whom I had heard Carl Sandburg talking in Taliesin, the man who had carried so many worries on his lean shoulders. I had had no idea that there was any dynamite in this project and certainly considered Lincoln a safe and glorious subject in this land of his. Quite suddenly I saw this assignment again with an entirely different background. A quarter of the nation might be against it, and many were probably less calm, educated, and cosmopolitan than this sad young man in front of me, whom I had come to like as so many Southerners before. Amazing what changing visions I had lived through in the last five minutes since that telephone message!

Mr. Riddick angrily wondered what I was to commemorate. He burst out with a tale of the military genius, and more than that, the gentlemanliness of Robert E. Lee, all that my young friend from Virginia had learned in grammar school about the shining strategic prowess of this hero. I gathered it was to *him* that the memorial should be dedicated. I remembered an architect must respect cerebral dynamics and read the old tracings within a soul. The client was here a whole nation which had long carried the word "united" in its name, and believing it, I was stumbling right at the beginning of my project, only a few minutes after the job was before me.

Meanwhile, Mr. Kingsley went on chewing his tobacco and, as from today's Texan empire, considered himself neutral while he watched Mr. Riddick, who looked so depressed, and several times seemed to grit his teeth. I felt with the sufferer, and placing my arm around his shoulders, I said, "Let's get into the car and drive on."

I remembered lush, beautiful Southern lands.

We traveled through the peaceful, silent desert. It had been there a long time, long before any Civil War, and far away from battle noise in Pennsylvania on the other side of the continent. How everything, even the most distant, gets close together in one human brain. I tried to think how to calm Mr. Riddick, who was driving on in sorrow and anger. Suddenly I felt melancholy myself, realizing that my 180,000,000 clients were not unanimous. What a complication to start with! Mr. Riddick was certainly no oddity. And no client should appear an oddity to his architect. In my heart I thought that Gettysburg, in spite of General Lee's courageous staff and men, had not been to himself a display of happy strategy. I remember my own military days and thought how heavy a battle pack is to carry uphill on an early July afternoon when three hundred pieces of artillery are belching at one from a higher ridge in front. And I remembered that an invasion army always has a good deal of dysentery and cramps and bellyaches after drinking water from strange wells and living off the land, which often means eating stuff one is not used to. I had heard that once when visiting Gettysburg together, Eisenhower and Montgomery themselves had had doubts whether the commanding generals at the dawn of that fateful day had really merited glory for their plan. I could not think so much of heroes, but rather of the many who in that messy situation long ago were doomed to bloody disaster. What was left of it? Old soldiers' boots and pistols were excavated from that battlefield and placed in a museum dedicated to their courage.

I did not say any such thing to Mr. Riddick. The Southerners may have fought like lions, but they had long and from many sides magnanimously been offered the sop of being heroes so as to bear a chivalresque defeat more gracefully. To me all this seemed a sanctimonious cliché, and I wanted to think of something else and more, which in the late light of today would speak in their favor. It would justify a historical truth in honor of which I was to build a monument. I said to Mr. Riddick, "Maybe I know the South—I mean, what meets the eye. I have traveled much with Southerners. I have had the honor of being a keynoter down there as well. In fact, I spoke before a large crowd of Gulf Staters only a stone's throw from Jefferson Davis's last dwelling place in Biloxi, and they gave me a big hand. Awfully nice people." He said nothing.

"Let's not talk of heroes," I went on. "I am not a militarist, and for sure, civil war, however fought, grieves me deeply and doubly. In the future all wars will have to be crammed under the tight blanket of one civilization with unequal bedfellows. But at close sight all will be brother killing brother. Do you know, I believe something truly very precious was lost to the United States when General Sherman marched across the land of the 'rebels,' with his famous boots trampling down the living and the past. Let me see how I can express it to you. I really ought to be a stranger to it all because I was born in faraway Vienna. Nevertheless, that was once the capital of almost a world on which the sun did not set, and I feel at home when my profession takes me to Mexico, Manila, Lima, Brussels, or Madrid to serve on some construction or give some advice or planning ideas. You know, we Viennese are cosmopolitan under the skin, and I believe we are also known for a certain urbanity that permits acclimatization and fast assimilation, in spite of a little left-over accent. Don't forget that it needed many nationalities, quarrels, and conciliations to make the Viennese.

"I believe those Southerners of old, too, had an unusual power of assimilation and quite a little capacity for heart-warming, maybe with strangers and savages who unhappily arrived haggard and in chains after an awfully rough voyage. I have recently seen La Gorée island, off the coast of Senegal. I have sketched a slaver's waterfront establishment, from the dungeons of which Yankee captains took the miserable black cargo into their holds for the painful trip to Charleston, now so lovely to another sort of tourist. Somewhat later, Yankees became terribly touchy about this black deal and the sons or grandchildren of their partners, the cruel Arabic slave hunters in Africa, have now, too, a lot of scorn for 'imperialistic commercial penetration.' Liberty has found so many strange advocates. The crusades of world history were occasionally quite soiled."

Mr. Riddick kept his eyes on the road and stepped on the gas.

I paused, then I went on. "I'll tell you something which comes to my mind. When I was six years old, my mother read me a story out of a picture book, a children's edition of *Uncle Tom's Cabin*. It made a deep impression on me, and I was taken in by all the characters. There seemed to be only a very few really bad ones. There were bad and good people, as in any other country. A lot of these scenes—black Eliza with bleeding bare feet crossing over the icy river—stuck in my memory, as did a wonderful little white girl who died, to the grief of her father's Negro slaves. I cried when my mother read it to me.

"Now, a few months ago I was driving through the Colorado desert, somewhat like this one here, and when I landed in a motel in the evening and, yawning, started to undress, I saw a couple of books on a shelf. I opened one, and there it was again—*Uncle Tom's Cabin.* Sixty years had passed since my mother read it to me from a German picture book. This time it was the original in English. I began the first page, curious about how much I remembered, but suddenly I marveled at how much I had misunderstood essentials."

The story started with a Mr. Selby, a plantation owner who is in financial difficulties and must sell some of his slave stock to keep above water. He is conversing with a slave dealer and describes a fellow called Uncle Tom, who is a wonderful, loyal worker, dependable and good to have around. He also is a good Christian already, although only three years out of the bush.

Here I stopped abruptly. All these years in America I had subconsciously nurtured my dream memory of "Uncle Tom"; when I first saw a kindly smiling Pullman porter of the Pennsylvania Railroad, I though I saw him, and this picture remained in my mind. I had completely overlooked that "Uncle Tom" had not been a Pullman porter, but had been a "savage," or at any rate a man from far away, who was only three years from the original tom-toms, but had already and incredibly fast become a good Southerner and, after a fashion, a Westerner. I suddenly saw the miracle of the amazing assimilation which that South of plantation mansions—as bitter critical Northern writers had to grant—achieved along the Mississippi in Louisiana and along the James River in Virginia. Being an architect—but one, surely, without any particular leanings toward quaint classicism—I had nevertheless immediately felt the uncanny convincing power, the assimilating capacity of the scenes in New Orleans's endearing Le Vieux Carré—so different from those in Detroit, where nowadays the long-free colored men and women may immigrate but never seem really to become "Detroiters." Why was it different with these

Negroes brought from the bush to become slaves of a distant civilization in a foreign land? Why was it so much easier for these utter foreigners to establish roots in the South than in the "free" North?

"Yes, we lost something in that Civil War—the South and, with it, the North," I said to Mr. Riddick. "Especially we should notice this quality now, when we want to lead the free world and need it most. The power of assimilation, of making foreigners feel close to us, is exactly what we should have." Even a great Northerner, a sensitive thinker like David Thoreau a hundred years ago, did not feel warmly embedded in his own bristling home civilization, and tried an escape to Walden Pond. Has our rushed, shapeless civilization become better since, or only more opulent on the installment plan? Everybody is free, but where does he find a free parking space for his soul? The United States once had a tradition for that sort of thing, but, it seems, more in the South."

We were driving along through the Saguaro cacti, and Mr. Riddick was silent. I went on: "Now we need it most, *warmth enough to assimilate*, like that Old World capital of Vienna, where Czechs, Poles, Croatians, Romanians, together with German-speaking Tyrolese and Styrians, were made to feel at home around St. Stephen's and between those fine pieces of human although palatial architecture which were owned by a few, perhaps, but loved by all as their home-town own. Here we have the cash, and are trying to influence and somehow run a whole free world. We should have the goods, too, to assimilate souls from quite primitive areas—countries in development—and from many highly cultivated ones as well. Such things cannot be done with force or dollars alone.

"What kind of a world do we offer ourselves? How does it look to others? I have been all around the globe in many places, and you know how they look at us? *They look at us exactly as Southerners looked at Yankees!* To most of them, to their critical or revolutionary papers and funnypapers, we are the ever-foreign, ridiculous, uncouth traders. I cringe when

I think of it. They do not know anything about how many splendidly educated, sensitive, and cultivated Americans there are. They see only our feet on the desk and a dollar-wise, brutal ignorance and lack of cultural sentiment and attitude. Perhaps we lend them money or leave travelers' checks, but otherwise, 'Go home.' I know, and you, an alumnus of such an erudite place as Columbia University, know that they don't see us quite right. But we are not speaking here of hidden truths and unappreciated qualities. We speak of how the others see us, and how glad they are to make their coarse cartoons of us still simpler. It is a pity to find, from Caracas to Copenhagen to Korea, more doubters than friends."

Mr. Riddick looked up from the steering wheel and nodded gravely to me when I repeated, "Yes, we lost something when Sherman marched to the sea: To the outer world we all became just Yankees—you included."

"It should have been possible to bring things to a more conciliatory, cosmopolitan conclusion. The outcome of the Civil War and Gettysburg doubly seems a turning point and a danger point a hundred years later, when Yankee America' is said to dominate the world, and the warmer, more urbane Southern admixture of yore has been dissipated or has dwindled in self-conscious defensiveness. The Southern regionalism has now shrunk possibly to an embarrassed, spiteful introversion which breeds race hatred hardly in keeping with the true memories of the South. Beyond that, Southern consciousness leads, in the midst of all possible industrial progress today, only a very reduced existence in old antique shops.

"Here is something to bring before the world once more: The United States is wonderfully many-sided, many faceted, and has profoundly more potentials and tributaries than foreigners, who are limited by their own four walls, may dream. Our country, with its population stemming from so many, often lowly, sources, should rightly have the best empathy and in-feeling.

"Lincoln, I think, had such a feeling. If one has it, one can be born in a log cabin by a prairie grove and yet fit into the White House on the Potomac. There are many diversified modes of living, and lots of habitations less weather-tight than log cabins left around the globe, and one must be able to feel oneself into them in order to do good and achieve anything. It is strange that a Northern woman writer was able to find such a homelike feeling even in the Southern cabin of Uncle Tom, so recently arrived under the deck of a bitter salty Boston slaver. What do you think? What do I know? I am a foreigner myself."

"Yes," answered Mr. Riddick, "but you are not a Yankee." He took a deep breath. "If anyone, you should build that memorial of and for reunification." He looked at me very seriously and yet happily.

"I thank you from my heart that you, too, now give me this assignment or gladly grant it to me," I said. Gazing out over the desert at the thorny cacti, I added thoughtfully, "I really know so little about these historical facts. I may be guessing awfully wrong. Lincoln finally did win a war, yet I believe he did not feel like a victor with a boisterous capital V. Nobody ever will be a full-fledged victor again in history to come. It was a precedent of wise humility for all the future, and for the whole split-up world, in need of union. Perhaps an architect and a building could help to signify the world's historical multinational necessities on a shrunken globe.

"I would like the museum exhibit sequence to have its climax in a dimly but solemnly illuminated 'rostrum of the prophetic voice,' to be seen from the auditorium which we shall build, as well as from a tremendous, gently rising outer gathering ground, in the shadow of Ziegler's Grove, the historic oak woods on Cemetery Ridge. Our building should play itself into the background, behind a pool reflecting the everlasting sky over all of us—and it will not shout out any novelty or datedness.

"Every year a great statesman from one of the nations of this earth might be invited to speak here. Even the hostile nations from the cold-war regions must have men worth hearing. As long as tensions need relief, a guest from somewhere, provided he tries to represent the best of humanity, should speak before thirty thousand people, there where brothers killed each other, about 'What Shall Not Perish from the Earth.' Lincoln's own words were not empty sound. They could lead to a long series of serious yet hopeful speeches throughout the centuries. The guest of honor might be India's vice-president, the philosopher Radakrishnan, who kindly talked to me in his house at Delhi; it might be Chou En-lai, if he bristles less than usual, or a man like Doctor Heuss, the former President of West Germany and a friendly patron of architects in the service of mankind—I know him; he always seems to find the right tone and conciliatory thought—or it may be someone who has not yet been born. The future is long, and it needs to be long to fuse and harmonize human beings.

"You know we are the species with a split lower end, on which we used to amble through the landscape before we got motorized; but we also have a split upper end—we are, with a touch of schizophrenia, the most brain-endowed, brain-burdened and -biased bunch that ever trod the earth, badly in need of unification, in need of peace within ourselves.

"We urgently need festive occasions to make peace and impressively celebrate union. We can commission an architect to provide the framework and setting for it. I should talk about this with the United States Secretary of the Interior, to whom this project is subject. Perhaps he can even step in on behalf of our international relations, where our Secretary of State sometimes is not so much of a success in calming the waves." Later, I did, in fact, use exactly the same words in speaking with the Secretary, and he listened graciously, as did our clients guiding the national parks, which all together represent an undisputed issue of humanity.

"We haven't money enough to seat thirty thousand people in American Seating Company plush chairs, but they can stand on a lovely landscaped natural gathering ground, somewhat like the solemn forecourt of the Shinto shrines of Ise, Japan. The visitors can stand up for one minute and forty seconds. Lincoln did not need more time. They can listen standing up to a thirteen-sentence message, such as his, about the ideals of mankind, which must endure. Mankind is the Greater Union which must be preserved over the sovereignty of any one political area, be it now Indonesia or Katanga, or, as then, Maine or Virginia. None of them must be allowed to split off, trigger disaster, and become cause for mankind to perish from the earth. Profound common interest must live on among men. For vital survival, mankind must bring about the end of an ever more terrifying force of arms which fills the future with horror and makes tiny this old battlefield, and heroism, useless. The Greater Union has become even more significant on this shrunken globe. The same issue is still with us and will probably be with us for generations to come. Lincoln was not a victor-speechmaker; he was a prophet, and his text still resounds."

I had talked my head off, but my host-chauffeur gave me a friendly side glance as we caught sight of the Mexican frontier guards.

About a week later, Mr. Riddick wrote me. I showed the revealing letter of the now very much exhilarated Southern patriot to the director of our National Park Service and to the Secretary of the Interior in Washington, whom I wanted to see served in the more profound sense of a broad, cosmopolitan audience. Beyond all external mechanics, the emotional becomes in building a propellant and steering wheel. The sad memory of an internal and still painful rift could, by the erection of a monumental building group on a battlefield and through its new dedication, commemorate what mankind must preserve as a common aim of harmony. I felt that the building program had now turned into an almost sacred task, not only a harking back to the past.

Architecture lasts too long to commemorate grim hostility and narrow ignorance of the fact that we are in the same boat, rolling and pitching until we reach firm, common ground. Architecture belongs on terra firma, is destined and apt to help find in sound settings a lasting balance for human souls, for single ones and for groupings and masses of them. This is the greatest know-how to have and to commemorate while we build something around us.

In the future, when building programs may be prepared through research on 'functions' and 'operation,' and by feeding equations into an electronic computer, then a multitude of variable parameters in the field of endocrine biochemistry will also be observed and considered. Looking only at outside determinants, no answer may be hoped for. Architecture stems from deep inside.

Our Fateful Setting

Human Cities

For years America has proverbially been the country of industrial, technological know-how, of which so much could and does apply to community management. Mayors, city administrators, and councilmen are at least made conscious of this ponderous wisdom, and may read with some profit to taxpayers the informative articles on so many subjects of "utility" which month after month *The American City* and other journals lay before them. Utility and economy of maintenance are stressed above all in the voluminous "ad" section. Occasionally the beauty of a street lamp, a bridge or a sewage plant, or the landscaped setting of a playground may also be mentioned.

Yet, as a whole, our cities are not a success. Their appeal is mixed; what they have to offer is confusing. "Soul satisfaction" may remain in a few green spots or on their fringes, but does not permeate throughout; and sometimes the fringes are the worst!

My suggestion has long been that the "biologically bearable" and maintainable be our guide, even in the heart or in the underground of our metropolitan civilization, where in a few decades we might have to escape from the supersonic boom of ever-increasing air traffic. What is tolerable to nerves and what possesses form and pattern are indeed positive biological determinants.

Nature is man's precedent, the point from which he started and from which he has, over tens of thousands of years, first by simple adaptation and later by ever more complex modification, tried to derive the current shape and shell of his existence.

We ought to have done better, especially these last generations, since some of our best scientific brainwork has been devoted to pointed and systematic research on the significant subject of human organic make-up. But the biologist is not yet the most weighty spokesman, even in great, singular urban offerings like Le Corbusier's Chandigarh or Costa-Niemeyer's Brasilia, which the decisions of visionary statesmen conjured up—with excavation machines that I saw rolling fast over verdant ground. These new towns do show a sudden colossal will to form.

Herein they might be the "singular turning points" which we have already considered.

Newly shaped cities once may have been in contrast with dragging on, left-over situations. Now they stand out in the midst of the tedious probability mathematics of ever more quickly piled up accidentalism. But nature—we can hardly overlook it, and yet we hardly ever fully grasp it—has startling shape, and no unhealed accident in her workings.

From Infusoria to butterflies and on any organic bracket, there is form. We today know much more than any previous generation about this intrinsic quality of nature as to consistent conspicuous form, and so should dread what may badly conflict with its frequent yet mysterious function.

Brain physiologists, reviewing our urban scene, think of this burden of manifold conflicts when they speak more specifically of "arrhythmic innervation." Dr. N. Ischlondsky, of the here-somewhat-waning Pavlov tradition, has at any rate collected and published striking tables concerning "civilization damage" and misery which the daily irritations of amorphous urban life hold in store for us. The jamming and occlusion of the coronary arteries and inner circulation seem directly related to outer traffic jams and confusion.

Our Fateful Setting 319

Chaos has long been recognized as man's concrete enemy, contrasted to *cosmos*, the Greek word for universal shapefulness. What we have called simply or vaguely nervous strain is largely a product of lack of formal definition, shape and shapeliness, quite general in our urbanized existence, not only in the life of megalopolis. Our civilization and the indifference to form and its underevaluation has conquered the flat country, the mountain resorts, the coast, and will probably penetrate under the seas. There is almost no refuge anywhere. It tends, like a neoplastic cancerous growth of the late stage, toward a malignant ubiquity through metastasis.

Shapelessness is peril. I am convinced of this, through a life of health and sickness, the fluctuations of its vitality, and by half a century of professionally interested watching.

Nevertheless, we do little to change the situation, for the "good" reason, such bond issues threaten to fail, even if projects are involved that aim at keeping organics intact. Past investment is "more practical" economy, and so daily mix-up remains sacrosanct.

Yes, our reasoning must be formidably, demonstrably "practical" to convince voters. But there is nothing more practical than life itself, nothing more impractical and costly than impaired vitality. Nervous disorders are the most insidious and costly camouflaged health hazards—at least until the sufferer is spotted, properly isolated, and institutionalized. That is costly, but cheaper than leaving him to his own devices. Perhaps there are many reasons why fourteen million Americans—or is it sixteen?—cool their too-hot heels in psychiatric waiting rooms annually. One wonders where they parked the car!

But perhaps that is it! They did not find a parking place for their car, nor for their soul; at any rate, no self-parking place.

The world of today, dressed up city-shape, or non-shape, undoubtedly has her share in this trouble. A cannibalistic hostess on all her continents, she daily invites more guests for a meal. Human beings, maybe, are fed, but they also are consumed by haste, confusion, and din, and by the synthetic, reckless anorganic color collision of neon lights which scribble over the wholesome darkness of night, or, in the daytime, by a dizzy network of wires overhead in the pale smog. Once upon a time a blue sky and a distant skyline, almost touchable, were our daily comfort.

I am writing this in Los Angeles, but it might as well be São Paulo, or the mainland industrial zone of Hong Kong, or anywhere from the cozy Paris sidewalk café, near the bus stop veiled in thin blue stinging haze, to the suburb with oil heating—wherever molecules of exhaust gases from only half-invented "climate-control" devices settle into our breathing tissue and swell pulmonary cancer statistics. Professor Paul Vogler of Humboldt University, living under the pine trees of Grunewald, has all the data at his fingertips, but the practitioners have often other interests than to pay attention.

"Progress statistics" becalm and befog our minds with reduced infant mortality, increased longevity, the impressive rise in population and ever-denser balling of humanity in cities and on the planet. But what are the parameters and the correct determinants of vitality? What keeps mankind, and its capacity to create, alive, and what protects it against withering in its essentials or becoming altogether fossilized?

What makes places like textile-industrialized Ahmadabad, India, or some of the miraculously fast-reconstructed European cities, or the new Tokyo—of how many millions?—so obviously amorphous to the naked eye? This is the most adequate expression for what one sees when the limousine brings one from the airport, past infinite traffic signals, to most any town. Even when seen at the side of a tantalizing "freeway," with clogged exit, why does amorphousness, frozen or in motion, give rise to a feeling of hopelessness?

We have voiced our message again and again. Man has lived among clearly ordered or grown forms, has used *Gestalt* and imagery to express himself and give messages, long before he could count to three. We must do our best to remember this always. Even now, some Straits islanders have difficulty with figures, but none at all with images. Their village has shape even if they have no population statistics and cannot count their belongings correctly.

Unfortunately, as I have also often before pondered and ever again spoken of, in English, the word *figure* means *two* things: "number" and "shape." Shape is an ancient asset, of long-proven but sometimes almost forgotten necessity. It is prehuman, primeval, eternal. Yet it is now often discarded for impressive numbers, especially big ones.

Every ten years urban life will absorb many more living millions, if you then can still call it life, as it once used to be. There are then corresponding quantities of cars, passing intersections, and freeway interchanges, tonnages of exhaust material smogging our air, into which loom millions of rentable square feet of "usable" space. Billions of dollars and rubles pay for it and "make good" for everything that had not been thought out beforehand. Lots of proud numbers characterize our metropolitanized civilization of glorious multiplication and geometric progression—many hard "facts and figures," ever more impressive, from one fiscal year to the next. To Americans and Russians, and every satellite of theirs, big numbers are coveted and inspiring. However, basically beyond individual grasp, they have a depressive tinge mixed in.

Instead of offering a merely embarrassing and unfathomable mass and mess of things, biology pleases, as stressed in these pages, by shapes and shapefulness, shows memorable and often easily remembered events of morphology, of morphogenetic context of forms and functions which we often comprehend at first glance. Parts of the brain, perhaps not those "in front," are activated a fraction of a second earlier, and *play way beyond that frontal lobe of conscious "mental strategy" manipulations, concepts, and numbers.* But practically, of course, all parts of this huge billion-cell bell are rung at once, while in ourselves something occurs which we in simple words might call our emotional life—altogether the most touchy part of us, and very consequential to boot. It lends the sounding bell its wholeness, the right tone and the true timbre.

Even—or, I should say, especially—famous "economic facts" seem in this light of *bio-events* less "hard," and about as resilient as brain tissue. Those facts fluctuate no less than other very dynamic organic happenings in us which go with all these cerebral events of fact evaluation and motivation. That last word, motivation, means clearly that logic is a byplay, not at all in a monopoly situation. Certainly it is so if we look at what building improvements we make or fail to make, letting old wrecks stand endlessly between shiny prides.

Shape is not sophistication but elementary. It must again be recognized in its relation to essential emotional swing, tested as a foundation of human life, and revalued, upgraded. The design of our man-made setting cannot and shall not foot on a formula mistaken as utilitarian, like "form follows function," as if form or shape were a follower, a hanger-on, something static, a rigid cart behind a dynamically pulling, functioning horse in front. Nothing of the sort. We have already rejected it repeatedly.

What in nature *precedes* some other thing? There does not really exist a linear causality of the one which stems from the other.

What has become a cliché of "cause" now is second best by far to everyday—not to mention to systematic—observation of the researcher. Form has a pronounced dynamism of its own that everyone may see, touch, hear, and follow.

A firefly zigzagging over the nightly meadow is not at all a static form. Its very motion constitutes a shape; like a dance, this is a locomotor shape, enriched by flickering illumination and intimately fused with it. Such illumination is in no way utilitarian, like headlights shining on the road on which one drives. It is a patterned, exciting message received by the she-glowworm. The two meet and mate, and characteristically the light goes out at this point. It is the shape, the *Gestalt*, that has brought about the fireflies' most vital function—the propagation and survival of fireflies. Utilitarian explanations for bird calls, with their auditive shapes, or for butterfly wings, with their visual charm, are nineteenth-century old hat. In those days proud utilitarian fanatics claimed to know the rhyme to everything. We do know now that in the long future ahead of us we simply must find a different rhyme, and *in our cities we must in no event be cluttered with chaotic sensorial litter*, which is such an obvious perverse detour from nature and the natural. Biologically intolerable, it must not close in on us. The machine-made setting, though technically feasible or commercially exploitable, carries no automatic insurance to be also, in shape or otherwise, biologically bearable. When this occurs here and there, it is merely accidental; more often, it does not.

It is easily proved that man cannot well exist in shapelessness. Laboratory experiments might demonstrate this, and that "large control group" of past human existence has proven that throughout history and prehistory man's habitat has been endowed with comprehensive shape in its components and in wide-span composition. As a matter of fact, shape in organic nature preceded man himself by billions of years; again, it is not just a beautician's frilly fashion. Further, history is here a test, and should be a warning.

In convincing the "practical man," we do better not to speak of so vague a topic as beauty. The jurist will also shrug his shoulder about framing or enforcing laws to create or protect it in the community. Neither the law, nor the legislator, nor the businessman, nor the censor or art jury, nor the politburo will save man unless they listen to the *naturalist*, well informed on contemporary terms, but able to translate elementaries into their language. Do not let us forget that the kindness which calms resentment comes from satisfying, gratifying insight into the nature of things human.

Once man was credited with five senses. In recent decades modern physiology has been busy discovering ever new sense endowment and receptors; we have spoken of it, millions of them are now known, but the "sense of beauty" has ever been revealed. We must again emphasize it. It is merely a figure of speech. It is vague and unprovable. Perhaps rightly, it does not, and never will, convince those practical myopic adversaries who set a forest of naked telephone poles in place of trees or in the speedy way try to squeeze extra revenue out of a square foot of real estate. Also, being myopic is a physiological condition to be understood, and sympathetic understanding seems almost an equivalent to Christian forgiveness. But beyond this, additional constructive steps might be required. This became clear to me before I reached the middle of my life.

Some such thoughts had by then grown and turned ever-recurrent to me. The conventional separation of mankind into "tasteful" and "purposeful" people has little meaning, physiologically speaking. Even within ourselves division is fictitious.

It merits repetition: By our nature we are whole, not split into various "departments." The same is true for the natural precedent around us. It would be hard to say where a tree stops being "utilitarian," "functional," or "operative," and where it starts being beautiful. The mere question seems ridiculous.

In attempting to weigh beauty versus utility, or vice versa, we merely create a false issue, an erroneous "strategy" to handle things. And if we contrast these two abstract "frontal-lobish" ideas, we simply stay precariously away from biological realism and from much more *molten-together* natural reality. Any such dual view on what is unity is unnatural, and only leads us into a blind alley of boring or pernicious clichés. It is best to break away from such fruitless habits of thought and come to ourselves, to the essential and most lasting in us.

A special "beauty committee," mayor-appointed as usual, an art commission with practically no budget, will mean nothing to the other important departments of municipal management which have to deliver prescribed "tangible" goods. They are by charter obligated to do so, but no intelligible legal clause authorizes them to "waste taxpayers' money on any wild long-hair ideas." Above all, they have no one on the payroll who would be qualified to suggest or carry out such ideas with any possible promise for convincing returns. For example, a harbor commission in a seaport town like Hamburg, San Pedro, Vancouver, or Athens would be charged with providing facilities for shipping that is needed commercially, increasing yearly gross tonnage exported, imported, and transferred from ship to rail, keeping the longshoremen and the shipowners happy enough not to wreck business by too-sharp dispute or competition, and performing cargo-to-freight and freight-to-cargo conversion and commutation successfully. If anyone demanded that the commission pause and see or symbolize a harbor as the busy, monumental gateway of a city or country—or, as in the new Cape Town, foreshore for a colossal new business-bristling continental area—and ask that it spend money on wide-span or even detail "beautification," the commissioners and the port manager would gasp in astonishment. After all, the taxpayers would justly become irate if port engineers engaged in expensive aesthetic improvements of which they would probably understand nothing, anyway. This is not the business the engineers are trained for; they are specialists, and proud of it. And specialists are the trademark of our "scientific age."

If a city owns its power and water supplies—well, its motive is obviously to furnish current and water at a neatly cut rate. The department concerned will be staffed with engineers who have passed civil-service examinations on their competence to design transmission lines and water reservoirs. How could such a department permit itself to make the power poles less "ugly" or to consider transformer cans in front of bedroom or living-room windows as anything else than good practical items?

That a large open-water area in a dense city means a priceless treasure of free space over a million-dollar mirror, reflecting clouds and hills and trees, all seems poppycock to some. In the fulfillment of its duties, the water department is an agency which, as an administratively endorsed obligation, keeps on its staff a nursery superintendent and plant expert. He must plant inexpensively maintained ground cover on slopes in order to firm up their surfaces and minimize erosion. A million automobiles pass the "lake," the waters of the reservoir, enjoying a glimpse of it in the daily tedious nerve-wrecking hour of commuting. Commuters would love to refresh themselves a moment by this vista, but enabling them to do so would be a rare, even crazy, afterthought for a municipal agency. Each American automobile on that lake road, fins or no fins, is designed for a large fee by a swanky industrial designer. The water and power engineers, on the other hand, have no legitimate budget for aesthetics. Even if this reservoir is only considered a "plumbing fixture" right in the heart of the city or a residential district, a tiny fraction of compensation is paid for design talent invested in it compared with what our plumbing-fixture manufacturers pay designers of their flashy lavatory fittings so that they can produce a more elegant bathroom than their competitors. The cost of a full-page colored ad to attract us buyers greatly surpasses what can be done aesthetically on behalf of us taxpayers, uninformed as to what we really need to shout for, as being "entitled" to it. And now we can hardly depend on kings and czars or even dictators to get cities in which one can live, satisfied in all one's senses. We must learn within a democratic setup to strive for this wholesomeness and agreeableness.

We could go down the line and touch on all the municipal departments and agencies, from public works to district school boards, which deliver pupil-hours in big numbers but for years could not well afford three different cans of paint to provide a little color variation; more than one paint can is simply too complicated and "unnecessary," and the same thing is true of tree maintenance or an increased janitorial expenditure if the blacktop is interrupted by ground cover, which, to please nature, ought to be kept growing. When birds drop something on the tops of teachers' parked cars, that can readily and radically be taken care of by cutting down the trees where birds may perch. All this I have painfully lived through; it is a nightmarish reality. Once I threatened a school board, in case they should actually go ahead and cut the last trees, that I would commit suicide and create a public scandal by leaving behind a letter of explanation for the newspapers. It worked—the trees are still there, and the birds in them, too.

School-desk units, on the other hand, have become much more "shined-up" and beautiful than they used to be. Their tilt, however, may not be adjustable, and the little close-to-the-desk fixed chairs may not swivel to fit two eyes wholesomely to a slanted paper on which to write without straining, so that the malpositioned children sometimes grit their teeth. For this, then, we have a school dentist to conduct a check-up and compile statistics, while ignoring causes.*

If there is a dualism and duplicity of utility and beauty, the latter surely comes out second best, and no art commission will help it. But to raise children in psychologically satisfactory surroundings and not have them warped by sensorial privation, by confusion and irritation to the eye or the ear or the nose or to inner body senses, all tied together with intimately related organic functions when they sit on the school benches, is worth while. To have them look out during intermissions onto a green ground, or into green foliage, or play in the shade of trees—instead of the board spending money on well-advertised aluminum blinds or electronically controlled awnings

---

*See also Richard J. Neutra, *Survival Through Design*, in which the author quotes Darrly B. Harmon, on whose Research Commission on School Design Mr. Neutra has been invited to serve, together with noted scientists of a nation in perpetual difficulty to finance such investigations without the subsidy of interested industries.

after cutting the trees and putting low-cost blacktop or glaring cement where there used to be grass to be watered every so often—all this worry is not just "idealistic." It is quite practical. *Proving* it is the problem! Yet fantastically difficult proofs have been found by science, provided the conviction exists that an entirely new vista will open once proof replaces opinion or even hypothesis.

Instead of discussing a contrast between the practical and the aesthetic, we must enforce the natural and therefore reliably durable. Is art being good to man as a whole, rather than long-hair interference to a numerical computer? Is it sustaining because it's natural to us? Even amid the ringing of a thousand cash registers, the ring of nature can still be discerned. It remains fundamentally necessary, and must be heard.

Man has been conditioned to form and molded by consistently shaped nature for a million years—and city administrations, if one looks at it right, have the job of administering those biologically bearable conditions to the citizens, young and old. In itself, this is an extremely practical consideration. Nothing is more so, and we must never get too tired to say it to ourselves and to others over and over again.

I have called it *biological realism,* or *biorealism* for short. It is reasonable, and, once more, "a must," to strive and profit in design from all current scientific information, and from actual application of it. Can an austerity program, for instance, turn against a program of our natural *"form necessities,"* which have been scientifically authenticated? Any walk through the woods or watching of "wild life" proves their endless precedents preliminary to our existence. The real "wilds" are not there at all, but in the midst of our downtowns, clogged with messy disorder. Having lived in the midst of "progress" after being born at the *"fin de siècle,"* at the exit of the nineteenth century, a time of grandiose progress in America, I came to the following conclusions.

First, we must agree and educate ourselves to admit that

there is nothing more practical or realistic than wholesome life, and for perfect realization our current sensorial and nervous loads must be relieved, in substantial measure, of irritation and clash. *Coute que coute*—any price will be a good bargain here. Our intake must be reasonably screened. Drug and food acts protect us only against dangers which threaten us when we put something into our mouths and swallow; but we have a vast multitude of orifices in our millions of sense receptors, and a creeping peril endangers us through innumerable channels. Perpetually it filters into us. Energy transactions and substances enter through our skin and mucous membranes, which are not merely barriers, but permeable as well. Surely there is entry through our eyes! Anybody can see that! Any "selectivity screens" which nature has, more centrally, grown in us give way under the pressure of an avalanche of visual horrors.

Second, we must not, when franchised to vote, just sidestep an essential issue, leaving it to a powerless "art commission." How can we "let George do it" when he is only superficially, if at all, informed about the facts of life? Beyond all bacteriology, a terrific propaganda effort was required to get cesspools moved away from wells. Combined, their excavation would cost less, though!

Third, each municipal department can and shall gain citizen support for the manifestations of its activity, if it is convincing. The citizenry must be won over not only by a balance sheet but by a performance acceptable to senses and nerves. Intramural public relations are indeed often better furthered this way than even by great technical accomplishment, unfortunately understandable to a few experts only. The *brain dynamics* of *communicating necessities* are behind and at the base of all democratic achievement. Also, the out-of-town national and cosmopolitan prestige that can be gained, and the emotive lift connected with it, will benefit a city; examples are the recently completed, magnificently art-enriched aqueduct terminals in Manila and Mexico City, municipalities so much less wealthy per capita than comparable cities in our country.

What is produced should also be, as to form, impressive. The American businessman is now brimful of this faith; the American *citizen* lacks it miserably.

Fourth, we must, after an understanding with the mayor and the council, prepare for a detailed talk with the city attorney to see how the legal obligations, authorizations, and qualifications of all city departments can be revised in order "to hold water" in the eye of the jurist, and we must find ways to enlighten the taxpayers and voters about what is really "good" for them. Or should, perhaps, the voters educate the legislature? What comes first—the chicken or the egg?

Among the goals of the revitalization of cities will be the organic psychological satisfaction of the inhabitants, which could be distilled as a clearly recognizable end result of the prebudgeted physical "improvement," not leaving human nature starved like a forgotten stepchild. It is our genuine, legitimate darling.

Presentation of the issue for municipal legislation must be clear, logical, and universally appealing—not comprehensible to only a few. It must carry along the many, for a majority vote. And the anticipated satisfaction will begin to find credence, first in important elemental sensorial matters which can be proven, as I said, most easily, often in laboratory experiments which simulate the proposed conditions.

Later, we might develop minute techniques to check into more complex inner repercussions of outer city planning features. An interesting array of telling physiological factors and an evaluation of varying determinants is ahead of us in checking and insuring in the future what otherwise might be depreciated as "only" intuitive, design. Variables and their categories within our skin appear, for most architectural tasks, to find less attention than the external ones. That must be revised.

All conditions around us alter kaleidoscopically, yet our capacity for adaptation slowly drags behind. We must supplement its measurable slowness by design. The grown and breathing individual must remain recognizable in the midst of abstract and concrete artificialities and synthetics.

A vast woods or even vast crowds are easier lived with than the metallic herds to be parked around a football stadium.

"Face-to-face" is noticeably different from "fender-to-fender." The first relationship has anthropologically a conditioning period of hundreds of thousands of years to back it up, and "ontogenetically" it is the earliest social experience emerging for an infant smiled at by its mother, WE HAVE GROWN FACES AND VOCAL CORDS BECAUSE THE SUPRA-INDIVIDUAL CONTACT IS PART AND PARCEL OF OUR INDIVIDUAL LIFE.

To search for elemental environment factors (interlinked with social ones) to which a human organism already has an adaptation of long standing, and fit them into our design, applying in all this the insight of the biologist, is our safest principle and approach.

This book, too, has turned into the autobiography of an idea, not rounded out like the great Sullivan's, but perhaps of a tight cluster of ideas and observations, grown together. It has started with the child on the apartment floor, abandoning itself to a lot of prime experiences which will always, even subdued, sound into the more vocal parts of the human life symphony.

Especially when we face complex and novel situations—of which there are more and more, faster and faster—we must not, in our enthusiasm for the novel and again for the "logically consistent," disregard the treasure of elemental tracings in our memory, nor adaptations which, properly honored and used, could better sustain the new design than can mere rationality. Fashion, novelties, do not count long here. Every city, by comparison with them, is an eternal city.

And again—we cannot state it often enough—form and shapely organization are more than frills. They have been well recognized as a survival aid by the naturalist, and no animal behaviorist questions that fact today. We have been sure it would be foolish to shoot rocket pilots to the moon or man a space platform without testing the sensory impacts and new organic adaptation problems of the conditions to be met. In *Izvestia* a Soviet engineer lengthily explained the crew's need to have a lilac sprig to take along on a space platform, or in a rocket capsule, to make it more homelike, and solved the problems of keeping the sap circulation going under those strange gravitational circumstances so that withering can long be delayed. In a sterile anorganic universe we are not only sentimentally attached to what is organic—we are ourselves of its vigorous but also tender kind. So, in space travel, one must have that flowering twig along from dear old Earth, and must also preserve a few other organic things en route.

There is indeed ample reason to assume that satisfactions, internal benefits, and strains and stresses produced within a human being do not have to be spectacular to be significant; they can be most insidious in a subtle form, and cumulative. The sufferings of those daily strap-hangers in busses, fast curving to the curb to stop abruptly, have something to do with the total organic response, set off in the inner ear by our acceleration sense, also known as our vestibular sense of gravity. Such impacts reach throughout our whole indivisible totality. The special receptor, the cortical organ, is only the starting point of a complicated chain reaction, which branches out until somebody with badly disturbed "enteroceptives," or intestinal nerves, must give up, might even have to vomit.

The same sense organ of passengers going out for a demanding workday in the crowded subway is quite differently and less severely affected by the much more gradual deceleration, acceleration, and the reduced centrifugal stresses that an electric train imposes, on its carefully traced tracks, with only large-radius curvatures. (Of course, here as there, the breathing air in a human crowd becomes rather polluted, which has another series of consequences).

The elevator, even in a sixty-story office building, provides still gentler treatment, provided it does not stop on a lot of floors. Our weight, so familiar to us, to our inner senses, grows heavy at every start, becomes light when the elevator suddenly stops.

There is so much more to it than meets the eye or ear. A good deal happens deep inside the outer ear. Of course, the visual impacts all around us might be more obviously significant and also pathogenic than we are prone to recognize.

There are few people starting in the morning on a trip to the moon, but many millions embarking for downtown. It should not be unfair to test their organic risks and realize that even from the point of view of dollar-and-cent realism, it would finally pay to understand clearly that fantastic losses must be faced through most costly irritations and premature fatigues.

Yet the cumulative effect of ignorantly glorified progresses which bump into each other and bring organic life into that daily jam cannot really be measured in money. Nevertheless, the biological wear and tear cause a downgrading of productive power, and maintenance costs are staggering in these, our know-how metropolises and modernized old towns, whose design often shows no awareness of its essential threats to vitality. This could be proven by many examples of well-known subjective feelings of being sick and tired of it all.

Beginning with the elemental, we would have to proceed to a research of the more complicated. Likes and dislikes of city fathers, the property or tax interests of their constituents, are only some of the influences the shaper of a city has to consider; but, unfortunately, they are the most easily emphasized and organized to oppose more provident measures. There are so many factors outside of public focus.

We have already hinted at it: microbes had first to be discovered, so that anxiety would force appropriations for grand-scale sewage disposal plants. Today, millions of dollars are spent on these miraculous establishments, at which I look with the hope that fear will bring us to voting for other scientific necessities, even if it costs money. It seems we need such fears to spread in order to see human biology win in financial and fiscal politics. Smug confidence statistics do not truly support vitality. All the effect they have is to create a threatening passivity in matters which call for urgent action. Artistic points of view concerning form have no currency value, but art in the design of our setting can provide relaxation in the midst of turmoil, in the focus of the urban scene of our civilization. The progress of biological insight can be brought to bear to convince the citizen who votes and to lead him to understand how to choose.

My life experience has been that we must usually face a long uphill struggle in the midst of parochial, old-fashioned, grimy, slow, still nineteenth-century-influenced mentality. Modern science has recognized many vital needs beyond the grasp of that old-hat, crude and limited, mechanistic brand of materialism. We do honor the fresh *avant-garde* of a hundred years ago. But today researchers have forced us to have a less flat-footed concept about what once was called so neatly and clearly "matter." Taking the lead in this struggle, and the initiative alone to tackle the problem with all expert circumspection employed, could be a feather in one's cap. Every smallest single step forward has its consequence; an individual in the right spot at the right moment might mean much beyond all estimated probability.

The mayor and the manager or director of practically every department of the city will slowly have to become part of this day and age, in organic reality and not merely technically.

In all this popular acceptance of an attitude is decisive. Public relations and community support are always necessary and bound up with the soul satisfaction of democratically activated voters, who, after all, are people, and who demonstrably do have human needs for form and shape. Mohammed, a successful reality-politician if there ever was one, said, "If I had two coats (and we have more in America than in Mecca!), I would sell one and buy white hyacinths for my soul." Mohammed had long hair pending from his chin. His beard has been recorded as auburn-colored, to go well with white blossoms. But this practical man must have had more in mind than a mere decorative color scheme. In his time he was amply shown to know what makes a human community vibrate in enthusiasm, and, with a fast schedule, go into a wealth of sweeping, constructive cultural action against shallow commercial interests and a *status quo* which had become impossible even to them. In old Mecca and elsewhere even the practical people must agree: The best customer is a live customer, who keeps vigorously surviving.

Life in empty space is killingly lonely, but there may well be organic vacancy also in the midst of our crowdedness still to come. There is no automation which enables humans to survive the din and turmoil of more and more inventive but unassorted "progress," indifferent to form, shape, pattern, and harmonization. On the contrary, it takes principled, co-ordinated attitude and skill to sustain life amid those our snowballing artificialities. *Psychosomatic design*, a devoted, well-fused understanding of the subtle organic in us, *implemented* by the tough technical around us—yet not overrun by it—is our hope.

Physiology is a term which the Renaissance man, Jean Fernel, physician to Henry II of France, first used four hundred years ago. One must comprehend it, he said, in its normalcy, if one wants to fend off morbidity in its smallest beginnings.

I believe that the Paris of about 1550 A.D., when Dr. Fernel lived, was more calm and less pathogenic than Manhattan today. In order to prepare oneself for the twenty-first century, one needs badly an attitude which is run by sound bio-principles and more cautiously tuned to perilous circumstances in progress.

A presentation of problems for urban regulation must be transparent and generally appealing. It cannot be comprehensible only to a few, but must carry along with it the majority and their sentiments. Thus it will find faith. After a fashion and forever we shall also live in an "Age of Faith." Such faith and sentiment are capable of being translated into primary patterns of action which can be practically proven beforehand. This is what we of our day have faith in—and also that a good deal could be tested even in the laboratory.

Such instructive experiments would have to isolate *principles* for an automatic convincing power and for a following in daily life. Conflict of sensorial situations could be imitated in a simplified manner, and certain inner repercussions of this or that planning decision searched for by watching large numbers of "subjects" exposed to its result on their inner function caused by outer arrangement and shape. Also, the *opinion* of human subjects could be polled to learn and sift something useful for the outer scene itself.

At least for carefully selected setups, reality could be sufficiently simulated so that one would not have to blunder into later real losses of staggering investments.

Pertinent physiological factors, and the evaluation of changes in effective determinants working on them from the outside, should be demonstrated. This will supplement and control intuitive planning in days to come. The variables which very much exist within our own skin seem, so far, for most planning propositions of this nature, to find much less attention than the so-called external problem which has *no meaning without our reaction to its solution**

Instead of merely saying that people get nervous in downtown traffic, one can test a man at the steering wheel of his

---

* Discussing a research program of the "Richard J. Neutra Foundation," A. E. Parr, senior scientist of the American Museum of Natural History, just told the author, while this book was in press, of his thought to use the wide motion-picture screen for visually confronting subjects with simple and complex environmental constellations, and from large control groups, reach conclusions.

automobile—one can then be more enlighteningly precise about it. Males and females in reliably large numbers, from adolescent hot-rodders to slowly reacting senior citizens, could be checked.

Testing could be quantitative, starting from the rate of respiration and pulse, up to the blood pressure, the percentile increases of blood-sugar content and a great number of endocrine-determined secretions. Some of the survey might be done from second to second, while the motorized guinea pig approaches a left-hand turn, in his subconscious or even conscious "anxiousness," and while he finally and actually then accomplishes this turn in the traffic jam.

On an attempted shopping trip in the midst of bewildering downtown traffic, someone with a sinking heart looks for a parking place, or, full of impatience and disappointment, he simply has, one time after the other, to miss a change of light. Everything, and especially cumulative inner damage to us, is an "urban affair," and is the biochemical, biophysical research field of the future. How else, within reason, should one tear down and redevelop wholesale an entire cityscape of ours, with billions of dollars of taxpayers' money? Don't we quite willingly experiment and find out in advance what physiologically will happen to someone on that distant space platform?

Our ancestors endured with comparative calm the accidents of life in the jungle. They did it with a fine balanced sensitivity, developed or evolved from tens of thousands of years of mneme, the engraving experience which preserves itself through long periods and achieves such inner balance. What we, too, need is balance and calmness, but it will not just happen; it will happen less and less! We won't survive, waiting so long for it just to come to us in our fast man-made trouble. Mohammed had to come to the mountain, do something about it, to have his enlightening revelation. Probably he had a safe inkling of it before he went. We have to come to grips with the massive speed-up of our anorganic civilization, try to weave into it, design into it, what is found and proven organically bearable. There is nothing automatic about it, except our extinction if we just wait.

All engineered conditions around us change fast, kaleidoscopically, and our adaptive capacity drags behind slowly.

Being informed, anticipating and aiming, intrinsically belongs to the human make-up. It is our survival equipment. Wild shooting around, mere prolific inventiveness, will wreck us.

Words like *mission* and *conversion* sound morally accented, but have their clear physiological "underwear" which can, and deserves to be washed, periodically, upon inspection, and must remain evaluated to its core.

Missions should be clean-cut for comprehension, not only cleverly conceived. Wherever today cultural effort and daily routine are transplanted, especially where built and planned accommodations are transferred to new areas, *it always concerns human beings*. Their "humus" must be most cautiously and without haste cultivated and "dug under," not carelessly spilled or disturbed; otherwise, it doesn't work. For my meeting human nature and even serving it in distant places and in different languages, I had a good deal of incidental apprenticeship.

To find examples through years in my life, I review before my mind the building procedure of housing colonies for thousands of families. I think of settlements in which I had to anticipate later development, had to dive as well as I could into a prognosticating creation. The situations were so different in four projects in Spain, from Sevilla to Saragossa, and of others in Boise, Idaho, in central and southern California, in Arizona, in Italy, in Guam of the South Seas, and in Germany.

Some of these housing projects aimed at permanent resettling, initiated by a socially concerned housing agency.

Others were for the armed forces and other special cases, which did not propose financial or biological *rooting*, but fairly temporary establishments, so to speak, of *long-term transients*, which in our world today are generally so much more characteristic than enduring rootedness.

Even so, there is always a soul-anchoring to be dealt with, which is never just for the moment, but has its mnemic lifetime extension. Children's souls grow a good piece in the two or three years during which their father, a petty officer, is stationed at a naval base, and lives, together with his family, near an elementary school furnished by a nearby civilian school board which, as on a recent occasion, was gracious enough to give my layman's name in beautiful lettering to that education facility for the up-and-coming. I was deeply touched. If surely I must be modest as a name-patron of a school and as a would-be educator, I try hard to recognize the deep responsibility of the architect in these matters as far as immediate and nearby surroundings of children in their conspicuous growth period are concerned. At any rate, *the school becomes linkage with the old settlers in the neighborhood* and, in this case, a tie between the military and the civilians. This is very necessary; otherwise, there develops so easily anywhere a two-camp tension and mutual resentment, reflecting on young minds.

Military personnel is, one could say, "commandeered," directed, and shipped to a point of world geography. The man has to go according to his pledge; his woman does not. In a measure, she volunteers. She has met him in a trim uniform and married him without knowing where, for heaven's sake, he was going. They do not love the place particularly; it is a military station and a fate to be accepted. The man flies a bomber to Tokyo on duty, and in the home the dust flies into the living room. The Army Engineers, in their simple geometrical grading plan, may have insisted on a Euclidian regularity of street network, simplified in tracing and leveling to place economically all appropriate underground utilities as an appendage beneath. In fact, the whole thing, however simply-conceived, or even simple-mindedly, still sounds controversial to the guardians of taxpayers' money and is hard enough to get off the ground before a Congressional appropriation committee "on the Hill" in faraway Washington, D.C., bristling with utilitarian austerity. The bulldozers have obediently ruined the topsoil for all organic phenomena. It will take years until something agreeably greens and grows; meanwhile, the housewife who married the trimly dressed officer, labors day in, day out, cleaning up her parlor. She becomes despondent on the "base," emotionally sick, and it might be small wonder should the armed forces be troubled by a high divorce rate. This is what, as a community designer, I ought and want to battle against: the divorce rate in general, family friction, depressiveness. I feel that a man, in cases of matrimonial tension, is for months ahead not quite himself. In his state one should not trust him to fly million-dollar equipment; taxpayers beware. But meanwhile the engineering economy continues to direct its bulldozers, perhaps, over matrimonial graves—which are not so fully private affairs as they may seem. A multitude of individual discomfort becomes public concern. Looking across the political curtain, some observers feel it might ultimately be decisive in the cold war world contest.

Even so, I have been deeply happy in the midst of all frustration to watch young couples and families, all decked out for the occasion, move in with really shining eyes when the admiral from headquarters had made his TV speech and cut the ribbon at the inauguration of a new housing project. It is always a heartwarming occasion to see something accomplished for human beings, even if it has to be a little wholesale.

As "housers," we were given a chance to study an entirely different and unusual sort of transient population when we were occupied in northern Arizona with the settlement of employees for the National Park Service at the twin parks of Painted Desert and Petrified Forest. As always, we familiarized ourselves with the needs of the women and children who would live in happy solitude near these nature parks. They love it. The man has chosen this profession and this life in undamaged nature; here they will *voluntarily* pass many years. Their income is surely not so great as to bribe them to stay on here if they didn't like it. They are thus ideal clients of an architect who himself feels nature bound; and their children, young and half grown up, are ideal clients, too. What a difference from any "commandeered populations," which deserve deep sympathy, too, but another kind of help.

Over this interesting wasteland near the Painted Desert blows a wind of thirty miles an hour, and sometimes it rises to a velocity higher than that. I was glad to find an encouraging archaeological and anthropological "exhibit" nearby, a prehistoric village of long-disappeared aborigines who had experienced and mastered this very same climate a thousand years earlier. Visitors, and I, particularly, now ponder their long-vacant townsite. Such strange and yet telling relics are heartrending, from Uxmal in Maya-land to Angkor Wat, or in the huge abandoned Mogul city, Fatehpur Sikri, once much more pompous than Pompeii, and four hundred years earlier, yet humanly ambitious like Brasilia or Chandigarh of today.

The Puerco Indians here had lived first fully underground, apparently due to the wind. I assume that when agriculture and maize were imported, they began to come up out of the earth and to build their crude stone-masonry walls high enough so that the ring-shaped settlement could protect a small maize patch against the wind, which would evaporate and blow away irrigation water in a moment. In the wind-shade, with air movement reduced, not all humidity would be dispersed. They needed it.

Only the "kiva," the council room of the elders, remained underground, perhaps in memory of the mode of living of the ancestors; but perhaps, also, because full wind-stillness is best suitable for thinking and counseling. At any rate, also in our fusion bomb future, cool-headed thinking about what next on the surface of the earth is best contemplated in deep-down cool underground shade!

This crowded way of settling in mutually protective surroundings, with inner courts to hold water for planting and plants, became the prototype of our design thought, borrowed from the prehistoric desert for the much-in-demand desert of today. It became a settlement which demonstrated how human beings more than a thousand years later could be guided by climate to similar ideas and similar ways of housing and living—a striking example of human constancy, man-nature constancy. And here, appropriately, it took place in a national demonstration nature preserve.

It was all very different from the real-estate speculation psychology, which in these days of overpopulation everywhere in the world leads and ever more will lead supernumeraries or surplus mankind into ever more arid areas: in northern Peru, Mesopotamia, Northwest India, even Kalahari and Gobi—everywhere population contingents flow where none have ever been before. Always, and especially in the western American arids, "the large piece of land which can be bought at low cost" becomes the bait to move men into the wide open spaces. It is quite natural that this should be so to land-hungry trans-settlers, coming from fertile but dense and tight "old countries." Yet it will not be simple to manage living the new life with irrigation-gardening. Though bought with avidity, land remains three-quarters unused, often abandoned to barren trash heaps of corroding children's toys, gardening implements, and cut nursery cans of plants which were planted but never grew.

And this again means that the chance is being passed up or missed to change the climate through landscaping and management. With united forces, just this could be slowly accomplished, but it will never be if the land is distributed wantonly and without regard or know-how of what to do with it.

When I first came to California, merely the green strip along the coast of the Pacific was settled. The desert inland, the "wasteland," was the playfield of the devil. Now it is added to the realm of the realtor. This whole vast territory is studded with industrial and military establishments, rocket-testing stations, and what have you, and housewives have resigned themselves to follow their men who are occupied here into this barren land. Every family has two cars which, glittering, then later fading out, stand around in the sunshine. And father, mother, and kids hang on a telephone plus its pole, standing against the sky like a sore thumb, so that from their grand property they can talk over the distance to other grand-property owners of half a neglected acre or more.

It is wasteful sprawl all over again, only more so.

Our colony at the Petrified Forest in Arizona was differently conceived and motivated. A wind-protected plaza, surrounded by school, multipurpose room, and visitors' center was made so wind-still that I could have shallow waters partially cover the ground—as they had sixty million years ago!

Small relatives of the giant horsetails, which once upon a time grew to looming heights and are now petrified to marvel at, could again be planted, together with certain club mosses which also once were found here. In a pool there was even to be a living lungfish, so that one could show it off to the visitors and give them the chance to grasp what this region had been like so long ago.

Weather is a good peg to pick to tie our today to how it all was yesterday. For me, the climate long before, and then again after the glacial periods, became in this national park settlement and estate the common denominator of explanation and interpretation. A nature park is not easily understood by ignorant "unnaturals" who come visiting from town. Perhaps one can interest them in how organic life has made its adaptation and assimilated itself to changes of climate, or how in general everything is tuned together in nature. Ecology—the balance or the equilibrium of the natural scene—is instructive and strange to us at the same time. It is strangely satisfying for anyone who comes from the wide unbalanced urbanism of our badly rocked civilization. He comes on a visit; he, who has begun to believe in chaos as man's fate, is restored.

Always there is, or should be, a new colony somewhere outside the old settling place; a tryout group to regain naturalness, to overcome the perverse which created those sinful towns, first mentioned in world literature, after the Creation went on the rocks of urbanism and had to be started all over again by courageous Noah. It was perversity which also, according to this tale, made those cities perish with all their inhabitants, without grace or charity, and in spite of all negotiations and dickerings of the well-meaning patriarch to save them. Against the perverse, Creation won. It had to be preserved.

Now those sinful towns have been recently rediscovered, with considerable salt water over their highest towers. We may assume that even Manhattan, with ten feet of salt water over the top of the Empire State Building, would be a calm and peaceful place.

Perhaps it can be done without salt water, but we have not yet learned how.

The housing colony for the State of Hesse, in West Germany—one of the three extensive but related projects I have worried about for "Bewobau"—was designed from a distance, in California, yet adapted to the pine and beech forest ten auto minutes south of the greatest airport of Europe, at Frankfurt. It has all the elements, in the good and in the best sense, to deal with and take a position in the employment market of a metropolitan city and an ever-growing industrial region. There is an urge to escape and flee from urban life and mass pressures in the direction of natural preserves. Simultaneously, these preserves are endangered by overpopulation which in the future becomes even less avoidable. All this seemed to be part and parcel of the background of such a task of settlement. On the railway from Frankfurt to Darmstadt, hundreds of trains morning and evening move the commuters to and from the urban centers.

Then there is also another need; namely the one to have this forest settlement tie itself to an adjacent little old town and to make and maintain sociopolitical peace with it. It all must be done with human skill. Accommodating men, women, and children by planning and building is a perpetual human issue. My previous life, as sketched, with all its byways, had slowly prepared me for it, at least somewhat.

The little town in the neighborhood is Walldorf, a community of almost eleven thousand, itself now fast growing and situated at an ancient railway stop, where a tired small depot is filled morning and evening with smoking newpaper-reading commuters. The town itself was founded in the last year of the seventeenth century by fifteen families of Waldensians, French Protestants who were told by a minister of King Louis to get out of France. They were not sent into gas chambers, but simply out of the country. Humanitarianism seems to have prevailed around 1700, and the *landgraf* of Hesse gave them a refuge south of the great commercial town of Frankfurt, to start a new life in the forest. Miraculously the forest is still there today, and, thank God, is well defended by the forest administration in Darmstadt—otherwise, it would be gone.

Bewobau, a building and trust company in Hamburg, acquired many hectares of this forest land between the great highway and the suburban train track, and had the idea of sending their directors to visit me in Los Angeles. I was to offer the Germans, who were getting together in this new employment market from all parts, after having escaped from East Germany or elsewhere, something improved beyond custom. I was to set an example in this quickly growing Rhine-Main triangle of industrial and population development. Each plot of justly valued land and the house were to cost together some $25,000 each for hour hundred settlers. But money figures are of such dubious significance, when seen over a distance. Life perspectives, slowly acquired, can bridge much.

From Brandenburg to Schleswig-Holstein and Hesse, where I have worked simultaneously, I found Germans neither more nor less conservative than other human beings. It is extremely difficult to give ethnic groups ratings in this respect, but mnemic conditioning rather similarly signifies everywhere human brains. Equal but opposed to it is their curiosity, which already erupted in paradise, and then illuminated even the exit, where an angel with fiery sword stood to let them pass for a trek into an unknown and hard world outside, wide open for curiosity seekers.

The urban life of Frankfurt overflows first in the direction of the Taunus heights, where, too, as a stranger from the other side of the globe, I have had occasion to make plans for a house with pleasant mountain views. South of Frankfurt, however, there is no distant vista into lovely valleys, but only one upward into a green umbrella of pine tops, screening off the swishing and droning of jets as they arise from the airport, flying into the wind and off to all the world, which they will reach in a few hours. But it is also a screen against the rare, sparse sunshine in the southwest, or from any direction, for that matter. There is a filtering in of daylight, but the south orientation of houses is more or less a meaningless custom under the broad shading conditions. Not a few imaginary "sun windows," but diluted daylight through a multiple of wide openings will have to make for the necessary vitamins. It is not customary though.

And perhaps here we have reached the main topic. Everybody is, a priori—to start with—organically entitled to habits. It is not judgment which sits on the coach seat right in front under the brain roof, but habit, or rather prejudice, preference, *partiality*, which the scientific observers will have to localize a little bit lower down, in the subcortical centers, in the "dien-cephalon," legitimately midway in all our thick skulls. This preference must be gently dislocated and quite slowly transmuted whenever a plan attempts to substitute the new for the old.

The German press chose to print broadly styled news items, as if I now would be an importer of blessings and wizardry, of American technological wisdom, of stunning economies and simplifications—of course, I would do all this in short order. It was certainly well meant and flattering, and, indeed, I was flattered to see how the value of my commission and assignment was interpreted; but, really, things lie quite differently.

I didn't come to Hamburg or Frankfurt because I could prove Americans different from and better than Germans, who were ready to learn from them through me. Quite the contrary, I came because, apart from minor wrinkles, Germans, and human beings in general, are rather, and in many respects, exactly like Americans. I could come with an expectancy of success because I had learned over here, in long effort, how to *overcome the same prejudicial preferences*, and *to transmute them into what is to follow*.

When I acted as a missionary forty years ago in southern California and later in so many different parts of the states, ever again anxious and worried local realtors spoke quite the same language as their brethren in Wiesbaden or in Walldorf. There, a quarter of a millennium after the persecution of the Waldensians, still live approximately 180 "Cezannes" and 250 "Jourdains"; they can't even speak French any more, but are proud of precedent. And they would have the job of accepting the new-settlement neighbors. One might think that they would find an easy way to do that, drawing on their own experience or that of their ancestors; accepting newcomers is an age-old problem. It goes with transplantation, just as the sun will set after every day of hard work.

The true value which I carried to Hesse, to South Africa, to Pakistan or Brasilia, or to any place on earth, was merely that I had earlier learned to know human beings in slow transmutation. It is this knowledge and experience which can also be applied south of the Frankfurt airport. Once more: my utility, my usefulness, does not derive from the fact that

Americans are mentally different, but, on the contrary, from the fact that we humans are similar in our organic make-up and hence *similar to each other in our growth processes and impediments.*

Said the Californians forty years ago, "We cannot live without a cellar; one has so many old things, you see, and food to store, and Coca-Cola cases and what have you."

The Hessians today say, "One must also lay in things for the kitchen—potatoes, preserved fruit, coal, and coke."

"Coal and coke? Haven't you any oil heating?"

"Sure, but what if an emergency suddenly occurs? I believe I told you we even want a place for a wood range in the kitchen beside the other new one—perhaps not a wood range itself, but at least a place for it—one never knows!"

Only loving comprehension, not shaking of the head, has helped me with the Californians who wanted cellars, or with the people in the German woods.

I visited many basements in early California, just as later the cellars of Hesse. Some of them were neglected, some clean, most half or three-quarters empty, or full of dusty trash. In such cases there was a lot of apologizing on the part of the housewife.

Well, cellars, then, are accepted by me as unavoidable for the moment, although now it is quite possible to install heating devices on the ground floor. But never, at least, would I admit to those cellar-wishers, "that a cellar doesn't cost anything, anyway." Both in America and in Europe I figured out for them the contrary; quite in vain, of course.

We then open the entry door, and a *windfang*, a wind trap, a space before a second entry door, is most certainly "a necessity." But I have built in cold Montana and in northern Iowa (so that Canadians could see it), and they, too, left out the second entry door. Yet here in mild Frankfurt it wouldn't do, says the realtor, shaking his head. It is evidently in the head, not in the climate.

Our Fateful Setting 349

Let us then go on, with our empathy, and see an entry hall, provide for it, of course, smallish; and it will be even smaller because so much space is taken out of it for wind defense and by the cellar stairway, "which must be enclosed, as it is an eyesore." And then there is, of course, also cramping the space, a full wall and a door between the entry hall and the living room.

First, you see, there was a draft in early California, and later in Hesse, just as in Schleswig-Holstein, even in the Ticino, Switzerland, south of the Alps, where, "in winter it becomes really quite cold, you know." (Doesn't it in Montana or Spokane where I have built? I wondered, without saying it, to avoid arousing doubts of my good will.)

But then, one also wants and needs privacy in a living room, so that not everybody who comes in at the door—let's say the milk boy, or any sort of delivery man, can immediately hear everything that is said in the parlor. I must think of the many people under Hitler who said the wrong things in the living room, were overheard by the milk boy, and landed in concentration camps. Nodding the head is much better in building than shaking it if one is inclined and ambitioned for reform, and perhaps only a little psychiatrically gifted for it. *Tout comme chez nous* is a better expression than one of amazement. Progress of mental adjustment is by nature not meant to be rash or rushed.

How then comes progress over people? It must be planned patiently on the basis of cerebral research. In this field valuable information is necessary. A strategist knows his theater of operations, where it is passable and where it is blocked. And a brain surgeon knows where and how he can cut without too serious damage, and where he cannot.

I described the procedure to the real estate man and his assistants. First let us in the basic building leave out everything that is worth leaving out, all that should be discarded, but then on occasion give in, until finally and happily everything is tested as to magnitude of resistance, or becomes in a measure acceptable. *Comparison with similar experience elsewhere* is next to the prophetic gifts through grace, which descend on the seer from above. Yes, comparison of human beings around the globe is the nearest to "knowing the shape of things to come."

Let us try then and leave out the *windfang*, for example, after we have placed the entrance-door on the lee side, or in the wind shade of an in-corner. Let's try it once, but for the real-estate salesman to fall back on, let us have a *windfang*, an inner door set, *neatly prefabricated*, and a ready stand-by, so that the thing can be seen by the purchaser in the store-room, as an example of our good intentions. Of course, it will have a very legible price tag. It becomes an *alternate*. In case you want this, ladies and gentlemen, it's an "accessory"—also according to price. It is at any moment obtainable on short order. There must be no sales impediment. The developer cannot afford that; not even a sales delay, since he must pay every day much interest on what he has borrowed.

Now, this entry hall, in the model house at least, opens directly into the living room—what do you say to that, Mr. *Immobilien Expert?*

The assistant of the realtor is called that in Germany. When he is taught to pull aside a beautifully woven warm-feeling curtain, one has an even still more beautiful view right into the spacious social quarters, and through it, onto the wide glass sliding doors, and in turn through them a glance into a green circumplanted garden patio, with lovely flowering perennials. They are pleasingly color-harmonized with the curtain.

"Very nice, but you know we want to have privacy."

Fine. "Here you see the prefabricated panel partition, with the door a part of it; all as you like it. You can immediately give the additional order—delivery time four days; price: sixteen hundred Deutschmarks." No longer a peep into living quarters—for now, at least.

The cellar, of course, cannot be delivered later; that won't work, and, as conceded, the sale of the house cannot possibly be endangered by something lacking that cannot be quickly added. Therefore, as we said, there is a cellar here. But the cellar stairway is not a concealed, cold, winding, utilitarian concrete contraption. It is an open, appealing, representative oak stair, with low-cut blond ash plyboard railwalls, and it doesn't need to be concealed. On the contrary, it is charmingly suggestive and seems to lead down to a playroom or a bar. A mirror wall doubles the entry hall, in the model house at least. All of it is a calculated attempt to convert the mind to the right faith, by a friendly bribing of the senses which are its outward tentacles.

Saint Ignatius Loyola was the great reflexologist, or soul-knower, of the sixteen century, and an expert in dedicated missionizing.

"Very, very nice; still, there may be a draft of cold air from the cellar."

"Of course, you can have here, too, a prefabricated wall and a door for enclosing that stairwell, price: fourteen hundred Deutschmarks. You can have the stairway separated from the entry hall, see! So to speak, get it out of sight. I mean, separate it. Well, for my part, I am for integration if it can be done. I don't really recommend segregation, but you can do it easily if you are already so used to that kind of ugly stair, and to covering it up. If one wants to be unwashed behind the ears, of course it is better to conceal it. As mentioned, fourteen hundred Deutschmarks extra, three days' delivery, any time.

"And the main basement cellar room, I must tell you, can be made marvelously comfortable. See this indirect illumination and the wood paneling here. Of course it is a model house, but you know you can order all these things later; they will fit neatly. It makes something really useful out of the cellar, which actually we have planned as a later expansion area; one lives for a long time in a house.

"The main room down there can be very neatly enclosed, lit up and furnished, as you see. No heating ducts are visible behind these easily put up, indirectly illuminated shelves. Arid that direct stair from above is really an asset, and it looks fine by itself. Tell me, do you really want to conceal it? Are you quite sure? And at fourteen hundred Deutschmarks extra? Can we perhaps look for some better use of that money?"

Then there is the carport, well open into the woods.

"Oh, no! We have a new Volkswagen. We want that car better protected." Germans are much more recently automobilized than Americans, who are old hands at it, and so more carefree.

"The people in America in recent years..." "No, I really want a closed garage."

"Well, you may see the front and the back wall here as a prefab; the fold-up door comes with it; everything obtainable at once, but naturally at additional cost. All of it is here, marked in our catalogue, page fourteen, Garage Fronts. We are particularly prepared to fill such special orders."

And so the "subcortical" realm, the emotional attic of the old Hessian or immigrated Silesian, reacts exactly like that of any other human being around the old globe, whatever the linguistic medium of communication here or there. Our readiness to serve individual aspirations and anxieties, sympathy for his personality, awakens in him a deep satisfaction. In the main it is sympathy for fears and desires, native or just customary, which throws a bridge for human beings to get together.

Let us say 70 per cent of the prospects may not get rid of all these fears at the first onslaught on viewing of the new. They would rather pay for this or that extra, but on one or another occasion the extras do begin to become educative, habit-breaking, and thus truly effective.

Similar extras for accessories are quite common in American automobile selling, in order to keep low the basic price of the car which is being presented, at least in first conversation, and raise it in the next half hour, bit by bit. Accessories are first gently and then urgently offered in proportion to the pocketbook thickness of the purchaser. One after the other is explained, presented, demonstrated, eulogized, in order to raise the profit. In this case we are using the same method of accessorial supplementation, *but exactly in the contrary direction.* All accessories are presented, without being lauded at all, and plus prices, extras, are being used as deterrents while they are being offered, in order to get the purchaser *not* to purchase! The purpose of the exercise is: Let the original clean-cut design alone.

So, let us assume that 30 per cent cannot resist their earlier custom of having the entry hall completely separated from the living room. This is thoroughly human, and thus easy to anticipate. But it is also human that these people will not stand still psychologically during the thirty-year amortization period of their house.

While they are paying off, they become acquainted with their neighbors, the Meyers, who have accepted the open spaciousness on first sight. The Meyer house looks bigger at every visit. You become worried and think you have probably made a mistake. Finally, after three years, you notice also that the Schmidts have had their prefabricated partition removed without difficulty, and the cellar stairway, too, has been made free and open, and they say they like the wider space. Two more years later you decide to try it, too; that is the way of the world.

One of the wall panels removed by the Schmidts has been put up in the cellar as a play table, where the children can sit by themselves, or they made of it a low occasional table for a cozy, pleasant secluded sitting corner where one can comfortably relax and chat, once one is out of the formality up there. One steps down the nice stairway, which doesn't look at all second class. It is astounding what the Schmidts have done with their cellar. Let's see—maybe we can do it, too.

So it goes. "One-after-the-other" is a totally natural pattern for brains and whole organic systems. They fit themselves to new things slowly, but resist sudden transformations violently. This I have learned in my profession of proposing new things, and it deserves to be understood by everybody, not just by experimental neurologists.

It is always good to provide and leave space in surroundings intended for the next thirty years, space for slowly sprouting afterthoughts. As a matter of fact, one could inconspicuously plan for them, *just like a real gardener who must know the pre-established pattern and future development of a tree* he is planting in an ensemble. He must foresee a lot of evolving.

All "sales tricks" are used only as financially devised steers for those to be housed anew. They are not real tricks, only friendly camouflage of the serious organic business of habit-changing. Conversion depends on it oftener than on magic revelation. By itself, this manipulation of prospects for a new life is way beyond superficial frippery. It is hearty insight.

The flexibility of the building concept permits another healthy adaptation at slow speed and a comfortable tempo in making up and making over minds. Soft music here cautiously follows the dancer. And yet many dances have turned out beautifully beneath the trees I love to build under, lastingly. It is all service to the person, service to the single individual, avoiding the *trauma of the organically too sudden.* It shows respect for nature, to give her leeway to grow.

Every chance of piecemeal change, every chance of avoiding shocks, is to be observed in the house as in the garden. Also there, "one after the other" is the need and promising program. Prefabricated screen panels come into use, around garden court and patio, varied in texture, color, and material, and help as screening panels and space builders for privacy and by concealment of visual nuisance. Together with varied plants and planting, they come into play, even in the smallest space, as instruments of individual expression.

Just this it is which signifies and offers physiologically sound and proven satisfaction, as it occurs already in prehuman, in animal behavior. Finding one's own individual spot has there certain very characteristic antecedents.

Personally—even the smallest space becomes larger for our "persona," our soul. It is not for the measuring stick of meters and centimeters to decide living size.

Over two meter-high partitions, six-foot enclosures of garden patios, one can look up slantingly onto the green roof of the dense high pine trees. This is in any case the only distant view in this woods, where straight ahead nothing could be admired except a driveway cut into straight trunks of second growth, and on it the prominently duco-finished car of a neighbor.

Whoever wants to become an architect must honor trees with an eye for their refreshing green; they are honorably constant and elevating, whether they stand beside or behind a house or spread over it. To make an end to them is sad, and here they fortunately already happen to spread over the houses to be.

As a young fellow I wrote in my diary of 1917, while many young men died in the war, something which I have found recently among old papers. Here are the fast-scribbled lines:

"Today I saw in the evening at the rim of our clearing, a fir tree of fifty years. She herself sees this nightfall, and the moon, for the last time setting behind the saddle between the hills over there, because she is already hacked on from all sides badly, and she will herself fall next morning at earliest. She stands ninety feet in her stockings—and is one of the last. Her comrades lie, skinned and pale, like giant asparagus on the slope. This fir has stood long in this spot, and tonight she tries in vain to draw her sap. Bark and inner bark and a good part of the corewood have been cut. It almost looks as if a light gust of wind might break down the colossal tree over me. I can say that sympathy with this tree, during the last short span of time before execution, melts my heart. In the morning come the lumberjacks, and the colossus breaks down. Crown and twigs swish and whistle through the air, the branches crackle and crash, just like the rigging of a ship's mast, cut in the emergency of a hurricane. Here was no emergency, but one suddenly looks, frozen, into the vacancy where for fifty years stood a green cone, the sound of the fall reaches one like the light detonation of a howitzer; all is over."

Howitzers detonated at that time frequently (it was in World War I), and they changed and ended much scenery and life. But this sharply observant remark, for which I found time at the deathbed of the murdered organism in the midst of a murderous time, seems when I now read it again by accident, characteristic of me; forty years before I thought of writing in a hospital bed my little book about "mystery and realities of the site."

Space-and-time around us are measured for the individual, operating in it every life moment by his inner nature. The land surveyor with his staking-out paraphernalia comes only a little before abstract Euclid himself, should he walk this earth; and the wrist watch he looks at is a more recent gimmick than his stomach, saying lunchtime.

Householding with space, understood also beyond all short-range consideration, on one hand, and on the other, *personality given to a narrow space*, in spite of mass crowding around it—this is the urgent project of a densely populated future.

But biological individuality has not been served either in the present era by any manner or means; even if each of us follows that latest issue of "House Magnificent," after a fast browser's glance, impressed by its enticements. The next issue will be out next month, and to be sure, will be more enticing. And variation of synthetic shingle colors of the subdivision developer from green here to novel pink on every third neighbor roof is far below what a biologically subtly advised future may do for the individual and his specific make-up. It will give his avid senses dynamic, variable refreshment also on small square footage. We must only take this seriously—technically there will be less difficulty to do it and be elastic in our offerings.

The attitude and thoughts, concerned with the beloved and better understood natural in man have accompanied me through a long life in a profession where, according to normal thinking, artificiality is specialty and daily fare. But to settle the living is above all the contrary from being dead-set and immutable. It calls for always reaching back beyond the rigid, mechanical, and artificial for the mutable of nature.

In human beings who squeeze daily into subways, brimful busses, elevators filled to the last square inch at the moment of office-closing, one may notice how they can relax even in the midst of their pressed situation of hampered breathing and tight discomfort. For a few moments, at least, they seem suddenly to be relieved of pure mechanics, almost purified and somehow helped *through the natural surroundings of expressive human faces.* Before human beings on closest range, they become contemplative and begin to get minutely interested in the physiognomies of their fellow passengers. It is something marvelous if one can escape all these other physical crowdings by taking into one's soul a human face. It is a bit of nature above the synthetically colored necktie or the low-cut blouse.

Epilogue to a Prelude

The great theme of our future *is the individual*—not liquidated, not lost in the shuffle, not regimented, in spite of all probability mathematics. Biologists call it the individual phenotype, the singly appearing specimen—it is by no means an unimportant minority report.

In biology, especially in the ever more complex systems which find their high point in the human cerebrum, the single voice of deviation can fatefully count. Organic variation and much of its consequences would be difficult to explain without it, and all evolution would be at an end, frozen stiff.

One, then, is more than just the lowliest number.

On the other hand, with all his specific characteristics and particular selectivity, the individual is unthinkable outside of his species, and never exists in a vacuum. No man can go it alone. Even if he walks on a desert island and talks to himself for twenty years, he talks to someone of his kind. If need be, he "anthropomorphizes," makes men out of animals near him, to have stimulated and stimulating company. For his arousal "of any companion" he needs emotion. "Comprehension" increases in a measure as it is supported by emotion.

It happens for all of us in the same measure as human individuals are brought together, and in mutual vitalization from one to the other, become richer. It is so when musicians in a quartet or an orchestra, by fractions of tone or time, are tuned into a cohesive, spontaneous group. For this, *team*, reminiscent of the rather uncreative horse job of pulling a carriage, is just an oversimplified word.

But in self-trained-together combination, soul and mind forces, as they are yielded by the so variously patterned brain action in every single skull, will be less used up by friction and interference. Sometimes seconds may suffice for a creative act. In a bisexual species like ours, a precious union of individuals is not infrequently proven to succeed for many years.

We just do not have such a simple nervous endowment as bees, nor hundreds of millions of years of beehive experience, worked out in reflexiveness. It is useless for us to envy bees or to sing the praises of their moral example. This is romanticism which the architect, especially, must avoid if he wants to house realistically human beings rather than bees.

As insight into nervous dynamics and the manifoldness of "biological individuality" increases, *can* individuals possibly be ever better tuned together? Can they, by study of all elements that contribute, be helped to subjective *and* mutual satisfaction? Nature's ties and guards of the individual, within his group and an artificial setting, must not be left to hazard. They again must be better known, more so, than as they once were by rote; and the architect of the setting can decisively help them along. What a task for a long future that, more than any earlier age, ours surely must solve! We face and will face increasingly massive and multipersonal transactions, especially in creating human environment. All of it means architecture, planning, design—ever more of it. Without design we shall not survive—only *through* it.

Clearly recognizing a total task like this, beyond all blunderings of patchy piecemeal progresses, however proud—honoring the urgency of wholesomely proportioned wholeness—must come first. Then action and results might follow, day by day.

To become convinced is an emotional event, and like the wise red Indians of America, Aristotle also voted, in his *De Anima*, for the heart as the seat of conviction. In this he contradicted his contemporaries and predecessors who localized the matter in the brain. Probably both, even much more of a spread, will ultimately be proved right. After all, localizing the soul remains always precarious! It is all *throughout* us.

Rejoicing in "feeling oneself into others," empathy, is a true promise for any personal solution. All solutions of an architect start here and from this very capacity.

Besides such a puzzling inborn, half-introspective capacity, there is also neat outward observation. Watching with care each individual, as he finds his right dynamic nervous patterns, his spot and mission in life, and so also his kind of feasible "emotional fill," will help usher even better each to his right path and place for partaking in the interplay. Without enjoyment, no play—nothing at all—turns out well.

For the clinical science of observing with sympathy—heartily attempted empathy—individual specimens of flesh and blood will help, be they ordinary or even exotic. They are what the architect needs to know in order to become better himself.

Large "control groups," as always, will round out the over-all experience of many individuals, as they reveal themselves in collaborative situations and a trusting mood. This *accomplishing things together* may be aided by thoughtfully set-up experiments in the lab; we have already said. I have long hoped for it: a science of and for the peaceful nurturing of collaborative brainwork, with more mutual feed-back than friction. The bearing subfloor of it all is the subbrain, the subcortical centers, where emotions have rooted, long before "clear concepts" ever sprouted.

It is in the trend of the times to study all this attentively. To decline any systematic trend in this direction would indeed be nihilistic. Statistics of observation should be carefully guarded, however, and never be allowed to get completely out of human hand, off into life-detached abstract speculation or self-satisfied electronically managed mathematics.

Rarefied abstractionists, as well as dollar-and-cent building economists, financiers, and fiscalists, must not domineer the scene which the planner and architect—a trained biorealist—has the never-ending task to set for organic human life, in town and habitat. His staging must be sensitively inserted into nature, must not be divorced from what is our primeval, unavoidable inheritance: nature, inside and out. We cannot let nature sink, or we are sunk. An entire life experience like mine is vividly behind this credo.

From the Emperor Diocletian, authorizing and building the same projects in Syria and Dalmatia, whose architect was a slave such as have been busy in imperial and caliph palaces, down to the king who was France, and in whose retinue an architect would work in one stretch for thirty-five years, and from now on, to a foreshadowed state of affairs where half a billion square meters of housing must be built annually for millions of occupants (and this must be raised to three-quarters of a billion square meters next year, at a unit price 8 per cent lower in spite of two added electric outlets per kitchen)—

what a change in my profession! There also has been a change away from deeper and deeper imprinted imagery to quite another standardization on one hand, and fast flashes of fashion on the other to counterbalance it. And statistical numerology has become tops. Numbers are our "stop" and "go" signals, says IBM, but I have to think that, maybe, it's not the entire story.

Allowing for all this, I then seem to have gone through my life during an "in-between period." I did not serve just one client or even one kind of client. Nor did I act among a vast regiment of busy readers of regulation bulletins on what was assured by a committee of upstairs sages as this year's or next year's "best for the most"—with these "mosts" and "bests" known to me only by round figures, handed down in inter-office communications, and perhaps by a bit of abbreviated hopeful speculation, slipped in clandestinely. Where is man the *individual?* Is he lost in this progress of the numerical, which sits somewhere in our frontal lobe? Is it truly an advance almost to ignore him, or is it perhaps a retreat from total life?

Besides projects for the United States Public Housing Authority, the Navy, and the Air Force, I have had the luck to confront that large control group of individual American schoolteachers, secretaries, band players, Americanized Chinese produce merchants, Nisei eye doctors, smallish professionals, and all sorts of people in our cities and distant development countries, who graciously gave confidence, last a small sprinkling of wealthy independents—I mean, independent of loan and average installment plan—who all make up our mixed society in the "free world." They were the ones who commissioned my life history as an architectural clinician of this perhaps passing day. It was above all a motley procession of very variegated experience, with many individuals from Montana, Connecticut, Switzerland, Ohio, Munich, Guam, Düsseldorf, Hamburg, and Caracas. Everybody was entitled to personal attention such as no architect of antiquity gave when he built a tomb for the Pharaoh or Polycrates.

Where or how will the practitioner of the architecture of the future individually have such experience? By good luck, it just happened to me during these few "in-between" decades. Maybe I have enjoyed one of the interesting interstices of history, even if it was not the golden age of *one* Pericles who fascinated a whole critical *politia* into grand expenditure to astound even foreign generations of several thousand years.

While it lasted, much clinical information has certainly been gleaned as it came my way. I have gathered it from a medley of individually diagnosed and prognosticated little clients, after the hand to mouth fashion of Hippocrates, who swore to be good, but had as yet no medical laboratories, cardiograms, or X-ray files at his disposal.

Individual, family, and later ever broader group psychology could first be purveyed on a small scale only, in case histories, family-doctor style—it had seemed to me. Meanwhile, the impersonal big curtain-walled steel cages would rise downtown and between them help jam the traffic of gleaming Detroit cars—smart applied-art objects on wheels—as they converge from suburbia or the outer landscape, from its cheaper and a bit more individual out-of-town sites; for there occasionally an individual shell could still have its single ring and sound.

Such a thing scarcely existed in my old-fashioned native Vienna. In the future, too, there may not be anything comparable, either, except a few *dachas* of ballet stars in post-Khrushchev Moscow. Mine was an instructive twilight period of a culture, sandwiched between other cultures, past and possibly in the offing.

Besides a natural nostalgic interest, though, I like to keep faith with it that there might be found in such a life's effort a telling documentary collection of individuals or individual families, anchored on individual lots of an often still somewhat recognizable landscape, with "psychotopes" to comfort them.

Some animal behaviorists, as my friend, Professor Hediger in Zurich, use this term for "soul-satisfying spot," or soul anchorage. An animal seeks out and defends such spots for nesting, breeding, feeding, and even for playing. Is that animal ever wrecked by it, as by a bad investment?

Maybe mass accommodation is the necessity and logic of the future; maybe artificial insemination, with all genetic parameters under control, will master safely population and propagation problems of the brave or grave new world. Yet love stories of bygone literature—and also the intuitive, the insightful planning of individual abodes here in a valley, there on some crest of rolling country—may, at least in retrospect, hold some interest, and perhaps more than that. Sympathetic stories are inspiring because they can still remind one of personality relationship in the original biological state. It was an age of greater human scarcity and of rootedness to a spot.

Individuality is prehuman. But human beings are undoubtedly more benefited, and also much more troubled, by it. There is rarely equilibrium within our brain roof, as Sherrington calls it. And beneath it is an attic room which listens and reacts most sensitively to the pattering rain above. From Asclepius to Sherrington, nobody really knows in which room the sensitive soul sits and listens, but our so-precarious brain-balance keeps us, as it were, in our own magic circle. Eminently human, it is by no means impenetrable, and often rattled by what penetrates it.

But Man is also left isolated, especially in critical moments of both letdown and creativity. Personally marked cerebral supremacy may yield, of course, the most famous examples of the human individual. Not even a queen bee has such a peculiar significance, or such a story of woe.

Archimedes wanted to keep his circles undisturbed, just at the moment when the lowbrow Roman legionary stepped forward, ignorant of marvelously distilled geometry and science, to crush in short order one of the best heads the world has ever seen. This sad story has long illustrated the lonely problem and the interferences in store for an absent-minded genius whose work remains removed and puzzling. He can't interrupt it; he is busy with himself and with his, speechlessly fast, inner mental processes. Neither his foes nor his friends understand, and only favorable publicity, coming for some extraneous reason, may sometimes legitimize the man so that he is tolerated outside an institution, outside society—or outside the grave. He has not provoked any real resentment, except the often-recorded reflexive hostility of the resorptive, but also sometimes repellent, swarm, the pack, the herd, often enough against someone different, be he so by deficiency or because of a fateful "plus" peculiarity. This is doubly true if the genius lacks any immediate and obvious signs of successful leadership. We mean here to emphasize only the somewhat uncanny *difference*, not necessarily superiority.

Frank Lloyd Wright told me, I think significantly, not once but on two occasions, the story of a monkey in Malaya. It was caught by a planter, roped around the waist, and tied to a post on his screened porch. During the night the monkey bit off the rope near the post, bit through the screen mesh, and escaped into the jungle to his fellows. But they were no longer fellows to a monkey with a peculiarity—with a rope around his belly. They regarded him with hostility for being different, "and tore him limb from limb." I still remember Mr. Wright's reverberating, almost trembling voice as he said this, and his baritone laughter which ended in a bitter smile. Frank Lloyd Wright did not simply have a strange rope around his belly—why did he link this story to himself? What really characterizes the relationship to others of the outstanding man, merely taken as the extreme case of a vital individual? Is it tragedy—not only necessity—that the individual, even the best, the most alive, is really not effective, not vital, in a vacuum? Always very soon, sooner or later, he must be involved with others.

Does the great individual, or top I.Q., *lead* the low I.Q.?

Such a question is easily misunderstood, or at any rate oversimplified. Limitedness in one may have to lead another less limited.

Once, as he was driving me to the airport, Joseph Koestner, director of the Natural History Museum which we designed in Dayton, Ohio, told me of a laboratory experiment with three rats. In it a rat had to tread on a switch to release a morsel of food. The treadle was placed next to, and close by, the alluring food. All three rats, one after another, learned to jump on the treadle to feed themselves. As I interpreted it, they were, and remained, three separate individuals even in a confined space, which in itself had not turned them into a *group* of combined functions. Mere physical nearness does not do that; it is not yet a genuine group-former.

But then the experimental arrangement was changed. The food was placed on one side of the cage, and the releasing treadle, diametrically opposite. Two of the rats were not brainy enough ever to connect the two distant events—treading here and getting food way over there. The third rat had the necessary intelligence, and had mustered mental "leadership" from the shortcomings of his companions. It stepped on the switch, but the other two fellows were naturally always a little closer to the food morsel when it popped up at the other end of the cage. They snapped it before the "wise leader" of rats could rush over to benefit from its own intelligent effort. This rat then became even wiser by necessity. First it had to step twice, in speedy succession, and while the other two members of the team were busy chewing their bites, it quickly jumped onto the treadle a third time, and then, unhampered, could itself capture its reward.

There is no moral to this story or justifiable gripe. It is merely an experimental picture of superiority feeding the less brainy and getting into a situation of working harder for its own sustenance and survival than anyone else. But what is strangely significant is that these three individuals have now, by inner and outer circumstance, been linked almost automatically into a sort of group action. Even intelligence—like a lot of lower brain benefits—does not breed independence but interdependence—often strikingly so.

Yet with more brainy humans the whole matter is sadly complicated by "thought-induced" glandular discharges and tricky emotions. The tragic point in human teams often arises because of mutual resentment. Resentment may be rife whenever contributing gifts are unequal. They could hardly be "equal" because they must be diversified, really, to be effective in combination. This has its significance for a working team, an architect's office, or a city council session where a regional plan or any important thing is up for discussion. Nevertheless, organized by insight into the true wonders of a team potential, and granted early nursery-school pretraining for it, I should say, success and individual reward *may* well come to an entire human group. It can be fused and bring happiness to each one, and something useful is then in store to be produced. I have hoped this all my life. And for stretches, unaccountable by the clock, people who co-operated were happy. An architect is a coordinator of many, and so lives enmeshed, never as a solitary monologuist.

In our age of ever-intensified colossal affairs, a lonely individual in the mass of linked contributors has become a forlorn agent and recipient of ever more meager satisfaction. But without any such positive emotion our world would stop. It is not composed of mathematically computed computers. Satisfaction is needed, emotive as it is, and an aim of the living.

Thinking of a future world, we had better avoid oversimplification and warn against it. Thus we should add one other train of thought, so as to illuminate the emotional stumbling blocks of human individuality, be it "great" or little. (The case of the genius is only somewhat conspicuous.)

The axiom of life reads: No individual is; he *becomes*. He oscillates while one watches or tries to adjust to his ever-varying phases and positions. To *travel* with him, orbit around him, the future may have to train as many skills as it will for interplanetary navigation. The ever-denser traffic of individuals needs, so to speak, its ordinances and licensing examination, based on deepened insight. The atmosphere around deviant, peculiar, forward, or specifically valuable individuals has its own air pockets. These individuals themselves often are characterized by their specifically marked graphs, curves, and velocities of vitality fluctuation. By these strange and unusually expressive accelerations and changes from depressed dark to exhilarated bright, their firing pattern becomes difficult to follow or to understand. Such people are hard to get along with, whether they are encountered by their fellow inmates in a psychopathic ward or whether, in the whirl of the outer world, they might even be somewhat credited by their contemporaries with, and for, an amazing production of one kind or other. All this does not occur with rats, or only in a rudimentary way. In brief, one commonly says so very tellingly that Man has a *soul*.

With complex humans, the physiological unusualness may easily amount almost to incompatibility. The "hardship in the group" for overgifted individuals is sharpened and intensified frequently by mutual flabbergasted responses or fearful friction.

To see one day a man walking on air, sky high, and then on the next—expecting him not only in the same dreamlike altitude, but at his height of true efficiency—to see him suddenly depressed, in the deepest ditch of operational ineffectiveness and despair, is socially indigestible—even to his loving wife, should he be able to keep one near him. And still, even a "mild case of Mozart," as I have called it jokingly, may yield such a social problem. Life is just a large bundle of rhythmical and other *unrolling* processes, with surprises rolled into them, for man, woman, and child—not to mention what faces their architect in the midst of all these happenings. From a safe, salubrious distance, geographical and historical, everything human, including architecture, may appear calmly leveled off. The continuous adjustments are no longer necessary; past lives—great and small—look rounded out and reduced to acceptability. Biology becomes becalmed when fossilized—and it is then often venerable but unexciting. There were more fireworks when unassorted saurians got in each other's way and into disputes outside of the museum.

The careful *observance of life-in-progress*, in action, and quite especially in the interaction of one biological individuality with others, may still reveal wonders for us. It may become the salvation of superbrained beings just like those who constitute our fascinating species which has been so long in the making, and most certainly still is.

In fact, with our swelling human multitudes our mutational opportunities might have an unprecedented increase, and evolution, a speed-up. Biological changes might not readily jibe with political economics! They will demand their right of way.

Man may now, in company of ever more population, no longer be able to muddle through without accommodations, subtly designed to be biologically fit. But with all those billions of brain cells firing, he will go on, we may hope, with an *increasing grasp* of his own natural needs. "Know thyself" still holds true. But now, on scientific terms, it must lead to survival through design. Live and let live, bearably housed together in buildings and towns—such is *our* necessary kind of survival.

It is a breath-taking task. If we want to go on and not perish from the earth, it will have to be done without reckless warpage or shrinkage of individual vitality. It must come to us without mutual defeat and without severe wreckage of the organic landscape—outside and inside our skin.

Bibliography

BOOKS BY RICHARD NEUTRA:
Amerika: Die Stilbildung des neuen Bauens in den Vereiningten Staaten. Anton Schroll Verlag, Vienna, 1930.
Architecture of Social Concern in Regions of Mild Climate. Gerth Todtmann, São Paulo, 1948.
Bauen und die Sinneswelt. Verlag der Kunst, Dresden, 1977.
Bauen und die Sinneswelt. Parey Verlag, Berlin, 1980. By Richard and Dion Neutra.
Life and Human Habitat. Alexander Koch Verlag, Stuttgart, 1956.
———. German translation: *Mensch und Wohnen.* Alexander Koch Verlag, Stuttgart, 1956.
Life and Shape. Appleton-Century-Crofts, New York, 1962.
———. German translation: *Auftrag für Morgen.* Claasen Verlag, Hamburg, 1962.
———. Spanish translation: *Vida y forma.* Foreword by Dion Neutra. Marymar (Arquitectura y Urbanismo), Buenos Aires, 1972.
Mystery and Realities of the Site. Willard Morgan, Scarsdale, 1951.
Nature Near: The Late Essays of Richard Neutra. Capra Press, Santa Barbara, 1989.
Naturnahes Bauen. Alexander Koch Verlag, Stuttgart, 1970.
———. English translation: *Building With Nature.* Universe Books, New York, 1971.
Pflanzen Wasser Steine Licht. Parey Verlag, Berlin, 1974. By Richard and Dion Neutra.
Realismo Biológico: Un Nuevo Renacimiento humanístico en arquitectura. Nueva Visión, Buenos Aires, 1958.

Survival Through Design. Oxford University Press, New York, 1954.
———. French translation: *Construire pour survivre.* Casterman, Paris, 1971.
———. German translation: *Wenn wir weiterleben wollen.* Claasen Verlag, Hamburg, 1955.
———. Italian translation: *Progettare per sopravvivere.* Edizioni di Communita, Milan, 1956.
———. Spanish translation: *Planificar para sobrevivir.* Fondo de Cultura, Mexico City, 1957.
Welt und Wohnung. Alexander Koch Verlag, Stuttgart, 1961.
Wie Baut Amerika. Hoffman Verlag, Stuttgart, 1926.
World and Dwelling. Universe Books, New York, 1962.

BOOKS ABOUT RICHARD NEUTRA:

BOESIGER, WILLY. *Richard Neutra: Buildings and Projects.* Girsberger Verlag, Zurich, 1950.
———. *Richard Neutra: Buildings and Projects. 1950-1960*, Girsberger Verlag, Zurich, 1959.
———. *Richard Neutra: Buildings and Projects. 1961-1966*, Girsberger Verlag, Zurich, 1966.
CASTILLO, JOSÉ VELA. *Richard Neutra: Un lugar para el orden.* Universidad de Sevilla, Seville, 2003.
DREXLER, ARTHUR, AND THOMAS S. HINES. *The Architecture of Richard Neutra. From International Style to California Modern.* The Museum of Modern Art, New York, 1982.
FORD, EDWARD R. *The Details of Modern Architecture, vol. 2, 1928-1988.* The MIT Press, Cambridge, MA, 1996.
HINES, THOMAS S. *Richard Neutra and the Search for Modern Architecture: A Biography and History.* Oxford University Press, New York, 1982.
———. Rizzoli, New York, 2006.
KOEPER, FREDERICK. *The Richard and Dion Neutra VDL Research House I and II.* California State Polytechnic University, Pomona, 1985.
KOKUSAI-KENTIKU. *Richard Neutra.* Bijutsu Shuppansha, Tokyo, 1953.
LAMPRECHT, BARBARA. *Richard Neutra: Complete Works.* Taschen Publications, Cologne, 2000.
LAMPRECHT, BARBARA. *Richard Neutra.* Taschen Publications, Cologne, 2009.

LEET, STEPHEN. *Richard Neutra's Miller House*. Princeton Architectural Press, New York, 2004.
MCCOY, ESTHER. *Richard Neutra*, "Masters of World Architecture." George Braziller, New York, 1960.
———. Italian translation. Mondadori, Milan, 1961.
———. German translation. Otto Mayer Verlag, Ravensburg, 1962.
MCCOY, ESTHER. *Vienna to Los Angeles: Two Journeys: Letters between R.M. Schindler and Richard Neutra*. Arts + Architecture Press, Santa Monica, 1979.
NEUMANN, DIETRICH (ed.). *Richard Neutra's Windshield House*. Yale University Press, New Haven, 2001.
NEUTRA, DIONE. *Richard Neutra: Promise and Fulfillment, 1919-1932*. Southern Illinois University Press, Carbondale, 1986.
SACK, MANFRED. *Richard Neutra*. Foreword by Dion Neutra. Artemis Verlag, Zurich, 1992.
WARSCHAVCHIK, GREGORY. *Neutra*. Museu de Arte, São Paulo, Brazil, 1950.
WIGHT, FREDERICK STALLKNECHT. *Richard Neutra: Is Planning Possible?* University of California, Los Angeles, 1958.
ZEVI, BRUNO. *Richard Neutra*. Il Balcone, Milan, 1954.

Index

Aalto, Alvar, 259
Academy of Modern Art, Los Angeles, 218
Addams, Jane, 180-81
Albania, 126-32
Aluminum Corporation of America, 261, 263
American City, 317
Amerika, see *Neues Bauen in der Welt*
Ammann, Gustav, 139-41
"Anita," 135, 136, 138-39, 141
Architect, attitude toward work, 8-9; importance of individual and group in work of, 61-62; as a clinician, 65-68; function, 274-76; relations with client, 302-4; necessity for empathy, 359-60
Architecture as a profession, 277, 279-80; apprenticeship, 90-98; education for, 92-93; one-man versus large firms, 201-206; relation with clients, 279-85; technical participation of clients, 282-83; case study of a $9,200 budget house, 285-91; human relationships, 291-92; case study of a failure through a marital disagreement, 293-302; the architect as a friend and adviser, 302-4

Arizona, trip of Neutra in, 305-16; Painted Desert and Petrified Forest housing project, 340-44
Arts and Architecture, 218-19
Baurat Bischof, 151, 153, 154, 155
Beer, Robert, 56
Bell, California, Corona Avenue School, 208, 216
Berlin, Germany, Neutra's work in, 149-51, 155-60; *Berliner Tageblatt* building, 156-59
Better Homes in America competition, 200-1
Bewobau Company, 344, 345
Blank, Dr. Friedrich, 89
Braun, Major General, 104
Brown, Harrison, 278
Building materials, Van der Leeuw house, 267-69

California, southern, idea of "The South" as exemplified in, 210-19; "The Past of Southern California," exhibit, 217; *see also* Los Angeles
Castelnuovo, Italy, 112, 116
Cetinje, Montenegro, 119-20, 125
Chicago, Illinois, 163, 171, 182-83, 196; World's Columbian Exposition, 163, 171, 203; Neutra's impressions of, 176-77, 189-90;

INDEX 373

Neutra's work in, 178-205; "prairie architecture" in, 178, 188-90; Neutra's views on buildings in, 181-82, 183, 202-3; Robie House, 182, 188; Palmer House, 195-97, 201-3; Monadnock Building, 200, 203; Industrial Art School, 263-64
China, 246-53
Civil War, Southern opposition to proposed Lincoln Memorial at Gettysburg, 305-16
City planning, see Urban planning
Cleveland, Ohio, 262, 263
Congrès International d'Architecture Moderne, 256
Corona Avenue School, Bell, California, 208, 216
Cristelli, Dr. Schrotter von, 63-65

Davis, Arthur Vining, 261
Dayton, Ohio, Science Museum, 88, 365
Delphi, Greece, 1-3

Eames, Charles, 280
Eckstein, Trude, 137, 139, 143
Ellbogen, Dr. Friedrich, 54
Elmslie, George, 187

Fisher, John, 179
Floors and flooring, in Neutra's childhood home, 37-38
Foerster, Carl, 139
Forrestall, James J., 179, 180-81, 195
Frankfurt, Germany, 344-52
Freud, Ernst, 78-80, 149
Freud, Sigmund, 90, 190, 259

Gardens, influence of Zurich nursery on Neutra, 139-40; in home planning, 355
General Electric Company, 200-1
Germany, housing at Luckenwalde, 151-55; housing colony for State of Hesse, 344-52
Gettysburg, Pa., Lincoln Memorial Museum, 305-16
Glaser, Regina (grandmother), 39, 50
Glass, use of, in Van der Leeuw house, 267-68
Gropius, Walter, 214, 264

Haifa, Israel, business center, 162
Harmon, Darryl B., 327
Harris, Harwell Hamilton, 261
Health House, see Lovell Health House
Hediger, Professor, 363
Heisenberg, Werner, 4n
Herzka, Ensign, 131-33, 134
Hesse, State of, West Germany, housing colony, 344-52
Holabird and Roche, architects, 195-97, 201, 203
Hollywood, California, Universal Pictures Building, 208, 221
Hong Kong, 230
Hotels, Palmer House, Chicago, 195-97, 201-203
Houses, Montenegro, 122; resettlement projects for industrial workers at Luckenwalde, Germany, 151-55; Robie House, Chicago, 182, 188; Taliesen, 189, 209, 306; Mosk residence, Los Angeles, 220-22; Lovell Health House, Los Angeles, 222-28; space planning in, 242-44; Van der Leeuw, 265-70; problems in design, 278-79; case study of a $9,200 budget house, 283-89; case study of a failure due to marital disagreement (Mr. and Mrs. O), 293-302; adaptation to national characteristics, 346-48; cellars, 348, 350-51; procedure for planning of, 349-52; carports

and garages, 352; *windfang* (wind trap), 348-49, 350; accessories in, 351-53; use of partitions and panels in, 350, 353, 354, 355

Housing projects, resettlement, Venezuela, 152-53; use of limited space, 277-78; resettlement, in Arizona, California, Germany, Guam, Idaho, Italy, Spain, 338-40; of military personnel, 339-40; Painted Desert and Petrified Forest, Arizona, 340-44; colony for State of Hesse, West Germany, 344-52; concept of space in, 356-57; *see also* Urban planning

How America Builds, see *Wie Baut Amerika*

Imhoff von Reutlinghof, Victor, 82
Industrial Art School, Chicago, 263-64
Ischlondsky, Dr. N., 318

Japan, Neutra's visit to, 229-30
Johnson, Homer H., 261, 262, 263

Kalischer, Edmund, 56, 78
Koestner, Joseph, 365
Kotor, Gulf of, 116, 119
Kravica, Serbia, 105, 106, 107
Krueger, Otto, 150
Kuras, Mr., 152, 153
Kwangtung, China, 246-53

Lake Titicaca, Peru, 120
La Paz, Bolivia, 124
Lastva, Serbia, 103, 106
Le Corbusier, 214, 256, 318
Lesh, Albania, 128
Libby-Owens Glass Company, 267
Lighting, Van der Leeuw house, 267-68
Lincoln Memorial Museum, Gettysburg, Pa., 45, 305-6; Southern op-osition to, 306-16
Loos, Adolf, 104, 144, 162-72, 191, 193-94
Los Angeles, California, opportunities for Neutra in, 209-300, 214; Neutra's practice in, 221-28; Mosk house, 221-22; Lovell Health House, 222-28; Van der Leeuw house, 265-70; *see also* California, southern
Los Angeles County Museum, 217
Los Angeles Hall of Records, 267
Lovell Health House, Los Angeles, California, 222-28; replica in Museum of Science and Industry, 261
Lueger, Karl, 69-70, 71-72

Macao, 230-33, 244-45
Maxwell, Clark, 10
McArthur, Albert, 184, 187
Mendelsohn, Erich, 155, 157, 159, 162
Merchandise Mart, Chicago, 207
Monadnock Building, Chicago, 200, 203
Montenegro, 108, 117-26
Moser, Prof. Karl, 140
Mosk House, Los Angeles, 221-22
Mosse, Lachman, 157, 158, 159
Mumford, Lewis, 10, 220
Museum of Modern Art, New York City, 260
Museums, Science Museum, Dayton, Ohio, 88; Vienna City, 71-72
Mysteries and Realities of the Site, 356

National Park Service (U.S.), 315; Painted Desert and Petrified Forest housing project, Arizona, 340-44
Netherlands, 258
Neues Bauen in der Welt (New Building in the World), 199-201
Neuman, Ludwig, 56

INDEX 375

Neutra, Dion (son), 209, 228, 259
Neutra, Elizabeth Glaser (mother), 45, 59, 148
Neutra, Frank L. (son), 209, 228, 259
Neutra, Josephine (sister), 52-54
Neutra, Richard Joseph
  Art and Architectural Works:
  sketches, 16-33; early drawings, 76-80; sketches during travels, 81-84; Lovell Health House, 88, 222-28; Science Museum, Dayton, Ohio, 88, 365; resettlement housing at Luckenwalde, Germany, 151-55; Luckenwalde Forest Cemetery, 154; *Berliner Tageblatt*, 156-59; department store buildings and houses near Berlin, 159-60; Haifa business center, 162; Palmer House, Chicago, 195-97, 201-202; Corona Avenue School, Bell, California, 208, 216; residences in Connecticut and Long Island, 208; Universal Pictures Building, Hollywood, California, 208, 221; "The Past of Southern California," exhibit, 217-18; Mosk home, Los Angeles, 221-22; Van der Leeuw house, Los Angeles, 267-70; Los Angeles Hall of Records, 267; budget houses, 285-91; house for Mr. and Mrs. O, 293-302; Lincoln Memorial Museum, Gettysburg, Pa., 305-16; housing in Arizona, California, Germany, Guam, Idaho, Italy, and Spain, 338-40; Painted Desert and Petrified Forest project, Arizona, 340-44; housing colony for State of Hesse, West Germany, 344-52
  Awards and Prizes:
  doctorate from University of West Berlin, 139; Haifa business center, 162; Better Homes in America competition, 200-1
  Ideas and Philosophy:
  outline of philosophy, 1-14; the architect as clinician, 65-68; function of eye and vision, 74-76, 84; apprenticeship in architecture, 90-98; time and space, 97-98; views on American technology, 191-95; southern California as an example of "The South," 210-19; Lovell Health House, 222-28; physiological background, 232-33; organic design essentials, 234-38; "Figure," definition of, 238; "Shape," definition of, 239-40; time-space relations, 240-44; enduring design, 266-70; design as a human issue (for life), 271-72; environment of the individual from embryo to birth, 272-74; function of the architect, 274-76; mass housing, 277-78; appreciation of clients, 279-80; relation of architect and client, 281-85; human relations between architect and client, 291-92; human interplay and environment, 293-303; architect as a friend and adviser, 302-4; commemorative architecture, 312-16; modern urban planning, 317-23; "shape," 321; beauty versus utility, 323-28; "biological realism," 328-31; environmental factors, 331; visual impact of surroundings, 331-33; attitudes of civic officials, 333-34; "psychosomatic design," 334-35; physiological basis of architecture, 335-37; adaptation to change, 337-38; meeting and serving human needs, 338-44; weather as a factor in planning, 343-44; adaptation to German national characteristics, 346-48; cellars, 348, 350-51; flex-

ibility in planning, 354-55; concept of space in housing, 356-57; individual as an element in planning, 357-59, 361; summary of career, 361-62; man as a complex being, 364-66; interaction of human beings with biology, 366-68
Life:
childhood, 34-61; father, 44-45, 49, 148; mother, 45, 59, 148; brothers, 46-50, 54; sister, 52-54; influence of Louise Schmidl, 54-56; early education, 56-57; youth, 56-82; influence of Arpad Weixlgaertner, 57-60; influence of friends of youth, 60-61; influence of medical practice on selection of vocation, 62-65; choice of vocation as architect, 68; travels during teen years, 78-81; studies at Technical University of Vienna, 79-80; prewar military service, 82; Archives on Neutra at University of California at Los Angeles, 83; education, 84-85; service in World War I, 98-132; journey to Switzerland, 133-34; stay in Switzerland, 134-47; work in Zurich landscape nursery, 138-41; first architectural work, 144-45; courtship of Dione Niedermann, 147-48; work with American-British Friends in Vienna, 148-49; architect in Berlin, 149-51; work in housing and design at Luckenwalde, Germany, 151-55; work with Mendelsohn in Berlin, 155-60; marriage and early married life, 160-61; arrival in United States, 172-73; life and work in Chicago, 176, 178-205; meeting with Louis Sullivan, 183-85; meeting with Frank Lloyd Wright, 185-91; writes *Wie Baut Amerika*, 196-99; writes *Neues Bauen in der Welt*, 199-201; magazine articles on work, 205-6; joined by wife, 209; move to California, 209-10; teaching at Academy of Modern Art, Los Angeles, 218; early practice in Los Angeles, 221-28; trip through Asia and Africa, 228-56; lectures in Europe, 256-59; New York activities, 259-62; "Pullmans of the Highway," 262-63; experiences with individual clients, 285-302; trip through Arizona desert, 305-16; Research Commission on School Design, 327n
Publications:
Survival Through Design, 88, 327n; *Wie Baut Amerika*, 196-99, 258, 259, 267, 270; *Neues Bauen in der Welt*, 199-201; magazine articles on work, 205-6; *Rush City Reformed*, 219-20; articles in *Die Form*, 229-30; Designs, text by Kameki Tsutsura, 230; *Mysteries and Realities of the Site*, 356; bibliography of, 369-70
Work as an Architect:
influences of childhood environment, 35-43, 50; influence of Otto Wagner, 68, 70; synopsis of development, 73-74; influence of teachers, 85-86, 89-90; influence of World War I experiences, 108-9, 117; influence of Adolf Loos, 162-72, 191, 193-94; influence of Frank Lloyd Wright, 173-77, 181-82, 185-91; influence of Louis Sullivan, 183-85

Neutra, Mrs. Richard, 145-47, 205; early married life, 160-61; *see also* Niedermann, Dione

Neutra, Siegfried (brother), 46-47, 48, 54, 55, 56, 57, 60, 63-65

Neutra, William (brother), 48-49,

INDEX 377

54-55, 60, 63, 75
Neutra, William (father), 148
Neutra, William (grandfather), 44, 62
New Building in the World, see Neues Bauen in der Welt
New Canaan, Conn., 208
New School for Social Research, 260, 262
New York, N.Y., 163, 164, 169-71, 172-73; Neutra's opinion on architecture of, 207-8
Niedermann, Alfred, 135-36
Niedermann, Dione (wife), 137, 142, 143-44, 145-47, 149-50, 160; see also Neutra, Mrs. Richard
Niedermann, Mrs. Lilly Antoinette (mother-in-law), 137, 142, 143, 147-48, 149-50, 209
Niedermann family, 136-37, 142-44

Office buildings, Monadnock Building, Chicago, 200, 203; Reliance Building, Chicago, 203; Singer Tower, New York, 206; Woolworth Building, New York, 206; Merchandise Mart, Chicago, 207; Universal Pictures Building, Hollywood, 208-21

Painted Desert and Petrified Forest housing project, Arizona, 340-44
Palmer House, Chicago, 195-97, 201-2
Parr, A. E., 336n
Pinner and Neumann, architects, 149-51
Playgrounds, of Vienna childhood, 51-52; in schools, 326-27
Pond, I. K., 185
Pullmans of the Highway, 262-63

Ragusa, Italy, 115

Regen, Dr., 85-87
Resettlement housing, see under Housing projects
Reliance Building, Chicago, 203
Residences, see Houses
Research Commission on School Design, 327n
Richard J. Neutra Foundation, 336n
Riddick, John, 305-16
Root, John W., 200, 203
Rush City Reformed, 219-20
Ruthe, Dr. Franz, 89

Saliger, Dr. Heinrich, 89
Sandburg, Carl, 189, 306
Sarajevo, Serbia, 99, 100
Schmidl, Louise (sister-in-law), 54-56, 60
Schools, Corona Avenue School, Bell, California, 208, 216; planning of, 326-27; Research Commission on School Design, 327n
Scutari, Albania, 126-27
Secretary of Urban Affairs (U.S.), suggested, 193
Semper, Gottfried, 134
Seymour, Ralph Fletcher, 184
Shaw, George Bernard, 10
Singer Tower, New York City, 206
Sister Elsa (of Staefa), 135-36, 141, 142
Southern California, see California, southern
Staefa, Switzerland, 134-37, 141-42
Sturm, Threska, 82
Sullivan, Louis H., 69, 104, 171, 183-85, 187-88, 195, 200
Survival Through Design, 88, 327n
Sweet's Catalogue, 199
Switzerland, Neutra's life and work in, 134-47

Taliesin, Frank Lloyd Wright's home, 189, 209, 306

Tharnay, Captain von, 104
Town planning, *see* Urban planning
Trebinje, Herzogovinia, 100, 101-2, 104-5, 109
Trenčín, Slovakia, 131-33
Trees, in home planning, 355-56
Tsutsura, Kameki, 230

Uncle Tom's Cabin, 45, 309-10
Universal Pictures Building, Hollywood, Calif., 208, 221
U.S. Public Housing Authority, 361
U.S. Secretary of the Interior, 314, 315
University of Arizona, Tuscon, 304-5
University of California at Los Angeles, 83
University of West Berlin, Germany, 139
Urban planning, *Rush City Reformed*, 219-20; space in, 242-44; Neutra's views on, 317-23; beauty versus utility, 323-28; water and power supply, 325-26; "biological realism" in, 328-31; attitudes of civic officials, 333-34; "psychosomatic design," 334-35; *see also* Housing projects

van de Velde, Henry, 256
van der Leeuw, C. H., 257-58, 265, 270
Van der Leeuw house, Los Angeles, 265-70
van der Rohe, Mies, 214, 264
Van Bergen, John, 184
Venezuela, housing projects in, 152-153
Vienna, Austria, childhood and youth of Neutra in, 34-82; Northwest Railways Building, 40; plan of, 52; City Museum, 71-72; Neutra's work in, 148-49
Vogler, Paul, 320

Wagner, Otto, 68, 69, 71-72, 103-4, 183
Wagner Richard, 53, 68-69
Walldorf, Germany, 345

Weixlgaertner, Arpad (brother-in-law), 57-60, 99
Wernli and Staeger, architects, 144-45
White Motors Company, 262-63
Wie Baut Amerika, 196-99, 258, 259, 267, 270
Windows, in Neutra's childhood home, 39-40
Woltersdorf, Arthur, 184
Woolworth Building, New York City, 206
World War I, Neutra's military service during, 98-132
World's Columbian Exposition, 163, 171, 203
Wright, Frank Lloyd, 104, 173-75, 178, 185-91, 204, 214, 222, 364
Wundt, William, 87, 90
Zurich, Switzerland, 134, 137-40, 257, 258

A STATEMENT OF PRINCIPLE*

FOR HALF A CENTURY all kinds of projects to accommodate man, woman, and child, their activities, and the entire community, have occupied my mind: neighborhoods, schools, hospitals, churches, theaters, colleges, embassies in foreign lands, buildings for business and insurance companies, and kindergartens. But nothing is as instructive to an architect as a client whom he can see in the flesh. Nowhere does an architect gain so much "clinical experience," as a doctor would call it, as when he sees the members of a family for which he is designing a dwelling place and making all physical arrangements for a long future ahead.

Happiness ever after is not easily insured, but it is achieved only by the greatest devotion and insight into what makes human beings tick happily—or hampers their heartbeat. An architect who practically applies life-science to life, best learns from home design. Such an activity will help him, and helpfully keep him going also on all the other projects which relate to human beings. All he creates is for an organic human welfare. In future, architecture, as I have looked at it also in the past, will depend on a deepened knowledge of nature, and of man's nature especially, however encroached on by his own patented artificialities. We must love and know him if we want to serve him.

RICHARD NEUTRA

*Originally appearing on the 1962 first edition's back cover.

www.ingramcontent.com/pod-product-compliance
Lightning Source LLC
Chambersburg PA
CBHW021828220426
43663CB00005B/172